The Price of Surrender

The Price of Surrender
1941: The War in Crete

Ernest Walker

BLANDFORD

A BLANDFORD BOOK

First published in the UK 1992
by Blandford
(a Cassell imprint)
Villiers House
41/47 Strand
LONDON
WC2N 5JE

Distributed in the United States
by Sterling Publishing Co., Inc.,
387 Park Avenue South, New York, NY 10016–8810

Distributed in Australia
by Capricorn Link (Australia) Pty Ltd
P.O. Box 665, Lane Cove, NSW 2066

British Library Cataloguing in Publication Data

Walker, Ernest
  The price of surrender 1941, the war
  in Crete.
  I. Title
  940.5421998

  ISBN 0–7137–22967

Typeset by Fakenham Photosetting Ltd, Fakenham, Norfolk
Printed and bound in Great Britain by Mackays of Chatham plc, Chatham, Kent

Dedicated to the memory of
my late wife,
Florence Evelyn,
who worried and prayed for me

Contents

Acknowledgments

To the late Mr K. C. Chant for his encouragement in the early days of my writing this story; to Mr R. F. Peachis, FRGS, for producing various maps of Crete; to Mr R. Frankland for going through the manuscript in search of bad grammar; and to Mrs Mary O'Sullivan for so painstakingly typing the manuscript. I would also like to thank Lesley Levene who edited the text so well, helping to bring my story alive.

Introduction

This is the story of the adventures of eight servicemen immediately following their capture by German paratroopers in the airborne invasion on Crete in 1941.

The writer of the story, Ernest Walker – known by the nickname Mike or Micky – a 34-year-old RAF reservist, one-time gold prospector, Antarctic explorer and freelance journalist, was the oldest member of the party. He was somewhat disabled as a result of the bad food (or lack of food) in the various POW camps in which he was imprisoned.

The story was drafted in note form between 1951 and 1953, but Walker could not find a publisher at that time because 'escape' not 'capture' stories were the vogue then and there was thought to be insufficient blood spilled! He wisely put it on one side rather than pad out his work with imaginary detail, in the certainty that the story would eventually be accepted for what it was – an accurate account of events as they really were back in 1941.

Crete – Background Information

Crete, the largest island in the eastern Mediterranean, lies about 100 miles south of the Greek peninsula. Until the Second World War, surprisingly few people in Britain even knew of its existence. Crete's industries are those common to most Mediterranean islands: the cultivation of vines, olives, citrus fruits and tobacco, and the production of wines, raisins and olive oil. In 1941 the island supported a mixed population of about a quarter of a million Christians, Muslims and Jews, most of whom were peasant farmers. Social life was primitive, and houses, shops and churches – except those in the larger towns – were of crude construction. There was no railway system and public services such as water supply, main drainage, electricity, gas and telephones, were seldom found outside the towns.

The island's known history dates back to about 2000 BC and many of the buildings and artefacts of the ancient Minoan civilization are still in existence. Most notable perhaps is the palace at Knossos, built some 3,000 years ago and considered today to be a masterpiece of early architecture; according to legend, it was here that Theseus met the Minotaur.

Following the Italian declaration of war on Greece in October 1940, the Cretan government passed a resolution of renewed allegiance to its mother country, Greece, and the island prepared for war. Air bases were quickly established by the Allies, and following the subsequent capitulation of Greece in April 1941, various Allied forces were drafted to Crete to strengthen her defences.

Although German military operations in south-east Europe had succeeded in establishing a valuable springboard for an attack on Egypt, there remained one serious obstacle: Crete. In the hands of the Allies the island was a menace not only to lines of communication but also to the Greek peninsula itself, and it guarded the entrance to both the Eastern Mediterranean and the Aegean, and the ocean route to the Black Sea.

A statement by the British Prime Minister, Winston Churchill, that Crete would be defended to the last man removed any doubt as to British policy. The task of making the island invulnerable to attack began.

In due course information leaked out about German preparations for an invasion of the island. Their plan was first to gain control of all aerodromes and landing grounds by the use of large numbers of paratroops, and then to land sufficient airborne troops to establish battle fronts. Further forces would then come in by sea.

General Student was appointed German supremo of the invasion of Crete, codenamed MERCURY, and the mainstay of his force was the XI Air Corps.

And on Goering's personal order he was also allocated the whole of VIII Air Corps, commanded by General Wolfgang von Richthofen, with its famous 'Stuka' groups, trained in close support, which had spearheaded the invasion of Poland, the Low Countries and Greece itself. The Corps consisted of three groups of Dornier Do 17 bombers, two groups of the new twin-engined dive-bombers, the Ju 88, one group of obsolescent Heinkel III bombers, three of single-engined fighters Messerschmidt Me 109s, three of twin-engined fighter bombers Me 110s and a variety of Fieselers and Do 17s without bomb-bays, for reconnaissance work. Backbone of the Corps and still the glamour crews of the Luftwaffe were the hundred and fifty single-engined Junkers Ju 87 dive-bombers. The dreaded 'Stuka' whose evil silhouette, high, square tail fin, fixed undercarriage, and jowelled cooling nacelle, had become a sign of ill-omen to refugees on crowded roads the length and breadth of Europe ...

The Germans had estimated the duration of the campaign at ten days, starting on 17th May. However, because of the impassability of the roads and non-existence of the railway system, it was necessary to bring the two and a half million gallons of aircraft fuel by sea in small boats down the Adriatic coast from Trieste, and the last consignment did not arrive until the 19th. The attack was accordingly set for the following day, 20th May.*

At the beginning of May 1941 German air activity over the island intensified. Previously, an occasional reconnaissance aircraft had flown over at great altitude, but these flights were now supplemented by others of a more lethal nature. Unfortunately, the lack of British air strength – it is doubtful if there were more than 40 operational aircraft on the whole island – seriously

* *The Fall of Crete*, Alan Clark.

weakened an otherwise well-organized defence. By 18 May these figures had been reduced. Losses in combat had not been made good; certain naval air units, together with anti-aircraft defences, were removed from the island; and the remaining aircraft of several RAF units were returned to Egypt for replacement. The situation at Maleme, the aerodrome at the north-west end of Crete, was acute, there being no operational aircraft whatsoever.

The Imperial forces (primarily Australian and New Zealand), under the command of General B. C. Freyberg, VC, numbered approximately 28,000; there were also some 6,000 Greek troops on the island. Many of these had been evacuated to Crete pending transport to Egypt. Most were inadequately clothed; some had no footwear. Arms and ammunition were in short supply, and food, beer, cigarettes and tobacco were scarce.

On 19 May German aircraft were particularly active over the whole of the island. Encountering little or no opposition other than a few anti-aircraft batteries, their raids were unusually audacious.

At seven o'clock on the morning of Tuesday, 20 May, a squadron of German fighter aircraft swooped low over Maleme and sent hail after hail of bullets into the base. The troops were at action stations and there were no casualties. At seven thirty the all clear sounded and everyone prepared for breakfast. At seven forty-five the alarm sounded again, and word went round that a large force of enemy aircraft was approaching from the north. At seven fifty an air raid of devastating intensity began, lasting for over an hour.

At approximately nine o'clock bombing ceased and, under cover of fighters, paratroops began to descend in areas to the south and west of the camp. Simultaneously, gliders containing from 10 to 15 well-equipped troops also landed. The invasion of Crete had begun.

The British defensive measures against the landing of paratroops were countered by the enemy's careful timing of operations. During the initial stage, the Germans not only destroyed many of the anti-aircraft batteries but also put down such a carpet of explosives that even the stoutest men took cover. The withdrawal of bomber aircraft was timed to take place at the same time as the landing German paratroops, while fighter aircraft continued offensive action. Thus the British were slow to notice the change in tactics and for the most part remained under cover.

The enemy landings at Maleme were under the command of Major-General Meindl. His orders were to attack and capture the landing ground. Several thousand paratroopers and airborne troops were put down by low-flying aircraft and gliders and, under fighter cover, formed themselves into combat units. Major-General Meindl was wounded during the first day's fighting and was relieved by Colonel Ramcke.

Although they were numerically inferior, the enemy had equipment vastly superior to that of the British. Each man was armed with an automatic pistol, tommy-gun, rifle, bayonet, large fighting knife, several hand grenades and stick bombs, and several belts and magazines of ammunition.

A force of over 100 men occupied Maleme camp. British and Dominion troops were established to the south and east of the camp. It was therefore inevitable that the initial German advance, coming from the west, should involve the airmen. As these personnel were, for the most part, ground staff and inexperienced in frontline fighting, they were at a great disadvantage. And yet, in spite of the their overwhelming superiority, the enemy had great difficulty in overcoming resistance.

Advancing eastwards from the camp, the German paratroopers encountered a particularly stubborn New Zealand unit holding out on the top of a hill (Hill 107). The camp sick bay, containing a number of sick and wounded men, had already been captured. The enemy, with cold brutality, forced every patient who could walk to advance up the side of the hill, a paratrooper sheltering behind each one. The patients were ordered to shout to the New Zealanders to surrender. They shouted - but not to surrender. Instead they called to their comrades to shoot regardless. In the skirmish that followed, some of the wounded men got away, though many were later recaptured.

German forces in the western area soon linked up with those in the south, concentrating the full pressure of attack on the camp. To the north was the sea, so any enemy landing to the east would now result in the complete encirclement of the British. In this knowledge, the British began a withdrawal to the east, in the direction of Canea and Suda Bay.

Meanwhile, a second German force had carried out an attack on Canea and its environs, including the 7th General Hospital. At eleven o'clock on 20 May paratroops were dropped to the west of Canea, and in a matter of minutes the hospital was encircled and captured.

> 10th Parachute Company landed directly on the undefended area of 7th General Hospital and 6th Field Ambulance. Here they forced the Commander Lieutenant Colonel Plimmer to surrender, and then shot him. The also shot about twenty of the patients and forced the remainder out of bed, using them as a screen in their advance against 18th Battalion positions at Evthymi.*

It was here, after some considerable difficulty, that the first swastika was raised on the island. The paratroops who made the first attempts were sniped by British troops and several were killed.

About 20 paratroopers occupied the hospital and immediately began to sort out the staff and patients who were able to walk. They were lined up and marched off in the direction of Galatos. Some distance from the hospital, a party of New Zealanders sighted the column and immediately began to pick off the German escort. The paratroopers mingled with the bandaged patients, but a New Zealand padre, under the pretence of giving orders to

* *The Fall of Crete*, Alan Clark.

13

the prisoners, shouted to his countrymen directions for furthering their good work.

Shortly after noon, enemy reinforcements landed in the hospital area. During a second sort-out of staff and patients, several wounded Germans, who had been receiving treatment, were discovered; on reassuring their comrades that they had received good treatment, the general attitude towards the British changed for the better.

By the evening, the hospital was again in British hands, the Germans having retreated in the face of a lightning British attack. All patients, including Germans, were now moved down to some caves near the shore for safety. A quantity of food and miscellaneous equipment was also taken, and after attending to the immediate comfort of their charges, the medical staff went to pick up those wounded in the recent fighting.

Around noon on 20 May the Luftwaffe carried out a blitz on Heraklion and the local aerodrome. Shortly afterwards, a force of paratroopers under the command of Colonel Brauer landed on the outskirts of the town. The few British tanks available immediately took up position and soon a full-scale battle was in progress. During the night the British forces turned to the attack, and succeeded in forcing the enemy to retire. Very soon the Germans were fighting a second foe – thirst! Apart from the litre of water carried by each man when he landed, no other supplies were available.

Before daybreak on 21 May the whole of the Maleme area was in German hands. Two solitary British guns shelled the aerodrome from a distance of some 4 miles, but apart from pitting the landing ground with large potholes, little damage was done.

A small stone building situated on the edge of the aerodrome was taken over by Major-General Meindl as his headquarters. It was in this building that a steel chest containing British secret codes was discovered by the Germans – a discovery which later decided the fate of the island.

Late that afternoon, a number of Ju 52s put down several hundred Alpine troops, together with light armoured vehicles and guns. Under cover of falling darkness, these forces penetrated to the extreme east of the island and, with little difficulty, surrounded and captured most of the Greek troops stationed in the area.

During the morning of 22 May the two British guns fired to such effect that the enemy was unable to use the landing ground, and but for a few dozen paratroopers who landed well to the east of the camp, German aircraft had to crash-land on the beach some miles along the coast. However, information regarding the two British guns had been passed to General von Richthofen, who was responsible for air cover, and by noon a formation of Stukas set to work. One of the guns was soon silenced, but the other continued to fire for several hours. However, as fast as a shell tore a hole in the surface of the aerodrome, a party of Allied prisoners was forced, at gunpoint, to fill it in.

In spite of the continued shelling, the German High Command decided to carry out its original programme of landings, and by sunset that day 98 wrecked aircraft were strewn across the small aerodrome, together with the burnt and mangled bodies of hundreds of German troops.

When I was in a POW camp at Belaria in Germany, the chief security officer was a Sergeant-Major Ricardo Scholz. He was a surprisingly friendly soul. During one of our conversations, he surprised me by saying that he had been in the battle at Maleme. He also told me that the Germans had discovered a steel chest containing British secret codes which was sent back to Berlin. As a result of this they were able to decipher British signals, one of which stated that the British intended to evacuate the island. At that time the Germans were in a very dangerous position, losing ground in most areas, and were themselves considering withdrawing all troops from the island. Suddenly a signal was received from Berlin, telling them to stay but not to attempt to evict the British, who were getting out. This is what they did and, in due course, the British ceased sending reinforcements, while the Germans started sending more men and equipment. On 1 June they were ready to accept the British surrender.

Tommy-gun: this weapon was in fact the German Schmeisser Machine Pistol. In effect it was little better than the Thompson Sub-machine Gun, having a range of only 30 yards. In consequence it was regarded by the Allies as a tommy-gun and usually referred to as such.

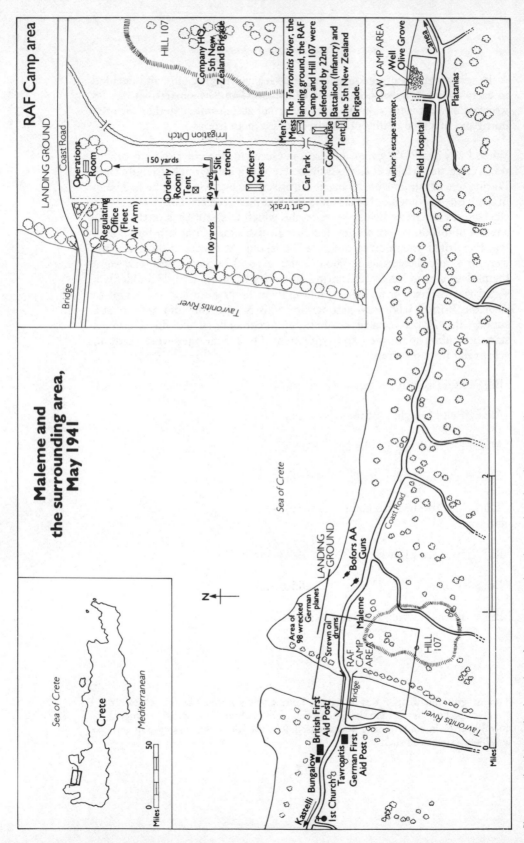

RAF Camp area

LANDING GROUND

Coast Road

Bridge

Operations Room

Regulating Office (Fleet Air Arm)

150 yards

Orderly Room Tent ⊠

40 yards

Slit trench

100 yards

Cart track

Officers' Mess ⊠⊠

Car Park

Cookhouse

Men's Mess ⊠

Tent ⊠

Irrigation Ditch

Tavronitis River

HILL 107

Company HQ 5th New Zealand Brigade

The *Tavronitis River*, the landing ground, the RAF Camp and Hill 107 were defended by 22nd Battalion (Infantry) and the 5th New Zealand Brigade.

POW CAMP AREA

Well

Olive Grove

Canea

Author's escape attempt

Field Hospital

Platanias

Maleme and the surrounding area, May 1941

N

Sea of Crete

Mediterranean

Crete

0   50

Miles

LANDING GROUND

Bofors AA Guns

Area of 98 wrecked German planes

Strewn oil drums

RAF CAMP AREA

Maleme

HILL 107

Bridge

Tavronitis River

Coast Road

Kastelli Bungalow

British First Aid Post

1st Church

Tavrogitis

German First Aid Post

0   Miles   1   2   3

Please note that this map has been drawn from memory and is only a rough guide to the events in the text.

List of Main Characters

Bill Austin ('Bunny') – Squadron Stores Accountant – 24

Albert Bell ('Dingle') – Stores Assistant – about 22

Albert Bond ('Lofty') – Aircraft Hand – 26

George Burwell ('Scruffy') – Aircraft Hand – about 26

'Darky' Dear (christian name not known) – Squadron Cook – age not known

R. J. Lawrence ('Lawrie') – Stores Clerk – about 24

Ernest Walker ('Mike/Micky') – Confidential clerk to CO – 34

Bill Williams – Fitter/Blacksmith – about 30

1

Surrounded

Inside the trench, conditions were grim. It was overcrowded, the air was hot and foul, and it was so dark we could see little more than the dim outlines of each other.

'I've had enough of this dump,' said Lawrie.

'We've all had enough,' I told him, wiping perspiration from my face. 'It's been the longest raid ever.'

He glanced impatiently at his watch. 'Half eight and no breakfast!' With a sigh, he moved nearer the entrance and looked outside.

I brought out a packet of cigarettes, then turned to Bill Williams.

'Smoke?'

'Thanks, Mike,' he said, producing his lighter. 'Nasty habit, smoking before breakfast.'

'So is no breakfast,' I replied, holding my cigarette against the flame. 'Have you no work to do?'

'Since they flew the kites to Egypt, no one has any work,' he said with some bitterness.

I nodded. I knew just how he was feeling. Less than a month ago, we'd been thrown out of Greece by the Germans. Officialdom had explained away the defeat easily enough, but we hadn't been convinced.

Now we were in Crete. Here, we were told, we would make our real stand against the Nazis; the defeat in Greece would be avenged. With more hope than faith, we watched, and helped, the island prepare for battle. Troops moved in by the thousand, anti-aircraft batteries sprang up like miniature forests, landing grounds were prepared, and all available aircraft were flown in. Here at Maleme, the most important landing ground on the island, was based our own squadron, No. 30, together with flights of Hurricanes and Fulmers from other units. Our confidence began to return; perhaps we *would* be able to avenge our defeat.

One day, to a trumpet accompaniment, it was announced on the radio that 'the island was to be defended to the last man!' Our reawakened faith immediately began to wilt. Simple souls though we were, we instinctively knew that neither wars nor battles were won by such wasteful tactics. Some of us were self-centred enough to wonder who that last man would be!

Our scepticism was amply justified. Just as preparations were supposedly nearing completion, nearly all our aircraft were ordered to Egypt, and most of our anti-aircraft defences withdrawn. But that was not all: officers and also men holding key positions were evacuated, there was an immediate shortage of food, communications began to break down and suddenly no one knew what he was supposed to be doing. It was now 20 May and except for two wrecked fighters, Maleme was deserted of all aircraft.

Here inside the trench I was suddenly reminded that there were plenty of aircraft *over* the landing ground. A series of high-pitched whistles heralded the imminent arrival of another stick of bombs. One of them landed nearby with a shattering explosion.

'Near one!' Lawrie exclaimed gleefully.

'I wish you'd keep under cover,' I said shortly. 'You'll get your head blown off.'

But I might as well have saved my breath. As soon as the smoke and dust cleared away, he was back round the corner of the trench again.

'That's the worst of the fearless types,' Bill said, wiping bomb dust from his face. 'They never know when to be careful.'

Glancing along the trench, I counted six other figures. No wonder we were overcrowded: the trench was built for five – now it held nine!

Presently there was a brief lull in the bombing. We edged out along the short top limb of our Z-shaped trench.

'Think it's over now?' asked Tom Yeomans hopefully, blinking in the hot sunlight.

'No, I don't.' Bill told him. 'Beat it back inside. When you're a bit older, you'll learn to appreciate a really good trench,' he added with emphasis.

I stood on my toes and glanced around. A little below us – our trench was situated on the side of a hill – I could see a dusty track which skirted the lower part of the camp and led to our landing ground. Down there in the camp was the air-raid bell. How soon before someone used it to give us the all clear?

My hopes were scotched by a sudden roar of aircraft and we ducked back into the trench. A moment later machine-gun and cannon fire told us that enemy fighters were back over the camp, strafing.

'What kind of raid *is* this?' Lawrie demanded with a puzzled frown. 'First it's fighters, then bombers, now it's fighters again!'

When the fighters had got rid of their ammunition, the bombers returned. A bomb from one of the first sticks dropped screamed down and landed close by. The earth gave a violent lurch, our trench rocked and the world went black.

While we were still picking ourselves up, Lawrie crept outside to survey the damage. The earth steps had collapsed and within a yard of the entrance to our covered trench was the rim of a 20-foot wide crater. We passed a message along asking how things were at Lofty's end. The steps at his entrance had also collapsed, but otherwise everything was all right.

'That should get you to keep your bloody head inside,' Bill said, looking at Lawrie's dirt-smeared face as he crawled back inside.

'It was rather close,' he admitted reluctantly.

'Too close!' I said.

For a time no one spoke. They all knew it was true. I tried to plot the course of the aircraft by the sound they made, but there were so many of them, I didn't have much success. Presently they began to thin out and the thundering roar gradually died away.

'I'll take another peep outside,' Lawrie said.

'Why not wait until the all clear?' I asked. 'You'll only get your nut blown off if you're not more careful.'

'Well, there's nothing directly overhead,' he said. 'But ...'

'But nothing,' I insisted. 'Sit down and exercise a little patience.'

For a brief moment Lawrie stared at me, pouting. Then, with a petulant shrug, he began moving towards the entrance. Had he stuck his tongue out at me, then said 'Shan't!' I wouldn't have been in the least surprised.

But I *was* surprised at his frantic next move. Before he'd taken three paces, he suddenly ducked down, then shot violently back into the safety of our trench.

'Germans!' he whispered. 'They're in the camp!'

I scrambled to my feet. 'Rot!' I said. 'Move over and let me look.' I pushed Lawrie to one side. He was right. Less than a 100 paces away, camouflaged and wearing dome-shaped helmets, were the enemy. They were moving up from the cart track at the bottom of the hill and were heading towards trees over by the landing ground. I stepped back, and as I did so, Bill pushed by me to have a look.

'Now what?' asked Lawrie in a strained voice. Almost as an afterthought, he added, 'Where d'you think they came from?'

'God knows,' I replied, taking a deep breath. 'But we better tell the others.' As I spoke we heard the crack of a rifle, and the tell-tale whine of a bullet as it passed.

Bill darted back inside the trench. 'To hell with this,' he said. 'I'm getting out of it.' Grabbing his battered rifle, he began to push his way to Lofty's end of the trench.

To step blindly out into the open seemed the height of stupidity. Quite

21

apart from inviting fire from any Germans in the vicinity, it would also give our position away.

'Don't be a fool!' I growled, trying to grab his right arm. But Bill rushed on, stumbling over bodies and legs as he forced his way along.

No one at the other end of our trench knew what was happening, but when Bill suddenly appeared in a blind panic, Lofty guessed that something was badly amiss and tried to block him. Again Bill dragged himself free, and in a moment was out of the trench.

'Stupid sod!' Lofty exclaimed angrily. 'He'll never bloody make it.'

Within seconds, we heard the chatter of a machine-gun. We didn't see him fall, but all knew that he had.

For a second there was silence. No one trusted himself to speak. We'd had fatalities in 30 Squadron before – aircraft had failed to return, crew had been brought back wounded or dead – but this was different; it was too sudden, too violent and too intimate.

Then I found myself angry. Why had be panicked? Bill, of all people! He wasn't a child. Not only was he the second-oldest man in the trench but he had served longer in the RAF than the rest of us. And where had he intended going? Certainly not to another trench.

A sudden outbreak of firing brought my mind back to the Germans – the enemy we'd been told was still in the south of Greece! Judging by the noise, they were already overrunning the camp. Lofty and Lawrie were on guard at each end, and between them they kept up a rather fearful running commentary. It was not long before we knew we were completely surrounded.

Just as suddenly as it had started, the firing died away. The quietness took the edge off my fear, and I slid back down the earth wall of the trench, until I came to rest on Lawrie's tin hat. Where had the Germans come from? How had they landed? What was their objective? The questions kept going round and round inside my head. We'd all heard rumours that the Germans were massing men and aircraft in Greece, but none of us had taken much notice – rumours were ten a penny. Now it looked as if they'd arrived. But how had they got here? Hell, they were walking about inside our camp! Then I remembered how close we were to the sea; a five-minute walk from the landing ground would take us to the water's edge. Was that the answer – a seaborne invasion?

I glanced up at Lawrie. He was leaning against the front wall of the trench, peering intently towards the entrance.

'Can you see anything?' I asked.

He shook his head. 'I think I'll crawl up to the steps. You can't see much from here.' Getting down on his hands and knees, he began to edge forward.

'Better be careful,' I said. 'There'll be more of the bastards about.'

Feeling afraid I stood up and watched him. He reached the collapsed steps, then slowly raised his head until he could see out of the trench. He beckoned me to follow him. Great! Bending low, I shuffled along cautiously until I was at his side.

'What is it?' I whispered, rising to my feet.

He didn't answer – there was no need. Just over the top of the trees near the landing ground, I saw hundreds and hundreds of parachutes descending. And attached to each was a small, dark figure. Paratroopers! The blood froze in my veins. We'd all heard about Hitler's paratroopers – his butcher élite. Rumour said they were as much at home with an open razor or a length of piano wire as they were with a gun or hand grenade. To be killed by one of them would be a painful and hideous experience.

Suddenly I wanted to close my eyes, crawl back into the trench and hide. I was horribly scared, but I was also fascinated. I'd never seen anything like this before. The sky was filled with them: pink parachutes (officers), black parachutes (other ranks), white parachutes (carrying weapons, arms and ammunition), and yellow parachutes (carrying medical supplies). And they were floating down to earth as innocently as soap bubbles.

Standing next to Lawrie, I watched parachutes drifting slowly out of sight behind the trees. So this is it, I thought. The real meaning of war loomed into my mind, and with it came the sick realization that it was not only other people who got mixed up in fighting ...

As the sky emptied, danger seemed to recede and I was no longer so scared. They're not supermen, I assured myself; they might be well trained and well armed but, like me, they must have their limitations.

Suddenly I was scared all over again. Like me ... Which one of them had only an old revolver and six rounds of ammunition?

2
Plans for Escape

The desultory firing which had been going on all around us for the last half-hour gradually died out. We heard voices – harsh, guttural voices – and the sound of wheels moving along the cart track at the bottom of the hill. Then silence.

Since the moment we'd known the Germans had invaded the camp, not a man in the trench had spoken a word about our precarious position. Doubtless each of us had thought a great deal about it, yet we all seemed content to accept the situation. Everyone had been very quiet – and perhaps very afraid. For most of us, this was our first close contact with the enemy, and everything had happened so quickly that we were at a loss about what to do. Still, it was high time someone decided on a course of action. If the Germans discovered our trench, we would be wiped out without the chance of a fight.

As I was pondering the situation, I suddenly realized why no one wanted to discuss it. Bill Williams! He was uppermost in my mind and I could be quite sure he was still uppermost in the minds of the others.

I tried to reason things out. When Bill first saw the Germans, he had immediately assumed that we were in danger of being surrounded. Naturally enough, he had wanted to break out before the ring closed. His mistake, though, had been in trying to run the gauntlet; he should have used stealth and cunning.

Well, presumably he was now dead, but we couldn't let that scare us into inaction. Rather, we should treat it as a lesson. I was beginning to understand the value of the old adage: 'United we stand ...'

United! That could hold for the 100 men in the squadron scattered through the camp. If we were united, something might be done about the Germans. Still, there seemed little chance of that now; there were very few covered-in trenches in the camp and it seemed obvious that the men in open trenches would have seen the paratroopers the moment they landed and retreated to safety. I heartily cursed myself then for having suggested to Lawrie that we put a roof on the trench. It may have saved us during the air raids, but now we were trapped.

Well, there was no point grumbling. The thing to do was to try and work out a plan of campaign. First, consider our position. The camp itself was on the lower slopes of a sparsely wooded hill designated Hill 107 which ran at right angles to the landing ground and overlooked a broad but shallow river. A little way up the hill was a 12-foot-wide irrigation ditch which wound its way gently through the lower part of the camp, and joined up with the river. At the bottom of the hill was the cart track, which led from the road by the landing ground to a small hamlet a couple of miles further up the river.

Our trench was in open ground, lying between the cart track and the irrigation ditch. The river, like the landing ground to the north, was hidden from our view by clumps of trees and the only covering for at least 100 yards was a small stone building, the one time Naval Regulating Office, now the Officers' Mess which was down by the cart track.

We had already seen or heard paratroopers all around us, and it appeared that they were fanning out into the whole camp area. Also it was likely that the Naval Regulating Office would by now have been captured and turned into a miniature fortress, blocking any attempt at movement during daylight.

So, that was the position. Now what about a plan of campaign? I already knew that between us we possessed only four rifles and a single revolver. There seemed but one answer: a furtive escape through the German lines. However, I didn't feel very happy about this. It seemed ignominious to think about escape before we'd even tried fighting, and in any case, where were we going to escape to? And how could we hope to remain undiscovered until nightfall? And how could we hope to fight unless we were all properly armed?

With a sigh I looked up at Lawrie, who was peering towards the entrance. Then I realized he was trying to attract my attention with his foot.

'What is it?' I whispered. I leaned over until I could look along the short limb of the trench. Then I heard dull footsteps, and a moment later I saw the lower part of the body of a paratrooper as he jumped lightly across the trench. I held my breath and the footsteps receded. Then there was a rustle, and I saw a length of rope being dragged across the trench. Suddenly it stopped, slipped back and formed a loop on the ground, less than 6 feet from where I was seated. There was a splash from the direction of the irrigation ditch and the rope began to move again, stretching taut across the trench. Then, with a swish, its tail-end whisked by.

25

Lawrie turned to me. 'Phew!' he whispered. 'I thought that was going to be the end of us.'

With a thumping heart I got to my feet. The irrigation ditch! That was it; that was how we would escape!

The idea had entered my mind a few moments before I heard the splash of the paratrooper entering the water. I knew that he would have to cross the ditch if he intended going up the hill, and I wondered whether the sluice gates were open and the ditch empty. In my mind's eye, I had visualized the German climbing over the low ramp and dropping down the steep sides into the ditch. The question was, would there be the tell-tale splash? There was. That meant the gates were closed. I offered up a silent prayer that they would remain so, then I settled down to work out the details.

First, though, I had to do something about the Squadron Operational Diary, which was folded and tucked away in one of my shirt pockets. Since being given the responsibility for maintaining the diary, I had been at a loss what to do with it. It had been given into my safekeeping several days before the last of our aircraft left for Egypt and although not many entries had been made, I was apprehensive about its safety. It contained duplicate pages of previous entries and would have been useful to an enemy, but there was nowhere safe to deposit it; the codes and cipher iron chest, where it was usually kept, had already been evacuated by the Cipher Officer, Flying Officer Speight, when he removed himself and the iron chest to Egypt. Ever since I had carried the diary with me. My first thought was to burn it, but I soon realized it would make too much smoke, so I decided to tear it into small pieces and bury them in the trench wall. I told Lawrie of my intention and he helped me excavate several deep holes in the sandy walls. I tore up the diary into tiny pieces, then inserted small piles of them into the holes. I have a huge sigh of relief when the task was done.

If we could hang out until dark, we could make our way to the ditch, slip quietly into the water and in less than half an hour be down at the river junction. From there it was only 1 mile to the sea. Once we reached the sea, there were all kinds of possibilities.

Some of the men were young and inexperienced, so I thought it would be better for us to go in pairs. We would have to make sure that one in each pair was armed. Our greatest difficulty was going to be remaining undiscovered. I glanced at my watch and almost groaned. It was barely ten in the morning and it wouldn't be sufficiently dark until nine at night. How could we possibly hope to hang out for 11 hours? We had no food or water, and it would get very hot later on.

A flash of light made me look along the trench and I saw that two men were lighting cigarettes. That decided me. I nudged Lawrie. 'Anything happening out there?'

He turned his head. 'No. Everything's quiet at present.'

I sent a message along to Lofty asking how things were at his end. Presently the answer came back: all quiet.

'I'm going to have a few words with the chaps about our position,' I told Lawrie. 'I've one or two ideas about getting away from here.'

He raised his eyebrows but said nothing.

'And I'm getting worried about the smoking. It'll give our position away if there are any Jerries about.'

He eyed me rather whimsically. 'You'll be lucky if you can stop them smoking,' he said.

With a shrug, I turned and looked along the length of the trench. At the far end I could make out the tall, lean figure of Lofty. With the advent of the paratroops, he'd assumed guard at his entrance to the trench and every few minutes he poked his head outside to see how things were. Next to him was a New Zealander, a rather quiet type of man, with the stub end of a cigarette between his lips. He and the Aussie who stood next to him were the only soldiers in the trench and until that morning had been complete strangers to me. The Aussie had propped his rifle up against the earth wall in front of him and his hands were deep in his tunic pockets. Little 'Dingle' Bell, pale and unsmiling, was squatting on the ground next to him. He wanted to stand up but there wasn't sufficient room, and every time the Aussie moved he knocked Dingle's tin hat askew. In the end he took it off and sat on it. 'Scruffy' Burwell, who was also rather short, squatted next to him. For his age – he was in his early twenties – he was somewhat hard-boiled, and boasted that he'd never been scared in his life. I didn't find it hard to believe! Tom Yeomans, the youngest man in the trench, was next to him. He was tall, quiet and sensible beyond his years. Now he was leaning against the wall, lost in thought.

I nudged Tom. 'Try and find room to sit down,' I said. 'I want everyone to hear what I say.' He raised his head in surprise, then sank down on his haunches.

I had decided what I wanted to say. The first matter concerned smoking, but suddenly I began to feel rather nervous. Would they stop smoking if I told them to or would they quietly ignore me? I glanced at Lawrie and our eyes met. 'It's still quiet out there,' he said. I took the hint.

'Listen, you chaps,' I started. 'I don't know what you think of things, but to me they seem pretty bloody.'

'Says you!' commented someone at the far end of the trench. The voice seemed unfriendly. Again I looked at Lawrie, who gave me a cold smile. I changed tack; maybe I could mention smoking at the end of my little piece, rather than the beginning.

'I've been trying to work things out. We seem to be surrounded by Jerries and I don't think we stand much chance of fighting it out with them with the few guns we have.' There was a murmur of agreement. 'This is what I have in mind,' I continued. 'If we can hold out until dark, we can sneak across to the irrigation ditch. If it's still full of water, we can float quietly through the camp down to the river. If we make that safely, we can drift or swim down to the sea – it's less than a mile. Once we're there, we can scout around and find a boat, then push off up the coast. We shouldn't have far to go before we meet up with some of our own people.'

I paused to give time for the idea to sink in. No one spoke, so I carried on. 'I think we ought to split up into pairs.' I suggested. 'Those of you who are young should join up with someone older.'

Lawrie turned his head. 'Dingle and I will pair off,' he said. 'We work together so we better keep together.'

'Right,' I said. 'And I'll take Tom.' Tom nodded his approval.

From the far end of the trench came Lofty's voice. 'Put Scruffy Burwell and me together,' he said. 'He's just about my weight.'

'All right,' I replied.'That means Aussie and Kiwi travel together. That OK with you two?'

'Yeh!' replied Aussie. 'We'll be OK.'

'Well, that's settled,' I said with some satisfaction. Things were going better than I'd hoped. The next point to decide was who should go first and who last. I didn't know whether to offer to go first myself. If it was more dangerous, then as the originator of the scheme, I should go. But was it more dangerous? What about the last pair to leave? Uncertain, I broached the subject.

'Who's to leave the trench first?' I had almost expected a debate to follow, but instead there was a long silence. I shrugged my shoulders. I would have to go first. But before I could say anything. Lawrie spoke.

'Dingle and I'll go first if no one else wants to.'

'And Scruffy and me'll go last,' said Lofty.

So I didn't have to offer to go after all! I suddenly felt humiliated. Had Lawrie realized that I was afraid? For a moment I almost hated him. Damn you, I thought, you're not going to be a martyr at my expense; I *will* go first.

'I think you had better let Tom and me go,' I said, somewhat airily. 'You and Dingle can follow if you like.'

He turned and fixed me with his blue eyes. 'If you really want to go, it's OK with me.'

'I do,' I said shortly.

I turned and looked down at Tom. 'You don't mind, do you?' I asked, and he shook his head. I took a deep breath, then glanced back at Lawrie.

He shrugged his shoulders and smiled. 'I don't suppose it makes much difference whether you go first or last. If the Jerries see us, we'll get it anyway!'

I had a sudden craving for a cigarette, and it reminded me that I had to say something about smoking.

'There are one or two other points we had better settle,' I said. Everyone continued to listen attentively. 'I suppose it will be hard to stop smoking, but we'll have to do something about it. The smoke drifts out of the trench and it'll give our position away.' I paused for comments but there were none. 'The best thing is to arrange that no two men smoke at the same time. When someone does smoke, he'll have to do it very carefully – only have two or three draws, then put the cigarette out. Do you all agree?'

There were three distinct grunts, presumably from the only other men in the trench beside myself who smoked. But there was no arguing.

'Then there's the matter of food and drink,' I continued. 'I've had a parcel from home – I've got some of it here.' Feeling in my tunic pocket, I brought out a small tin and two paper tubes. 'I have some Ovaltine tablets and thirst quenchers. We'll be glad of the quenchers during the day, but we'd better keep the tablets until tonight. I'll dole them out before we leave.'

I slipped the tin back into my pocket, then opened the tubes and shared out their contents: three quenchers to each man.

'What happens if we want a riddle?' someone at the far end of the trench asked.

'Use your hat,' I replied. Then I sat down and tried to work out what we would do if the Germans opened the sluice gates and let all the water out of the irrigation ditch.

3
Surrender

At about noon Lawrie asked me to take over watch. After thrusting the large revolver into my hand, he slumped down to the bottom of the trench, dead beat. I rested myself against the front wall of the trench, like Lawrie keeping my head to one side so that I could get a good view of the entrance and its immediate vicinity without exposing myself.

Over by the landing ground I could see the trees waving gently in the breeze. Everything seemed quiet and peaceful. It was hard to realize there was a war on and that we were in the middle of it. Then I began to wonder why things were so quiet. Had the Germans left?

I shuffled carefully round the corner of the trench and listened. Still no sounds of war. I moved towards the entrance and peered over towards the cart track. No sign of anyone there. I turned and looked up the hill. The ramp of the irrigation ditch cut off the view of the lower part of the hill, but further up I saw smoke rising, as if the undergrowth were on fire. Then I heard footsteps, so I ducked back into the trench.

A few minutes later I heard the sound of firing coming from the main part of the camp, further up the hill. Most of it was small-arms fire but the occasional crack of a hand grenade added to the noise. Then came the blast of a whistle and the firing suddenly ceased. A moment later the voice of someone shouting in English reached us. 'Hallo. Hallo, Tommy! Why don't you surrender, Tommy? We have you surrounded.'

The atmosphere inside the trench was tense. Had we been discovered? I turned quickly and looked at Lawrie. Then I shook my head. A moment's reflection convinced me that we were still safe; the voice had been too far away. As if to confirm my conviction, we heard an answering shout. It was an invitation to the Germans – in true service parlance – to go away and play. There was a loud cheer, then firing broke out again.

All was quiet except for the occasional distant firing. In time even that ceased. The sun had worked its way round and was now lighting up the dark patch of trees by the landing ground. I strained my eyes, but there were no lurking paratroopers to be seen.

Then I heard voices and footsteps. The sounds came so suddenly that I gave a start. I backed further into the trench and brought the revolver up in front of me. The footsteps drew closer. I put my right foot out behind me and gave Lawrie a light kick. He understood and passed word along to the others to keep quiet. Holding my face close to the wall, I moved slowly along until I could see the entrance. My heart missed a beat and I quickly drew back. A few feet from the entrance were two paratroopers, both looking down into the trench. For a moment I listened intently, hoping that I hadn't been seen. The Germans were talking but seemed to be making no effort to enter the trench. I judged that we were still safe.

My mind began racing. I had no doubt that they'd try to enter the trench and already I was deciding how to kill them with the minimum of danger to ourselves, and how to dispose of their bodies. What of the noise, though? The revolver would make an enormous row! I began to wonder whether killing them would be quite so easy. What if I succeeded only in wounding them? I'd never have the heart to shoot them a second time.

Again I peered towards the entrance. Perhaps they wouldn't try to enter after all. I got a snapshot view of them and saw that they'd moved closer. They seemed to be having a quiet discussion. What about? I tried to put myself in their shoes. Booty? The dangers of deserted enemy trenches? That was it – they were wondering whether it contained a booby trap!

Pressing close against the wall, I moved my head so that I could keep half the short limb of the trench in view. Then I waited. They would have to enter singly, so I would allow the first to come along until he was within a yard of the centre section, then I would shoot him. As he fell, I would take a quick pace forward and fire at his comrade. With these thoughts in mind, I raised the revolver until it was at heart level.

While I waited, my conscience began to trouble me. I found that I didn't want to kill the second German, but there seemed no alternative; if he turned and ran when he heard the shot and I didn't do something about it, he would fetch reinforcements. I smothered a sigh. This was going to be something that would give me nightmares for the rest of my life!

Suddenly the trench darkened. I drew a deep breath and strained my eyes to stop them from blinking. The first paratrooper was making his way awkwardly down the steep incline into the trench. Apparently his equipment impeded his progress and I could hear him wriggling his way along noisily.

When he was half-way he got stuck. There was a coarse laugh and his comrade shouted words of encouragement. Freeing himself, he started to move forward again.

I glanced along the barrel to make sure that it was level, wondering at the same time whether I ought to aim at his left breast or at the middle of his chest. I decided on his chest. Then his comrade shouted again, this time in urgent tones and the man stopped moving. I could feel beads of perspiration breaking out on my head and face, and every muscle in my body was taut. The man I was about to kill was less than 2 yards away.

The paratroopers appeared to be holding another discussion. From their tones it was obvious that the man outside the trench had suddenly developed cold feet and was trying to dissuade his comrade from going any further. For a few moments they argued – and I prayed! Then caution prevailed. The paratrooper tried to turn and retrace his steps but again got stuck. Breathing heavily and muttering to himself, he finally succeeded in getting free. This time he didn't attempt to turn round but lurched out of the trench backwards.

The sound of receding footsteps told us that our immediate danger was over. I gave a sigh and, lowering my right arm, noticed that it was shaking violently. A moment later I was trembling from head to foot.

Lawrie got to his feet and relieved me of the revolver. 'Better sit down,' he said. 'I'll take over for a while.'

The hours dragged slowly by. It was now after five o'clock and although the sun had lost much of its heat, the trench was like a miniature inferno. Much of the time had been spent discussing our position and our plans for escape. And what had happened to the rest of the squadron? Had they fought it out with the Germans – and lost? Or had they made good their escape? We went round and round in circles, trying to guess what orders we would have received had the powers that be been in a position to give orders! Would they have told us to fight to the last man?

Now we were all huddled uncomfortably close together on the sandy floor, sweating and completely exhausted. We no longer talked, but each man had his thoughts, and the focal point of each mind was zero hour: nine o'clock. While there had still been several hours to wait, nine o'clock had been sufficiently remote to cause us feelings of apprehensive impatience. Now it was less than four hours away, it was beginning to take on a new significance. Only four more hours to remain in hiding; only four more hours of this insufferable heat. Yes, we could comprehend the exact length of four hours. Nine o'clock was sufficiently close to bring an almost exhilarating stab of fear to our hearts.

I looked along the length of the trench. Tom had keeled over and was leaning heavily against my left side. Through the earthy darkness I could see the outlines of the others. Dingle was huddled up, chin on knees, hands clutching at ankles. Scruffy, no longer perky, lay on his side with his legs drawn up. The Aussie was laid out almost flat, his head and shoulders resting against Scruffy's ribs, his feet reaching to where Lofty stood. Kiwi, his back to the Aussie, was resting on one foot and one knee, and he and Lofty were talking quietly together. Every few minutes, Lofty would peep outside to see whether anything was happening; he had been checking all day long and had refused relief.

The minutes ticked slowly by. The sun was already sinking low towards the horizon and the sky had begun to grow red. In the distance could be heard the drone of an aircraft. The sound grew closer and was soon overhead. Lofty crept out to identify it; it was a reconnaissance aircraft flying so low he could see the pilot.

The air in the trench was getting damp and chilly, and spirits were rather low. One by one we rose awkwardly to our feet, cold, stiff and very grimy. Brushing loose earth from our clothes, we somehow contrived to make ourselves tidy.

I felt in my pocket and brought out the tin of Ovaltine tablets. After issuing each man his share, I ate my own and advised the others to do likewise; we were going to need every ounce of energy we could muster when we left the trench.

I looked at my watch: one hour and five minutes to go. I leaned back against the wall of the trench and closed my eyes. Outside the sun was setting. My imagination painted a picture of a sunset at home: a large fiery orb, balanced on the very rim of the earth, set in a sky of crimson and gold. For a moment I forgot all about the dark, foul-smelling trench, and my fears and discomfort; I was at home, happy and contented. Then the colours faded and the picture slowly dissolved, leaving me in darkness. The sound of explosions broke in on my train of thought and I stood upright.

'What's going on out there?' I asked Lawrie.

'I don't know,' he replied, looking down towards the entrance. 'It doesn't sound too good to me.'

I knew that we were all getting rather het up, so I tried to dismiss the matter from my mind. In any case, we had been hearing explosions of one kind or another all day. For want of anything better to do, I began to go through my pockets. Two unopened packets of cigarettes; I put one in each of my shirt pockets, where they might keep dry there. A half-empty packet, together with a box of matches; these I left in my tunic pocket. My keys, wallet, sun glasses, fountain pen, knife; all in their proper places. I decided that the matches would be better in a breast pocket and was in the act of transferring them when I heard Lofty cry out. His voice was loud and urgent, and its effect almost paralysing.

'Look out, boys! Look out. Here they come!'

There was a sudden ear-shattering chain of explosions, and the trench was immediately filled with flying earth and smoke. Everyone surged to our end of the trench. As they did so, there was another burst of fire.

'For Christ's sake do something,' Lofty shouted wildly. 'They nearly got me that time!'

There was another surge of bodies, and Lawrie and I were squeezed into the corner of the trench. The noise and panic made it hard to think clearly, and the sudden pressure against my ribs winded me. I started to wriggle clear and force a way into the short limb of the trench. When I was free, I stood on my toes and looked around the corner – just in time to see the results of another burst of fire: the wall at Lofty's end was caving in and the roof was about to collapse. Then everything was hidden by smoke and dust.

My mind raced. What had happened, and what were we to do? The answer to the first question came like a flash. The Germans were mopping up the area and had come across our trench. The previous explosions had been hand grenades; now, for some unknown reason, they were using their tommy-guns. So much for that. But what were we going to do about it?

My mind raced on. Grab the revolver from Lawrie and open fire on the Germans from this end of the trench. But wouldn't they know there was a second entrance? Of course they would, and any minute now they would be attacking us through it. Well, there must be something we could do! For a moment I could think of nothing; we seemed trapped. I began cursing myself for devising a plan which had kept us in such a dangerous position for so long – I must have been mad. But because it was my plan, I had to do something, and do it quickly.

The Germans were now keeping up an almost constant stream of fire, and soon Lawrie and Tom were forced out of the centre section into the short limb.

'We've got to do something,' Lawrie shouted above the din. 'We can't last much longer.'

I nodded anxiously. It was impossible to fight from Lofty's end because it was under concentrated fire, and at any moment the Germans might start using hand grenades. I turned and looked at our own entrance. Why weren't they attacking us through it? Was it because they thought it was a dug-out with only one entrance? Whatever the reason, this was our only chance.

Suddenly Scruffy Burwell and Dingle appeared in the short limb, and I saw that the rest were now crowding into the corner directly facing the entrance. One short burst of tommy-gun fire would mow all eight of us down! Dare we start fighting now from this end of the trench? It would be suicide, but there was no alternative – except surrender.

I almost gasped at the word. We couldn't surrender! We must fight it out! But how? Then I heard a violent explosion. It shook the trench and earth from the roof started to fall in on us.

'A hand grenade!' Lawrie shouted.

That decided me. We just couldn't fight; we couldn't even move! Then I remembered; paratroopers don't take prisoners. But it was already too late. Another hand grenade exploded and the trench began caving in.

There was a brief lull in the confusion of noises. That was my chance. 'All right, chaps,' I shouted loudly. 'We've got to surrender. Follow me and do as I do.' Without waiting to see their reaction, I turned and walked to the entrance. Then I raised my hands high above my head and staggered out of the trench, into the open.

4
Suspended Sentence

As I lurched awkwardly up the crumbled steps, I suddenly felt an almost overpowering urge to run – I suppose it was the instinct of preservation asserting itself. Somehow, though, my legs refused to move any quicker and I continued in what seemed like slow motion.

At last I stood on open ground and paused. The firing had ceased and everything was very quiet. For a brief moment I experienced a deep and morbid sense of loneliness – I was alone in the world, facing some indefinable horror; time stood still, and I was lost.

Then I was convulsed with a violent shudder, and returned to the world I knew. I was conscious of a feeling of coldness in my back. With that sensation came the knowledge that a dozen tommy-guns were pointed at me. I remained motionless, my arms still above my head. The approaching twilight made everything but the sky dark, and all about me was very still. I was almost afraid to move, to break the spell of this strange silence.

Out of the corner of my eye I caught the dull flash of moving steel. My head followed the direction of my eyes: a few feet away a paratrooper was fingering his tommy-gun menacingly. Beyond him, and forming a semicircle around the trench, there were ten Germans, each holding his tommy-gun or rifle ready for action.

Impelled by some unknown force, I started walking very slowly towards the furthest German. His comrades, curious, watched me, all the time keeping me covered. When I was within a yard of the him, I stopped. For a moment our eyes met, then I lowered my head abjectly. The fact that I had not been shot down as I emerged from the trench had encouraged me to believe that paratroopers were, after all, human, but apart from shape, there seemed little human about this specimen. He was of medium height, thick-set, with the face of a pockmarked ferret, and he had the most evil eyes I'd ever seen. He greeted me with a savage scowl and, as I lowered my head, gave me a violent blow on the side of the face with the barrel of his tommy-gun.

I closed my eyes. So this was the price of surrender!

There was a disturbance behind me and I instinctively turned my head, anxious to know if everyone had left the trench. The movement was cut short as the muzzle of the paratrooper's tommy-gun was pushed roughly against my stomach. I drooped forward, my aching arms sagging low over my head.

I heard footsteps and heavy breathing, then sensed that someone was standing next to me. I glanced furtively to the right and saw that it was Tom. With an angry shout, the German stepped forward.

'*Schweinhund*!' he bellowed. Drawing back his hand, he gave me a resounding smack on the cheek. The blow sent me reeling. As I regained my balance, I gave him a withering look.

'You bastard!' I spat out the words, caring little whether he understood or not. But I had been able to see that all eight of us were present.

We were formed into a line, about 2 feet apart and with a paratrooper standing guard over each of us. A small *Unteroffizier* (corporal) was in charge, and after shouting some words of instructions to two paratroopers over by the trench, he strutted along the line in my direction.

'*So!*' he said, coming to a halt in front of me. '*So*, we haf *der Englishcher flieger, ja*?'

I shrugged my shoulders. I didn't know what he was talking about and just glared at him, insolently.

The *Unteroffizier*, his feet well apart and hands on hips, smiled pleasantly. The smile almost warmed my heart and I suppose my face lost some of its sullenness; he didn't seem the type who would knock prisoners about. For a moment we looked at each other. He had a young and very dirty face and his helmet was pushed to the back of his head. His tommy-gun was slung over his shoulder and around his neck were draped two long belts of ammunition.

Suddenly he moved closer to me and without a word started going through my pockets. At first I gaped in surprise. Then I realized there was nothing very extraordinary about being searched; it was an elementary pre-caution – I might be armed. Almost the first thing he found was my wallet. He flicked it open and peered at the photograph of my wife.

'Is dis your *frau*?' he asked.

'It's my wife,' I said quietly.

He nodded and, after another glance at the photograph, closed the wallet and slipped it into one of the large pockets of his smock-like tunic.

I opened my mouth to speak, then thought better of it. Obviously he was no better than his underling and would bash me over the head as soon as look at me. One by one my possessions were transferred to the same voluminous pocket, but when the half-empty packet of cigarettes was dragged out, I could keep quiet no longer. Sun-glasses, fountain pens and wallets were perhaps fair booty, but when it came to cigarettes ...

'Do you usually take cigarettes from prisoners?' I asked contemptuously.

He looked up in surprise. I don't think he had fully understood, but he knew it was to do with the cigarettes. For a moment he hesitated, and I thought he was going to return them. Then he deliberately added them to the rest of my things. 'You vil not *zigaretten* need vair you go,' he said grimly, and continued the search.

As the cigarettes vanished from sight, my feelings of contempt turned to anger. You miserable little sawn-off runt, I thought. You're the kind of rat who'd rob the dead! By the time he had finished with me and moved along to Tom, I was in a really fine rage. Slowly, though, my anger began to subside, and, as my mind grew calm, I found myself trying to remember the exact words the *Unteroffizier* had used when he had taken the cigarettes. He had said something about not needing cigarettes where we were going – yes, that was it. Then the implication hit me right between the eyes.

For a moment I was in a panic. 'Christ!' I exclaimed aloud. 'Did he really mean that?'

Ferret Face waved his gun. '*Ruhig*! – Quiet!' he snapped.

I eyed him malevolently, then looked around for some means of escape. If we were going to be shot, it was almost worthwhile making a dash for it; it was better than standing still and letting them shoot. But that tommy-gun was pointed straight at my chest; he couldn't miss at 6 feet! Suddenly I grew very calm, and found myself developing a feeling of complete indifference to the whole affair. If we were to be shot, let them get on with it. It wouldn't help them win the war, and one day they'd get caught out themselves – perhaps sooner than they thought.*

To show my indifference, I lowered my hands until they rested on my head. I was almost disappointed when Ferret Face ignored me. My tunic got rucked up and I glanced down at it. I realized that the *Unteroffizier* had overlooked the two packets of cigarettes tucked away in my shirt pockets, and less than 4 inches from my left ear I could hear my wrist-watch ticking. He was not a very efficient German, I thought.

Further along the line I could hear an argument developing between Lawrie and the *Unteroffizier*. Why the hell doesn't Lawrie pipe down, I thought; he's only prolonging the agony. Let them shoot us and get it over. I'd hardly got the thought off my mind, though, when I appreciated how stupid I was being. You should thank your stars that someone has the guts to

* This treatment would have been contrary to Article 4 of the Geneva Convention.

start a delaying action, I told myself. Don't forget that it was you who got us in this mess!

Lawrie's voice grew louder. 'But you can't shoot us,' he was saying with great emphasis. 'We're British airmen and you must bring an officer.'

Ignoring the possible consequences, I moved forward a few inches and turned to watch what was happening. Fortunately Ferret Face was just as interested and was also listening to the argument.

Again came Lawrie's voice. 'Well, why do you want to shoot us?' he demanded. 'Do you always shoot your prisoners?'

The *Unteroffizier* fumbled for words – his knowledge of English was obviously very limited.

'You haf ... you haf,' he stuttered.

'We have what?' asked Lawrie impatiently.

'You haf our vounded ... How you say? You cut dair ...' He drew a finger across his throat.

'We've what?' asked Lawrie incredulously. 'We've killed your wounded, is that what you mean?'

'*Ja!*' said the German. 'You kill our wounded, now ve kill you!'

So that was the trouble: we were accused of slitting Germans' throats! The image of two paratroopers, each shot through the chest suddenly appeared before me ...

Lawrie was too dumbfounded to answer. He just stood where he was, eyes goggling, mouth agape. The *Unteroffizier* took a few paces back and called out an order. Immediately the paratroopers began shepherding us closer together, indicating that we were to move further back. Obediently we shuffled backwards until we came to the edge of the large bomb crater close to our old trench. So this is it, I thought. We just topple over into a ready-made grave. All very neat.

Suddenly all my feelings of indifference left me and I grew afraid of death. I had read about people being lined up and shot. Of course, nothing like that would ever happen to me, I had told myself; I was immortal. But now I was beginning to realize that such things could happen; there, at my feet, was my own grave!

In the distance I could hear Lawrie's voice again. 'But you can't shoot us,' he was insisting. 'You've got to get an officer.'

I was past hope now. It would take more than Lawrie's efforts to save us; it would require a miracle. I closed my eyes tightly and tried to concentrate on the picture of my wife. I'd go out thinking of her.

However, Lawrie's defiant voice kept breaking in on my thoughts. 'I don't care what you say. Bloody well go and find one!'

I opened my eyes. Surely that wasn't Lawrie; he never swore! I leaned forward and looked along the line. It was Lawrie, and he was still arguing with the *Unteroffizier*. The German was shrugging his shoulders and looking bewildered; he'd run out of words. After a short pause, he made a final effort

39

to convince Lawrie that no officer was available; this was a battle area and he didn't even know where to look for one. But Lawrie was adamant: no officer, no shooting. And to show that he meant what he said, he deliberately lowered his arms and folded them across his chest. The *Unteroffizier* suddenly gave in. Perhaps he had never before met a man who refused to be shot, but he accepted defeat – or was it only a temporary set-back? – with good grace, and dispatched one of the paratroopers to find an officer.

Since leaving the trench, none of us had spoken a word to each other – with such hostile guards it would have been dangerous even to have tried – but the moment the *Unteroffizier* yielded to Lawrie's demand, the tension snapped. The air of melancholy gloom didn't completely disappear, but we had been temporarily reprieved. The important question now was what the officer – if one could be found – would do.

The paratroopers moved slowly away from us and formed into small groups. Their tommy-guns still pointed in the same direction! I turned and looked at Tom. He was staring down at the ground, lost in thought.

'How're you feeling?' I whispered.

He glanced up. He might have been on church parade so far as his face expressed his feelings. 'Not so bad,' he replied quietly.

'Did anyone get hurt in the trench?' I asked.

'Lofty stopped a few small splinters. Everyone else is all right.'

'Is he hurt much?'

'No. He'll be OK. But it's a wonder we weren't all killed.'

For a moment we looked at each other silently. 'Why don't you rest your hands on your head?' I asked. 'It's easier that way.'

He lowered his arms, then gave a deep sigh. 'I didn't know arms could ache so much.'

I looked along the line. Everyone was ignoring the Germans and having a quiet talk.

'I suppose you know what they plan to do with us?' I said.

'I can guess. A bullet in the back of the neck.'

I gave an involuntary shudder. I hadn't expected him to put it quite so crudely.

'I feel bloody sorry,' I told him. 'It's really my fault.'

He shook his head slowly. 'No, it's not your fault. It's just the luck of the game.'

'We shouldn't have stayed in the trench so long,' I said. 'It was asking for it.'

'What else could we have done? We'd nothing to fight with. And you know what happened to Williams when he put his head outside.'

Quite suddenly everyone stopped talking. Out of the shadows appeared a solitary paratrooper – our paratrooper. He had returned much quicker than I had expected and the fact that he was alone was ominous.

After a brief discussion, the *Unteroffizier* walked across to Lawrie. '*Der ist* no officer,' he told him, almost apologetically.

Lawrie had his answer ready. 'Well, send someone else to find one,' he said curtly. Then he turned his head away as if he had no further interest in the matter.

The *Unteroffizier* clenched his fists. 'Dis is imposs-eble!' he said angrily. He was not going to be told what to do by a prisoner.

Lawrie swung his head round and glared at him. Neither spoke. Then, with a shrug, the German turned on his heels and marched back to a group of his comrades. A few moments later we saw another paratrooper go off.

The minutes slipped by and darkness began to fall. Presently there was a disturbance and we knew that the paratrooper had returned. He was alone.

The silly little pantomime started all over again.

'*Der* is no officer!'

'Well, you better go and look for one yourself.'

'*Ach*! Dis is imposs-eble!'

'You can't shoot us without one!'

'You Engleesh ...'

'Well, what are you going to do about it?'

The *Unteroffizier* was clearly undecided. There was a painful silence while he made up his mind. The paratroopers began to spread out again – an ominous sign – and I started to quake in my shoes. So this is it, I thought. But I was wrong.

The *Unteroffizier* unslung his tommy-gun. '*Raus! Raus!*' he shouted, moving backwards. '*Recht* – Right march! Ve all go find an officer!'

And Lawrie, as a sign of approbation rather than respect, again raised his hands above his head.

5
Adventures in a Village

The paratroopers ranged themselves on either side of us and, with the *Unteroffizier* leading, we set off down the hill towards the cart track. At first we walked slowly, but by the time we reached the road by the landing ground, the pace had increased almost to a run. With our hands still raised, we found the going very hard, but we received scant sympathy from the paratroopers; any signs of lagging brought a vicious jab in the ribs from a gun.

I was at the tail-end of the party, with a paratrooper on my left and another behind me. Fortunately for me, Ferret Face was up in front with the *Unteroffizier*. As we left the area of the landing ground, my spirits began to rise. I felt that the further we got away from the scene of our capture, the less hot blood there would be. If we could find a German officer, we would make out a good enough case to avoid being shot.

Presently we came to a bridge. It spanned the river down which we had planned to drift to safety. At that very moment, had all gone well, we should have been on our way to the sea!

A guard halted us, then held a brief but animated discussion with the *Unteroffizier*. The bridge was under fire from the British and if we wished to proceed, we would have to go further down-river and wade across. Such solicitude seemed strangely out of place.

We left the road and walked some distance along the river bank. Then the *Unteroffizier* stopped us. After a short discussion with his minions, he ordered those prisoners still wearing steel helmets to throw them away – to a paratrooper, a tin hat was apparently a lethal weapon! With some reluctance his orders were obeyed.

The river was less than 100 yards wide and fortunately not in flood. It was by now too dark to pick out an easy route and the *Unteroffizier* just splashed straight ahead. The rest of us followed in his wake. The water was icy cold and by mid-stream we were all shivering. Still, we were not too cold to enjoy dipping our faces into the water and drinking it.

When we were within a few yards of the opposite bank and had reached shallow water, the *Unteroffizier* stumbled and went right in. He had fallen over the body of a paratrooper. The man's head lay against a small jagged rock and one of his legs was bent to such an acute angle that it must have been broken. A tattered parachute, entangled among nearby boulders, told its own story.

The *Unteroffizier* was on his knees in the water, trying to discover whether the paratrooper was dead or alive. He soon found out that the man was alive but in need of urgent medical attention. He gave brief orders to the other paratroopers, who immediately ripped the belts off our tunics, using them to strap the injured man's legs together. After a dressing had been applied to the back of his head, four of us were detailed to carry him. He was a heavy man and, because of his injuries, difficult to carry. Tom and the Aussie took the upper part of his body; by slipping their arms under him and holding hands, they took most of his weight. Lawrie and I took the lower part, each wrapping an arm around one of his thighs.

Almost before we were ready to move, the *Unteroffizier* was rounding up the rest of the party, and, after ordering one of the paratroopers to accompany us, he and the rest pushed on.

After what seemed hours, we reached the main road. The unfortunate German was having a very rough journey. Through lack of support, his head was sagging downwards and almost trailing along the ground. We tried to keep in step but occasionally one of us tripped, with the result that the man was badly shaken and would moan in pain. We staggered slowly along the road. The trees on either side formed a black canopy overhead and it was so dark that we could no longer see where we were going.

'Holy hell,' panted the Aussie as we stumbled from one side of the road to the other. 'Where're we taking this guy?'

It was a question each of us had asked ourselves more than once during the past half-hour.

'I think there's a village a bit further along,' Lawrie told him.

'There is,' I confirmed with an effort. I wanted to tell them that the first houses were less than 100 yards away but I hadn't the breath.

We tottered along a few more paces, then stopped dead.'Drop him,' I said. 'We've just got to have a rest.'

We lowered the body to the ground. The paratrooper began to jabber and was slow to realize that none of us could – or wished to – understand what he was saying. Then he started to rattle the magazine of his gun to frighten us. But we were past being frightened and just stood where we were, panting and wheezing.

Lawrie was the first to recover sufficiently to speak. 'We better try carrying him some other way,' he suggested.

I looked down, and could just make out the outline of the injured man against the white dust of the road. He was very still and I thought he might be dead.

'I reckon I could carry him on my back,' said the Aussie. 'It'd be easier that way.'

'No,' said Lawrie after a moment's hesitation. 'He weighs about 12 stone and your knees would go.'

Then the paratrooper chipped in. '*Raus! Raus!*' he said, rattling his gun. '*Schnell!*'

'Him and his bloody *Raus*,' grumbled the Aussie. 'It's all he can say!'

We picked up the body, this time Lawrie and I taking the upper part and Tom and the Aussie the lower. We struggled slowly and painfully along. The man's head was still trailing a few inches above the ground, and he was cold and stiff. So far the paratrooper had seemed quite indifferent to the suffering of his comrade. Now, for no apparent reason, he slung his tommy-gun over his shoulder and raised the injured man's head until it was level with his body.

'We must be near somewhere,' commented the Aussie when he realized what had happened.

A few yards along the road, a house suddenly appeared out of the darkness. Yellow light was leaking through chinks in the shutters and from under the door.

'Is this where we go?' asked the Aussie breathlessly.

'*Hier! Hier!*' said the paratrooper, as if answering the question.

We reeled towards the house, a mean-looking two-storey building with a low veranda running along its entire length.

'This used to be a wine parlour,' I said, breathing heavily. 'You could get drunk for fivepence!'

As we stumbled up the rickety steps of the veranda, the paratrooper let go of the injured man's head and opened the door. We shuffled into the room and, without waiting for an invitation, lowered our burden gently to the floor.

The room was large and almost bare of furniture, lit by a single oil lamp suspended from the cobwebbed ceiling. Around the room were the bodies of a dozen or more wounded paratroopers, some propped up against the wall, others laid out flat on the wooden floor. Seated by a table under the oil lamp was a man in a white smock – the doctor. The paratrooper clicked his heels and proceeded to tell him all about the injured man. While he was still speaking, the doctor walked across to the prostrate figure. Going down on one knee, he rolled back the injured man's eyelids. Then he got to his feet and returned to the table for a pannier. The four of us moved back towards the door. The doctor had not even noticed us and the paratrooper was too busy talking to worry about us.

I saw the Aussie glance furtively around the room. All the wounded men were either asleep or unconscious.

'I guess this is where we slide,' the Aussie whispered to Tom. 'Pass the word to the others, then follow me.' He quietly opened the door and slipped out. In a matter of seconds we had all followed him. I was the last to leave, and as I closed the door behind me, I heard the others going down the veranda steps.

'Where're we going?' I asked in a loud whisper. I was blind in the sudden darkness and didn't wish to lose them. I moved forward a pace, then, with a clatter, fell down the steps into the road.

'Come on, you noisy sod,' I heard the Aussie say. I scrambled to my feet, cursing myself. In the fall, I'd grazed my knees and they were very sore, but I was more concerned about the noise I'd made and hoped that it hadn't alarmed the paratrooper. To my relief, no one came chasing after us.

Led by the Aussie and keeping in single file, we moved stealthily through the village. Everything was quiet; not even the rustle of a leaf disturbed the silence. After we had covered a short distance, the Aussie called us to a halt. We grouped around him, anxious to know his plans – if he'd been able to make any in so short a time.

'Listen,' he whispered. 'I don't know exactly where we are, but this might be the only chance we'll have of making a break for it. We'll have to get clear of the village, and that might take a bit of doing because we don't know whether there are any side turnings, or how many Heinies are here. Once we're out of it, though, we'll make for the hills. And while we're going through the village, be as quiet as you can – especially you, Walker!'

I swallowed hard but said nothing.

'Why make for the hills?' asked Lawrie.

'Because there's nowhere else to make for – unless you fancy swimming to Egypt.'

'But what about the rest of the troops on the island?' Lawrie asked. 'Can't we try and join up with them?'

I heard the Aussie breathe heavily. 'You tell me where they are and how to reach them,' he drawled. After a pause, he added, 'Anyone got any more silly bloody questions?'

No one had and, after listening carefully to make sure that everything was quiet, we continued on our way. Very soon we reached the centre of the village and were passing clusters of small, dingy houses on either side of the road. Everywhere seemed deserted. A little further on we heard the Aussie swear – he had walked straight into the stone casing of the village well! He felt his way clear of the obstruction and led us to the opposite side of the road.

We had gone only a few more yards when the silence was broken by a gutteral challenge: '*Halt! Wer ist dort?*'

We stopped dead. For a moment everything was still, then out of the darkness a figure approached. A torch flashed on us and in the reflected light we saw a paratrooper.

'*Ach! Der Englischer gefangener!*' he said, with some surprise. He moved closer, then shone the beam of his torch on us each in turn. I was last in line. When the beam caught my face, I was blinded and closed my eyes.

'*Noch nicht erschossen?* – Haven't they shot you yet?' he growled.

I noticed the sudden change in his tone when he spoke to me, but it was not until he deliberately lighted up his own face that I understood the reason. It was Ferret Face!

He doused the light and rattled his gun. '*Kommen Sie mit mir!*' he snapped. 'March!'

We marched back through the village, each of us lost in deep thought. What luck! We passed the well and the deserted houses, and when we'd nearly reached the wine parlour, we turned down a narrow lane. Its surface was wet and slimy and smelt like a farmyard. A short distance along we came to a cowshed, with two paratroopers on guard. A few words were exchanged and the doors were opened.

'*Komm!*' said one of the paratroopers.

Obediently we trooped inside. By the light of two smoking candles, I saw that we were not alone. Standing idly around, or seated on the floor, were about 20 other prisoners, mostly airmen.

'Come into my parlour said the spider,' greeted a cheerful voice. 'Where did they bag you lot?'

I looked in the direction of the voice. It was Tim, one of the flight fitters I knew rather well, and he wore a grin which stretched from ear to ear.

'Hello,' I said, trying to smile. 'How long have you been here?'

'Bloody hours and hours,' he replied.'I'm the oldest inmate – I've been here since this morning.'

My eyes wandered around the shed. One side was fitted with stalls, the other stacked high with bales of straw. I looked at each of the men, but though I recognized some of them, I couldn't see Lofty or any of the others.

The Aussie found himself a square of clean floor, and, after removing his wet boots and socks, lay down on his back. He had apparently had enough for one day and wasn't looking very sociable. The three of us squatted down close beside him. I think we felt rather embarrassed and for the present preferred our own company to that of the other inmates.

For a time we sat in silence. Subconsciously, I was living again through the day's events: the air raid and the landing of the paratroops; Bill's death; our plans to escape; and our surrender. And now we were locked up in a cowshed!

I began to wonder what was going to happen to us. Was the *Unteroffizier* out trying to find an officer, or was that phase of the business over and forgotten? And what of my wife – how would she get to know what had happened to me? How would anyone get to know? And what would they say if they knew? Surrendered ... But perhaps they would never get to know. They wouldn't if we were shot!

I turned to Lawrie. 'D'you think this means that we've been reprieved?' I asked.

For a moment he pondered the question, then he shook his head. 'I'm hanged if I know,' he said. 'If we can get through tonight, I think we'll be safe.'

'What about the others?' I asked. 'What d'you think has happened to them?'

He kicked his heel against the floor. 'If only we knew where they were ...'

'I reckon we'll be all right,' said Tom cheerfully. 'They won't shoot us now.'

'Melancholy bastards!' muttered the Aussie as he turned on to his side.

One of the candles, burned to its stub, began to flicker, then went out. The gloom of the place increased and it seemed to grow suddenly colder. The door of the shed opened and a dozen more prisoners walked in. I turned to see whether Lofty was among them. While I was still looking there was a terrific explosion and the remaining candle went out. There were shouts from all directions. The door opened again and a light was shone inside. It was one of the guards. He shouted something in German, then slammed the door.

'It's all right,' said a voice with a Yorkshire accent. 'The Jerry says it's our blokes shelling the bridge. That one landed on the farmhouse!'

'Well, it's a pity they can't shoot a bit better,' replied another voice in disgust.

Someone found the candle and relit it, but the wick had broken off short and it gave a very poor light. I again looked round at the faces, but Lofty wasn't there.

'Who's got a fag?' asked the Aussie, getting to his feet. His hair was rumpled and he looked thoroughly dejected.

'You can't smoke in here,' shouted Yorkshire Accent.'The Jerries told us they'd shoot the first man they caught smoking.'

The Aussie cleared his throat noisily. 'Well, that'll be me, not you!'

No one gave him a cigarette, so he sat down on the floor again.

I turned to Lawrie. 'D'you think we're here for the night?' I asked. 'If we are, I'm going to take my shoes off.'

'The Aussie seems to think so,' he replied, glancing at the bared feet.

I looked around the shed. No one appeared to be making any effort to get really comfortable.

The Aussie stood up again. 'Has anyone got a drink?' he asked.

47

Someone held up a tin mug and pointed to a bucket. 'Here you are, cobber. Come and get it.'

The Aussie collected the mug, then, picking up the bucket, came back to us.

'I guess I need this,' he said, filling the mug and raising it to his mouth.

We each had a drink and felt better. Just then the door opened again and the light from a torch shone inside.

'*Komm*! *Komm*! *Alles Raus*!'

'That means we've all to get outside,' said Yorkshire Accent.

The Aussie gave a deep sigh, then began putting on his boots and socks. 'Bloody *Raus*! Bloody *Raus*!' he muttered. 'I wonder where they're taking us this time?'

6
Night in a Church

We were made to fall in in three ranks, then a paratrooper began counting us. This was no easy task because, apart from the darkness, we seemed to be milling about all over the place. But he kept his temper and in the end got our number: '*Fünf-und-dreizig* – 35.'

Other paratroopers, who were to act as guards, had already appeared on the scene and were getting into position around us. When the counting was finished, someone gave the order '*Links* – Left march!' With little precision, we all turned left and began walking up the lane towards the road.

Lawrie and I were together in the same file. Neither of us was feeling very happy, and added to our mental discomfort was the unpleasant feeling of the cold dampness of our footwear and clothing.

When we reached the end of the lane, we turned right and continued through the village. Half-way along, we were shepherded over to the other side of the road to make way for a long column of German soldiers marching in the direction of the landing ground.

Soon we left the village behind us and were in open country. Now that there were no houses or trees, it seemed much lighter and we could almost see the faces of our guards. About 1 mile along the road we came to a small church. It was newly whitewashed and looked somewhat ghostly in the semi-darkness. Surrounding it was a low stone wall. We were told to halt and two of the guards walked up the pathway towards the church door. Presently they came rushing back and this time we were told to move in close to the wall and kneel down.

I was gripped by a sudden spasm of fear. This was why we had been brought so far from the village – they were going to massacre us! My heart began to pound against my ribs and I wanted to vomit. Dazed, I moved slowly over to the wall. Then, like the rest, I went down on my knees.

There were two flashes and two ear-splitting explosions, and I thought the end of my world had come. But as I was in no pain, I half-opened my eyes and found myself peering at the outline of the man next to me. To my astonishment, it was a paratrooper. Before I could work this out, someone shouted. 'All right, blokes, you can get up now!' I rose to my feet and followed the moving crowd up to the church. As I entered, I noticed the doors were badly splintered. Then I guessed the meaning of the two explosions: hand grenades had been used in lieu of a key!

The church was approximately 40 feet long and 15 feet wide. At the far end was the altar, furnished in simple style with crucifix and two candelabra. There were no pews or other furniture.

A guard had already lit the candles and once we'd all entered, he told us in broken English that we were to stay in the church all night and could now go to sleep. During the next few minutes, everyone was busy staking out his claim to a plot of floor on which to lie. By the time we had settled down, we formed two rows, one on either side of the church, with a clear space running from door to altar.

Lawrie and I chose adjoining plots next to the altar. There would be no draught from the broken doors and it was light. I sat down on the cold, hard floor and, after removing my shoes and socks, leaned back against the wall.

'I've slept in some strange places, but never in a church before,' I said.

Lawrie turned and smiled. 'What makes you think you're going to sleep in a church?' he asked, patting the floor with the palm of his hand. I glanced down. It was bare concrete!

Opposite us was the Aussie. He had managed to get a cigarette from somewhere and was now propped against the wall, smoking. A little further along I could see Tom, lying on his side, talking to a young and very pale-faced soldier. Everyone had something to speak about – usually how he had come to be a prisoner – but the buzz of conversation gradually died down and presently I heard a quiet snore coming from nearby.

'It sounds as if someone can sleep,' I remarked to Lawrie.

He nodded his head. 'I feel too tired to sleep.'

The candles began to flicker and smoke. Turning, I saw a paratrooper framed in the doorway.

'It is not permitted to smoke,' he said in a loud voice. There was a brief pause, then, 'In five minutes the lights will be put out.' He withdrew and closed the door.

'Well, that settles it,' I said to Lawrie. 'We'll have to try and get to sleep. We can't sit up all night in the dark.'

Then the door opened again. The paratrooper had returned. 'I have an important announcement to make,' he said in a pompous voice. For a moment he surveyed his audience, then he drew himself up to his full height and patted his tommy-gun. 'If any man attempts to escape, he will be shot. Do you all understand?'

There were a few grunts and titters, and someone shouted 'Yes, we understand.'

'Good-night!' said the paratrooper.

'Good-night!' chorused his audience.

I turned to Lawrie. 'I'm far too tired even to think about escaping.'

'So'm I,' I said, stretching out on the concrete floor.

After buttoning up my tunic, I lay down beside him, crooking an arm under my head as a pillow. For a time we both wriggled about, trying to get comfortable. The floor was terribly hard and in desperation I turned over on my back, but I was still too uncomfortable to get to sleep.

Presently there was a scuffle at the door and a guard came in and snuffed all the candles. The minutes seemed like hours. As they ticked away, I began to shiver with cold.

'Are you asleep?' I whispered.

Lawrie moved uncomfortably. 'No,' he replied wearily. 'I'm too cold.' I rolled over on to my side and, drawing up my knees, snuggled up close. Gradually we grew warm and our bodies ceased to ache. We were on the verge of sleep – peaceful, restful sleep – when, like a blast of cold wind, we heard the sound of that familiar pompous voice.

'I have an important announcement to make!' it said. 'Are you all listening?' There was no answer. 'For every man who escapes, one of you will be shot. Do you understand?' There was still no answer. 'Good-night.'

After he had gone, everyone started to grumble, and someone lit a cigarette.

'For Christ's sake, put that fag out,' a voice shouted. 'D'you want to get us all shot?'

'And you remember where you are,' someone else shouted.

A small red glow indicated the smoker's feelings of indifference to mankind in general, and to Germans in particular.

Everyone settled down again and, except for a snore or the scraping of a boot, all was quiet. Then I fell asleep.

A sudden wave of cold air entered the building and I awoke with a start.

'I have an important announcement to make,' said a voice. 'Are you all listening?'

The reaction was immediate and very noisy. Everyone shouted out at the same time: 'Why don't you take a run at yourself?' 'Bloody well beat it, you noisy sod!' 'Scram, you Jerry bastard!'

The German unslung his tommy-gun and rattled the magazine. Everyone was suddenly quiet again. Then he began all over again: 'I have an important announcement to make. Are you all listening?' No one spoke. 'If one man escapes, you will ALL be shot. Do you understand?' Still no one spoke. 'Good-night.'

7
Half-hearted Rebel

I awoke early but was surprised to see that quite a number of the others were already up and about. Lawrie was still asleep, though, and without disturbing him I began putting on my shoes and socks. During the night my shoes had dried out. They had also shrunk, and the leather was now so hard and inflexible that they hurt my feet. At last I got them on and, feeling very shaky, stood up. I glanced at my watch and saw that it had stopped. I stooped down and looked at Lawrie's; his also had stopped.

After an uncomfortable night, made worse by bad dreams, I was feeling very irritable. I glanced around and decided that I didn't want to speak to anyone. Instead, I began going through my pockets. The two packets of cigarettes were still there, though badly crumpled, and in my trousers pocket I had a handkerchief. That was all I could find.

'Having a roll call?' asked the Aussie from the opposite wall. He was leaning back, smoking.

'Yes,' I replied. 'That little swine of a Jerry took nearly everything I had.' Moistening the handkerchief, I began cleaning my face.

'He pinched my fags,' the Aussie remarked sourly.

Lawrie awoke. He sat up and glanced at his watch. He didn't believe what it told him and he shook it, then held it to his ear. With a grunt, he began winding it up.

'What time is it?' he asked gruffly.

'I don't know. I forgot to wind mine.' I turned to the Aussie. 'D'you know?'

'Nope. I haven't got a ticker.'

'It's twenty past six,' volunteered the man next to him.

We set our watches going.

'How do you feel?' I asked Lawrie.

He yawned and pulled a wry face. 'Rotten.' He looked as irritable as I was feeling.

When I'd finished cleaning my face, I put the handkerchief away. Then I found myself wanting a smoke. But somehow it didn't seem right, smoking in church. I looked around. Nearly everyone who was awake had a cigarette going. I rolled my tongue round the inside of my mouth. It tasted filthy. That decided me: I wouldn't smoke until I'd had a drink.

At eight o'clock we heard a commotion outside and everyone rushed to the door. A party of paratroopers had just arrived and was now being formed into two lines facing the church.

'Looks like a shooting party to me,' drawled the Aussie.

My heart began to pound and the awful sense of fear returned. Had the *Unteroffizier* come to collect us? Without a word, I went in search of Lawrie. I found him talking to Tom.

'I think they've come for us,' I said nervously.

'Come for who?' he asked.

'Us – you, Tom, the Aussie and me.'

A look of surprise spread across his face. 'Why us in particular? What have WE done?'

'Last night,' I said. 'You know what the little *Unteroffizier* said – they're going to shoot us.'

He smiled. 'You ought to forget all about that. I expect he was only bluffing anyway.'

'You know very well he wasn't,' I replied. 'And what's this bunch of Jerries come for?'

'To take us all away to work,' he replied. 'You don't think they're going to let you sit on your bottom for the rest of the war, do you?'

My heart stopped pounding, but I was still feeling very apprehensive. I didn't trust that *Unteroffizier*!

The crowd at the entrance had begun to filter out through the doorway and down the path, and the church was gradually emptying.

'Come on,' Lawrie said. 'We better get moving.'

Down at the gates stood two guards. As each man passed, they ran their fingers lightly over his clothing. 'Have you any firearms, matches or pencils?' they asked, parrot-like. 'Have you any firearms, matches or pencils?' The incongruity of the question was amusing, but one look at the guards' faces was sufficient warning of what would happen if we displayed any wit or humour.

Out on the roadway, we were herded together between the two lines of paratroopers. Lawrie and I managed to keep together, but Tom and the

Aussie were pushed further along. When everyone had fallen in, we were counted, then the order was given: 'Left turn. March!'

We moved off down the road and, for the sake of ease rather than discipline, we all marched in step. We reached the village. From its appearance, it had been taken over by the military authorities. Every house seemed to have its quota of soldiers; we could see them at the windows and doors, and in the gardens.

As we left the village, we heard the sound of guns in the distance, and in the direction of the landing ground several large black columns of smoke were rising high into the air. Apparently it was under fire. Overhead a solitary Ju 88 was on patrol. We crossed the bridge. When we were nearing the landing ground, a German on a motorcycle overtook us and we were called to a halt. Then we were told to turn about, and we left the road and went down to the river bank.

By now, shells were landing all around us and the guards, no less than their prisoners, were getting scared. After we'd been standing idly about for a few minutes, an English-speaking paratrooper appeared and told us to scatter and lie down. Everyone made a dash to find shelter, and Lawrie and I got separated. I looked around, trying to find someone I knew. Then a paratrooper began to bawl at me, so I made for a small rocky alcove, occupied by a soldier and a paratrooper.

As I lay down on my side, the paratrooper gave me a whimsical smile, then waved his gun at me. I shook my head. All right, Jerry, I thought. I'm not likely to run away with all this coming down. I looked at the soldier. His face was dirty and he needed a shave very badly. My hand stole up to my own face; it felt like coarse sandpaper.

'Nice state of affairs!' I remarked. I could think of nothing really appropriate to say.

'Huh!' grunted the soldier. 'Got any fags?' He was lying full-length on his belly, idly throwing small pebbles at a nearby bush.

I glanced at the paratrooper, wondering whether he would object to our smoking. Then I took out a packet of cigarettes and held it out.

'Thanks,' said the soldier. 'Better bribe the Jerry with one – we'll need a light.'

I handed the open packet to the paratrooper.

'Cigarette?'

'*Nein, nein,*' he said excitedly, and feeling in his pocket he brought out a metal case. Then he suddenly remembered. Rising to his feet, he looked carefully around, then he bobbed down again.

'Crafty little sod!' remarked the soldier.

I nodded. 'They're all scared stiff of each other.'

The paratrooper opened his case. '*Zigaretten?*'

I took one, and again held out the packet. '*Danke,*' he said, taking one. Laying down his tommy-gun, he deliberately broke off the cork tip and threw it away. Then he winked and began searching in his pockets for his lighter. For a time we smoked in silence.

'These aren't bad cigarettes,' I said to the soldier.

'Bloody ersatz, I expect,' he remarked deprecatingly.

I grunted. Perhaps he was right, but I wouldn't mind a few packets of them just the same.

A shell exploded less than 50 feet away and we all ducked. When the air had cleared, I took out my handkerchief and wiped my face.

'Where're all these shells coming from?' I asked.

The soldier heaved his shoulders. 'I reckon our Bofors have the aerodrome taped,' he said.*

'How many firing?' I asked. 'About a dozen?'

'Hell, no. Two or three, that's all.'

'Well, they're putting enough stuff down!'

'Not bad, considering they're 2 or 3 miles away.'

For a time neither of us spoke. I wasn't enjoying being shot at by our own guns, but the soldier was quite unmoved.

'Where did they nab you?' I asked him when I'd finished my cigarette.

'In a trench near the Naval Ops tent.' After a pause, he added, 'They lined all the Navy blokes up and shot 'em!'

'Rot!' I said scornfully.

'They bloody well did,' he said with emphasis. 'They hadn't got their jackets on, and seeing them in collars and ties, the Jerries said they were civvies and shot 'em.'

I let out a deep breath. 'What a shower of bloody barbarians they are.'

There was a long minute's silence.

'Where did they get you?' the soldier asked.

I told him.

'And you wouldn't believe me when I told you about the Navy blokes!' was his comment when I'd finished.

Shells were still falling, but they were now further away and the earth no longer shook when they exploded. I glanced at the German. He was sitting cross-legged and, except for his tommy-gun, he looked for all the world like a fat little joker out of a pack of cards.

The soldier moved uncomfortably. 'What d'you think they're going to do with us?' he asked.

'Make us work,' I replied. But I knew that wasn't what he wanted to know. Like me, he was anxious about the future, and he wished to be reassured. But my hopes were no higher than his and I knew perfectly well that if I

* I learnt later that although we had some Bofors, the present shelling was probably being carried out by several very old artillery pieces situated on the other side of Hill 107. The Bofors were eventually silenced by Stuka bombers, and their crews killed. They had a range of 4.3 miles.

started discussing the future in my present state of mind, we would both end up thoroughly miserable.

'Yes, they'll make us work,' I said. 'It'll help pass the time.'

He looked away, and threw another pebble at the bush. Presently a flight of Ju 87s roared by overhead.

'Dive bombers,' I said, looking up at them.

'Yes, and you know what that means?' he said, nodding his head in the direction of the landing ground. 'They're after those Bofors.'

I looked at him, slowly nodding my head. Poor beggars, I thought. They'll get hell knocked out of them.

A few minutes later we heard a series of high-pitched whines as the bombers dived down on their targets. Then came the explosions. We both glanced at the German. His face was set and expressionless.

The shelling ceased. Then there was a shout, and when we rose to our feet we saw that everyone else had fallen in. We limped stiffly across the uneven ground and tagged on to the tail-end of the column.

A paratrooper started to count us: '*Ein ... zwei ... drei ... vier ...*'

They were certainly taking no chances with us. When the counting was over, someone gave the order 'March!', and we set off up the bank and towards the road.

When we reached the corner of the landing ground, we were again halted. Then I felt a tap on the shoulder. I turned my head. '*Komm!*' said a para-trooper. I exchanged glances with the men on either side of me. One of them gave a watery smile; the other, a soldier, scowled – he also had been tapped on the shoulder. Together, we followed the paratrooper on to the landing ground.

'What's this in aid of, cock?' asked the soldier as we tramped across the sand.

I glanced down at him. He was a short, plump figure, with a complexion like an overripe crab apple.

'I don't know,' I replied shortly. Then I suddenly realized that I didn't like him. This was quite unreasonable, but I objected to the way he'd called me 'cock'; he was being much too familiar.

'My name's Walker,' I told him with bile in my voice. 'Don't call me cock. I don't like it.'

Almost as soon as I'd spoken, I relented. After all, he'd not meant to be offensive. 'What's your name?' I asked in a friendlier tone.

He eyed me suspiciously. 'It's Bill – and there's no need to get huffy.'

'I'm sorry. I didn't mean to be.'

He didn't answer and we walked on in silence.

The landing ground was roughly rectangular in shape, and to prevent aircraft landing in a north–south direction – AA guns had covered the east–west approach – several rows of empty 50-gallon petrol drums had been laid down the centre. As we approached, I saw a figure moving among the drums.

When we got closer, I saw that he was rolling the drums to the edge of the landing ground.

The paratrooper slowed down, and when we had caught up with him, we all stopped.

'So that's the bloody game,' said the soldier, realizing what work we were expected to do.

The paratrooper pointed his gun to the drums. *'Arbeit!'* he growled, *'Schnell!'*

For a moment we looked at him and at his gun. Then we ambled off in the direction of the nearest drums. I was feeling rebellious. Why should we be made to work on the landing ground? It was a battle area, and by clearing the drums away, we were making it serviceable for German aircraft. I walked a few more paces. Why should I help the Germans? It was all wrong, quite wrong. And if the Air Force got to know ... That decided me. I wouldn't do it.

I stopped and turned around. The paratrooper was watching me. As I began walking towards him, I saw him raise his tommy–gun. My legs began to grow numb from fear. With a mental effort I forced myself forward. He can shoot me if he likes, I thought, but I'm not going to move a single drum.

I found myself counting each step, and as I counted, the world began to grow dim. Now I saw only the muzzle of the tommy-gun; inside me was nothing but fear. I saw the spurts of yellow and blue flame; heard the rat-a-tat of the explosions; and saw the ground erupting at my feet. I stopped walking and, for a moment, closed my eyes. If I take one more pace forward he'll kill me, I told myself. Then I knew how much I wanted to live. I opened my eyes and, turning about, walked back towards the drums.

'You trying to get yourself shot?' shouted the soldier.

I heard him plainly enough, but didn't bother to answer. Now that I was alive, I wished that I were dead.

I heaved against the drum. Like the rest of them, it was full of bullet holes – the result of ground strafing. It wouldn't move, so I bent down and put my shoulder against it. As it fell over on to its side, a jagged spur of metal ripped through my sleeve and tore deeply into the flesh of my right arm. I cursed it and felt very angry, but because I was angry I ignored the pain and blood, and began venting my spleen on the drum.

Somehow I got it rolling, and set off across the landing ground. Because of the uneven surface it wouldn't go straight, and every few yards it crashed into one of the other drums. Regardless of the damage done to my hands by the jagged bullet holes, I heaved and pushed and managed to keep it rolling. When I was half-way across, I heard someone shouting. I stopped and straightened up.

'Why don't you use your feet?'

I looked across at him, a tall, thin figure of a man, dressed in khaki shirt and navy-blue trousers. His face seemed strangely familiar.

'Use my feet,' I said, almost to myself. I glanced down at the drum, then gave it a push with my right foot. It swivelled round and one end of it hit my leg. 'Damn!' I exclaimed, rubbing my shin. I looked at the man again.

'It's easier with your feet,' he said. 'Keep trying.'

Then I remembered where I'd seen him before. 'You're Fleet Air Arm, aren't you?'

He nodded.

Then we heard the German shouting at us.

'Better get under way,' said the sailor. 'See you later.'

At the edge of the landing ground, I gave the drum a final push and it went careering down the slope. Then I spat after it. 'That to Hitler and his gang of bloody cut-throats,' I said. 'May they rot in hell.'

On the way back I passed Bill, the soldier. He was already trundling his second drum, but now he was moving very slowly.

'Roll out the bleedin' barrel!' he said grimly as he went by.

As I walked along, a gun suddenly boomed out, and a moment later I heard a strange whispering swish-swish-swish rushing by overhead. Instinctively I ducked, and as I did so, there was a loud explosion over at the far corner of the landing ground. 'Those damn Bofors again!' I said to myself. I looked around for Bill and the sailor. Bill was nowhere to be seen, but the sailor was kicking a drum along as unconcerned as if he were on a football field.

I got to my feet. I hope we're not going to have any more of those, I thought. I pushed another drum on to its side, then got it rolling. In the distance I could now see the short, fat figure of Bill, still struggling with his drum. Then I heard the German shouting again. I stopped and looked across at him. Was he telling us to '*Schnell*!' or was he calling off work in case the shelling started again? Whatever he was saying, I would ignore him. He could go to hell; I was having no more to do with Krauts. I took off my shoes and emptied out the sand. Yes, to hell with Krauts – and he needn't keep shouting because I wasn't moving until I was ready. Slowly I put my shoes on again, tying the laces in neat bows. It made me feel better. Then I got the drum rolling again.

There was another boom in the distance, and again I heard the swishing sound overhead. I dodged down behind the drum. This time the explosion was much nearer and I felt its blast. Suddenly I felt cold and started to tremble. This is all wrong, I told myself. What kind of bastards are they, making prisoners work under shell fire? Minutes passed before I could screw up sufficient courage to get to my feet again.

I glanced around. The sailor was busy with a spade, digging a hole, the German looking on. And Bill was on his way back for another drum. I set off towards the edge of the landing ground, my ears straining to pick up the tell-tale sound of the next shell. It came as I was giving the drum its final shove down the slope. For a moment I stopped breathing, then dived after the drum. The shell exploded 20 yards away and covered me with dust and dirt. I stayed where I was until I heard Bill calling me. Then I got up and we both went back for some more drums.

The gun kept up its fire, shells landing regularly at five-minute intervals. The swishing as they passed overhead soon ceased to worry me and gradually I lost all fear of the explosions. If the shell had your number on it, you got it – an illogical but none the less comforting philosophy I learned from the sailor.

8
A Sort of Salvage

At the end of three long and painful hours, the sailor and I rolled the last drum from the landing ground. It was a combined effort: there was only the one drum left and we didn't know whose turn it was, so we joined forces. As the sailor gave it a final kick down the slope, part of the sole of his left boot broke lose.

'So much for using your feet,' I remarked. 'Now what're you going to do?'

He looked down at the boot and shrugged his shoulders. 'I'll have to try and scrounge another pair from somewhere.' But he didn't sound very hopeful.

We limped wearily towards the road. When we were half-way there we were joined by Bill and the German.

'I've moved 31 of those bloody things,' Bill said, looking at his lacerated hands. 'I reckon they ought to pay us off for the rest of the day.'

'You've got some hopes,' said the sailor. As he spoke, he tripped and fell. 'Damn these bloody boots!' he said. I helped him up. Then he noticed my hands. 'Just look at your mitts,' he said. 'They're worse than the soldier's.'

'They'll be all right after I've washed them,' I told him. But I knew they were going to need much more than soap and water.

We turned left along the main road, which ran parallel to the landing ground. Nearly every yard of the ditch on one side of the road was strewn with abandoned cartridge cases, hand grenades, gas masks and even oddments of uniform. Then we came to a dead horse lying in the middle of the road. We gave it a wide berth – it was already putrifying and covered with flies. Soon after passing the dead horse, we left the road and went along a narrow, winding footpath in the direction of the hills. Then we began to climb, and the path got rocky and broken.

'I can't go much further with this bloody boot,' said the sailor, coming to a halt. We were in single file with the sailor leading, then me, then Bill and the German.

We climbed upwards until at last the landing ground was nearly lost to sight behind the crest of an adjoining hill. The path swung to the left and brought us to a long, narrow gully, with trees growing on one side. As we reached the gully, the sailor again tripped up and landed on his face.

'*Schnell! Schnell!*' screamed the German, going up to him and brandishing his gun. '*Schnell! Schnell!*'

The sailor got to his knees, then looked up at him. 'Balls!' he said with contempt. Then he leisurely examined the boot. The sole was held on only by the instep. 'Who's got a bit of string?' he asked.

'*Schnell!*' screamed the German again.

Ignoring him, Bill and I felt in our pockets. 'This any good?' I asked, holding out my dirty handkerchief.

But Bill had a better idea. 'Hang on a minute,' he said. 'My buttons are laced on. You can have the lace.'

He untied the knots and one by one the buttons fell off, leaving him with over half a yard of leather lace. By the time the sole was tied on, the German was stamping his feet and threatening to shoot us.

We set off again, and when we were nearing the top of the hill, the sailor suddenly stopped again.

'Bloody O'Reilly! Look over there!' He pointed to the wreck of a glider on the opposite side of the gully.

For a moment we all stopped and stared – even the German was interested. The glider had apparently crashed head-on into a tree, and its fuselage was completely crumpled. One of its wings had come off and was now down at the bottom of the gully. So they'd used airborne troops as well as paratroops in invading the island.

'I wonder how many got out of that alive?' I said, peering over the edge to see whether any bodies were in sight.

'None, I hope,' said the sailor shortly. 'I haven't forgotten what the bastards did to our blokes down at the Ops tent.'

We continued on our way, and the path began to level out and get wider. Bill caught up with me and for a while we walked on in silence.

'I say, Walker,' he suddenly said. 'Why don't we do this bloody Hun in? There's no one about.' He glanced around at the German. 'What about it, eh?' He seemed ready to set about him there and then.

I turned and looked at the guard. He was following close behind, his tommy-gun ready for action.

'Just take a look at his gun, then think again,' I said.

He flashed me an angry look but didn't speak.

The path left the gully, and wound in and out among the trees until it finally led us to a small clearing. As we approached, I realized that we had come to the end of our outward journey. Lying on the mossy earth in the centre of the clearing were about 20 German wounded; over by the trees, huddled together, were a similar number of British wounded.

As we entered the clearing, I heard someone shout, 'Hi'ya, Mike!' It was Lofty Bond.

'Well, look who's here,' I exclaimed in surprise. Somehow this was the last place I had expected to find him. Ignoring the noisy protests of the guard, the three of us ambled across to where Lofty was standing.

'What happened to you last night?' I asked, taking hold of his hands and shaking them.

He grinned broadly. 'They locked us up in a cowshed. Don't come too close to me – I stink!'

'Did you get hurt much when those hand grenades went off in the trench?' I asked, looking him over for signs of wounds.

'Only a few small splinters in my hide,' he said, rubbing his backside. 'But we were lucky to get away so lightly. They used enough ammunition to wipe out a regiment.'

'We were lucky in more ways than one,' I told him. 'I only hope we don't meet that little *Unteroffizier* again. He might still be set on shooting us.'

'Sod him,' he said shortly. 'I hope he's bit it. He was a nasty little bastard.'

'And that goes for Ferret Face,' I said. I looked around. 'See anything of Lawrie or the others?'

'They're somewhere sculling about,' he replied. Then he turned to the sailor. 'I know you!' he said, giving him a quizzical look. 'You're Thompson – Fleet Air Arm!'

The sailor nodded. 'That's right. And you belong to 30 Squadron.'

Lofty smiled. 'You mean I *did* belong to it. It's been all shot up.'

'You better meet Bill,' I said to him. 'That is, if it's not beneath your dignity to hob-nob with a brown job – he's in the Army.' They grinned at each other and exchanged how-do's.

I glanced around the clearing, with its gloom of green light and dark shadows. 'What's happening up here?' I asked. 'It looks like the aftermath of the Battle of Waterloo!'

'That's about what it is,' Lofty said. 'We're supposed to be carrying all these wounded Jerries down to the bottom of the hill. They've got lorries taking them back to the village.'

'How d'you get them down?' I asked. 'It's pretty steep, isn't it?'

'Stretchers,' he replied. 'Four men to a stretcher. But it's hard graft; nearly pulls your guts out.' He raised his right knee stiffly. 'I went arse-over-tip the last time – nearly took my kneecap off. Now I'm having a rest.'

'Which way do you go down?' I asked. 'We didn't see any lorries on the road when we came up.'

He pointed over his shoulder with a thumb. 'This way – down the other side of the hill. It brings you out close to the cart track, not far from our trench.'

'Anyone we know?' I asked, nodding in the direction of the trees. I wasn't anxious to be reminded of that trench.

'Yes,' he replied. 'They're nearly all from the old squadron. Come on over.'

The wounded men were in small groups. Several were covered with blankets, but most of them had greatcoats thrown across them. As we approached, one of them raised himself on an elbow. 'Hello, Mike,' he said. 'I thought you'd have got away.'

I stopped and for a moment stared. Then I recognized Bert Lewis, a friend from one of the squadron flights.

'Hello!' I said, surprised. 'I thought you were supposed to have gone to Egypt.'

He let himself sink back to the ground. 'I was. But it's the usual story – no room on the kite.'

I nodded in sympathy. At least 50 men from the squadron who had been ordered back to Egypt had been unable to find space on the few available aircraft.

'Like another drink?' Lofty asked him.

He nodded. 'Yes, but you'll have to scrounge some more from the Jerries. We finished the last lot.'

Lofty glanced across to where some Germans were standing, close to their own wounded. 'I'll see what I can do,' he said. 'Where's the water-bottle?' He found it, then set off across the clearing.

I looked down at Bert's pale, grimy face. 'How long have you been here?'

'Since yesterday morning. We got surrounded, then they shot us up.'

Bill leaned his arm against the tree. 'Have they given you any treatment yet?' he asked. Bert shook his head.

I looked across at the German wounded, all laid out in a neat row. The methodical German mind, I thought. They looked like corpses awaiting burial. Then I glanced at our own men, bunched together in untidy groups. At least they looked like live human beings.

'What about that boot of yours?' I said, turning to the sailor.

He raised his foot. 'If I could find some string ...' He pulled at the sole. 'It won't last long as it is.'

Bert raised his head. 'Broken lace?' he asked.

'No,' I said. 'The sole of his boot's coming adrift.'

'Well, he'd better have one of mine.' He heaved himself up on an elbow, then turned and looked at the sailor's feet 'What size do you take?'

'Hell, no,' said the sailor indignantly. 'What d'you think I am?'

'Don't be so bloody fussy,' Bert said. 'I can't walk, so it's no use to me.'

At that moment, Lofty returned. 'Look what Fritz has given me,' he said, holding up a large wicker-covered bottle. 'He gave me a packet of fags as well.' He rummaged about under the edge of the blanket and produced a battered enamel mug. Half filling it, he handed it to Bert.

Bert took a sip and licked his lips. 'What's this?' he asked in surprise. 'It tastes like lime juice.'

'Don't ask me,' replied Lofty. 'Whatever it is, it's very likely poisoned.'

We all had a drink, then Lofty handed round the cigarettes. 'Who's got a match?' he asked. Bert handed him a box.

Bill squatted down on his haunches. 'What're these called?' he asked, sniffing disparagingly at his cigarette. 'It smells like a smouldering mattress!'

'"Privat",' said Lofty, blowing out a cloud of smoke. 'It's a bloody good name for them.' Then he caught sight of the sailor's boot. 'Cripes!' he exclaimed. 'What've you been doing?'

The sailor drew up his leg and tried to hide the boot. 'It's nothing,' he said casually. 'The sole's a bit loose.'

'He means it's falling off,' I said, smiling at his discomfort. 'Bert's offered him his, but he's too proud to take them.'

Lofty took a pull at his cigarette. 'What size d'you take?' he asked. 'I know where there's a dead Jerry.'

The sailor scowled. 'I'm not wearing boots off a dead Jerry.'

'Bull!' said Lofty. 'You can't walk around in those.' He bent down and caught hold of the boot. 'Size ten.' He stubbed out his cigarette. 'We'll bloody soon have you fixed up.' Without another word, he strode off into the woods.

'He'll be getting a bullet in his arse, strolling off like that,' said Bill.

We heard a babel of voices coming from the opposite end of the clearing.

'Here comes the strong-arm gang,' said Bert. 'What a noise they make.'

'You mean the stretcher-bearers?' I asked.

He nodded. 'You'd think they'd be too short of wind to talk, coming up that hill.'

Almost before the first of the stretcher-bearers had appeared, a guttural voice was shouting out orders. Bill got to his feet. 'Come on,' he said. 'Let's go and see what's happening.' I nodded goodbye to Bert, and the three of us set off towards the Germans.

When we were half-way across the clearing, Lofty caught up with us. He was carrying a pair of brown boots and grinning all over his face.

'Where did you pinch them?' I asked. 'They look like Aussie boots.'

'They are,' he replied, handing them to the sailor. 'But they didn't come off a dead Aussie.'

The stretcher-bearers – British soldiers, with a sprinkling of airmen – were already re-forming into teams, waiting for the Germans to load their stretchers.

Looking round to see if there was anyone I knew, I caught sight of Lawrie and Dingle, so I hurried across to them.

'So you've joined the strong-arm gang!' I said. 'Any room for me?'

'You bet,' said Lawrie. 'Come on, chaps, make room for Hercules!' They'd already made up a foursome, but one of the soldiers offered me his place.

I saw Lawrie looking at my tunic.

'What've you been doing?' he asked. 'You look as if you've been in a fight.'

I held up my arm. It felt stiff and sore. 'They had us rolling all the drums off the landing ground,' I told him. 'I fell over one of them.'

He folded back the torn cloth and exposed the raw and inflamed flesh. 'You ought to have something done to this,' he said. 'It's going septic.'

As I brought out my handkerchief, he saw my hands. 'You can't carry a stretcher with hands like those,' he said in a shocked tone.

'You'd better tell the Jerries that,' I replied. With difficulty, I ripped the handkerchief in half and handed it to him.

'You won't last one trip,' he said as he tied them up for me.

A German shouted for us to go over to where the wounded were lying. While we were sorting ourselves into parties, we heard the roar of aircraft, this time coming from the sea. Up on the side of the hill we felt reasonably safe. We would be a difficult target to bomb. But if they were fighters, they could quite easily get us with their guns.

Suddenly they came into view – Ju 52 troop carriers, flying at almost sea level and presumably coming in from Greece. As they drew close to the landing ground, they broke formation and the leading aircraft made a circuit preparatory to landing. For a time we watched them. The landing ground was pitted with bomb and shell craters, and each time an aircraft landed all eyes focused on it. Would it land safely or end up in a crater? The first five succeeded in avoiding trouble, but the sixth touched down on the very lip of a huge crater and went straight over on its nose. A moment later there was a muffled explosion, followed by a cloud of black smoke.

'Why the hell don't they get out?' I said. 'She'll be going up in flames in a second.'

'Let the bastards burn,' Bill said callously.

There was a sudden flash, more smoke, then flames shot high into the air.

'Just as it bloody well should be,' murmured Bill approvingly. 'Let the bastards burn.'

I turned my head away from the scene. Perhaps he had good reasons for hating Germans, but . . .

The sound of tearing metal drew my attention back to the landing ground. Another Ju 52 had put down, and as it ran along the ground, brakes full on, one wheel ran into a crater. The machine swung violently around, breaking part of the undercarriage. Then it keeled over and one wing hit the ground.

The wing buckled and broke off, then crashed into the side of the capsizing fuselage. There was a dull explosion, and almost immediately the aircraft was hidden from sight by smoke and flame.

While I was still watching it burn, there was another crash. Smoke rising from the first wrecked aircraft partly hid it from view, and another troop carrier had landed right on top of it. I strained my eyes to see if there were any survivors but saw none. Soon it was burning fiercely and I could hear the crackle of exploding ammunition.

Within minutes the landing ground was enveloped in a thick cloud of black smoke. The chances of the remaining aircraft making safe landings were now practically nil. The pilots could see neither craters nor wrecks, and every few minutes a crash told us of another casualty. To add to the pilots' worries, the Bofors AA gun had again opened up and were scoring direct hits on aircraft on the ground and in the air. Then the Germans started loading our stretchers, no doubt anxious to get the job of moving all the wounded finished.

A young, pale-faced officer with two broken legs was lifted on to our stretcher. He winced at every movement but didn't speak. When he was in position, one of his comrades covered him with a blanket and strapped him down. I looked at the officer. He was little more than a boy, and very handsome. As if to shut out the world of pain, he was holding his eyes tightly closed. For a moment I felt sorry for him. Then he suddenly opened his eyes and looked at me, and I saw an expression of hatred and contempt spreading across his face. After that, it was difficult to pity him.

'Right,' said Lawrie. 'Let's start. One, two, up!' We all lifted together and, following the party in front, set off across the top of the hill. Dingle and I led the way, carrying the foot of the stretcher. Though it was the lightest end, I found the going very hard and before long felt that I'd had enough.

'Can't we carry it on our shoulders?' I asked. 'I don't think I can go on like this.'

'No,' answered Lawrie. 'We start going downhill in a minute and it would slide off.'

We plodded on a little further.

'What we need is a bloody good meal!' wheezed the soldier of the party. 'I've not had a bite for two days.'

I slowed them down while I turned inwards and took hold with both hands. The pieces of handkerchief began to move and I felt the skin on both palms being twisted and torn. I carried on for a few more yards, then slowed down again. 'We'll have to stop,' I said. 'My hands feel as if they're in shreds.'

We lowered the stretcher to the ground.

'I told you that you wouldn't be able to cope,' Lawrie said. 'Let me look.' He took hold of my hands. The sight of them made me feel sick and they felt as if they had been in a fire. He shrugged his shoulders. 'No more carrying for you.'

I turned and looked at the German officer. Sour-looking bastard, I thought. Just sitting there like a bloody slave-driver! Then I felt sorry for him again. At least he wasn't complaining.

Dingle got in between the shafts. 'You steady it as we go down the hill,' he said as we started to move again.

I walked at the side of the stretcher, feeling very miserable. We followed the track down the side of the hill. It was steep and broken, and because of its narrowness, we couldn't rest for long without causing a traffic jam. Half-way down, the soldier and Dingle changed places. The officer had closed his eyes again, his face screwed up with pain.

At last we reached the bottom of the hill and two paratroopers took the stretcher. After unloading the officer into a lorry, they handed the stretcher back to us; presumably we were to return to the clearing.

'Better show your hands to the Jerries and see whether they can't do something for them,' panted Lawrie. 'We can't go on like this.'

I raised my palms; they looked like blood-soaked sponges. 'What can they do?' I asked. 'They can't even cope with their own wounded.'

'Well, at least you can ask them,' he replied irritably. 'It's no joke carrying one of those stretchers.'

I took a deep breath. I hated the idea of asking these barbarians for anything, but I realized that something would have to be done. With a sidelong glance at Lawrie, I walked slowly towards the lorry.

The two paratroopers were still loading wounded brought down by other parties, so I decided to hang about until they had finished. I felt tired and weary, so I sat on the running board by the driver's cabin. From where I was seated I could hear the German wounded talking among themselves. I tried to pick out words from their mixed conversation, but except for an occasional 'Englander', I could understand nothing of what they were saying.

I leaned my elbows on my knees and rested my head on the backs of my hands. I wanted to smoke but I'd no means of getting a light. Anyway, it might not be a very tactful thing to do – they might think I was deliberately dodging work. But I wanted to smoke so badly that I put a cigarette between my lips. My mind drifted back over the events of the day, of the night and of the previous day. What a hell-on-earth life had suddenly become. Then I began to think about the future, but unless I could escape, there was no future. Life under these conditions was not worth having.

I was so engrossed with my thoughts that I didn't hear the paratrooper approach. '*Was ist lose?*' I heard a voice say. I looked up, and took the cigarette from my mouth. Then I got to my feet. The paratrooper was a thin, straw-haired youth, with a mean-looking face. '*Was ist lose?*' he repeated. I held out my hands, palms upward. The cigarette was still between my fingers, but broken in half. For a moment he gazed at my hands. Then he turned and pointed to the path. '*Arbeit!*' he said. I shrugged my shoulders and started to walk. Then I felt a kick. It caught me on the base of the spine and sent me writhing to the ground. Pain and humiliation filled my eyes with tears. 'You bastard!' I muttered. 'You German bastard!'

I remained where I had fallen. Each time I attempted to move, the pain in my back seemed to pin me down again. Then I heard the lorry start up and move away. When it was gone I began to feel better. There would be no one to kick me around, and being kicked was what I now feared most.

I must have fallen asleep or passed out. When I regained consciousness, it was to find a paratrooper tapping me in the ribs with his boot. With a sigh of relief, I realized it was not the one who had kicked me. I tried to get to my feet. When he saw that I was having difficulty, he helped me up. I staggered to the lorry, which had now returned, and he assisted me on board. Exhausted, I lay down. Then I saw I was lying in a pool of blood. At first I thought it was my own. When I realized it wasn't, I began to vomit.

I dozed off to sleep again and didn't wake until they began loading wounded on board. The Germans looked at me sourly, but no one spoke. When the lorry was full, we moved off. Several of the Germans began to groan with pain. Because the road was in a bad state, we were bouncing about a great deal.

It took us 20 minutes to reach the village. We stopped outside one of the houses and, after the Germans had been taken off, the driver helped me down. He pointed to another house a little way down the road, indicating that I could get medical attention there.

I stumbled painfully across to the First Aid Post. To my surprise I found the Squadron Medical Officer, Flying Officer Cullen, was in charge. He looked harassed beyond words: wounded and dying men covered every inch of floor space, and the place reeked of blood and filth. The Medical Officer seemed to be ignoring me, but I saw Norman Darch, the Squadron Medical Orderly, so asked him if there was any chance of seeing the MO.

'He's terribly busy,' he told me. 'Is there anything I can do for you?'

'I want him to have a look at the base of my spine.' I told him. 'A bloody Kraut gave me a hard kick and it feels as if he's broken something.'

'I'll try and attract his attention in a minute,' he told me. 'Does it hurt much?'

'Not as much as it did. I could have killed the sod. I'd been helping bring Jerry wounded down from the hills and that was the thanks I got.'

Presently the MO was available and Norman told him in a few words what my trouble was. He told me to strip off, then he examined me. To my consternation, he found nothing more serious than a large bruise.

'Lucky for you that paratroopers wear rubber boots,' he remarked. 'If the one who kicked you had been wearing heavy army boots, he might have done you some real damage.'

He told Norman to help me on with my clothes, then said I'd better hang around for a couple of days to give my back time to settle down. I showed him my hands.

'Can you give me anything for these?' I asked. 'They're terribly painful.'

He shook his head sadly. 'We've used what few bandages we had, and also all the sheets and curtains we could lay our hands on.'

He walked across to a table and scooped out a spoonful of yellow ointment from a large jar. 'This is the best I can do for you,' he said. 'Rub it in lightly, then cover your hands with paper, if you can find any. It'll help keep the flies off.'

After thanking him, I asked if there was anything I could do to help.

'I'm sure Norman can find something useful for you to do,' he told me.

I was to go round with a bucket of water, giving the wounded drinks. But first I had to go to the village well in the middle of the main street and queue behind a batch of Jerries who were filling buckets and water bottles. For the next few hours I was busy doling out water and doing odd jobs in the 'hospital'. The doctor had hardly any surgical equipment. Eventually he came to an arrangement with the German doctor regarding the one instrument that was in constant use by both sides – a surgical saw. And whenever a wounded man died, his bandages were removed, sterilized and used on someone else.

At eight o'clock an English-speaking German visited us. He demanded lists of all the wounded and hospital staff. Norman and I set to work and when the lists were completed, we handed them over. Then he and the doctor visited the patients, and the German tied a label saying '*Verwundet*' around the neck of each seriously wounded man. When they had finished, those without labels were herded outside. Then the Germans demanded to know the qualifications of each member of staff. I was the only one of the three who appeared unable to satisfy him, so I also was chased outside. After posting a guard on the door, the German told us to follow him. He led us to a small one-room stone building a few hundred yards up the road. When we were all inside, he locked the door on us.

The room was about 15 feet square. What light there was filtered in through a small window set high up in the wall. For furniture, we had an outsize kitchen table, two chairs and an empty 5-gallon oil drum.

The table was allotted to six of the wounded men and everyone else just sat or lay down where he pleased. Before we had got properly settled down, the door opened and another half-dozen wounded men trooped inside. We had hardly absorbed these when about 10 more joined us. Two of them, 'Bunny' Austin and Stan Hog, I knew quite well. As both of them were rather badly wounded, room was found on the table. The rest just ended up on the floor. During the next half-hour, 15 more men were crammed in.

By now there was insufficient space for even the wounded to lie down, and 32 out of our total of 46 were wounded. What with the darkness, the smell and the heat, conditions were beginning to resemble those of the Black Hole of Calcutta. During the night, one of the allegedly lightly wounded men grew delirious, so we pounded on the door to attract the guard's attention. After an interminable time, the door was opened, but not to take out the sick man! Instead, a Cretan peasant was pushed in among us. His entry nearly started a riot. Half the prisoners were prepared to accept him, but the others wanted him moved, partly because he was a civilian and partly to let the Germans know that we were already hopelessly overcrowded. We redoubled our banging on the door and everyone began to shout. We might as well have saved our breath, though, for the door remained locked. Shortly afterwards, the delirious man died, but despite more banging on the door and shouting, we received no answer, and he remained dead on the floor until morning.

Somehow, everyone managed to find himself space to sit down and after a time things grew quieter. From sheer exhaustion, most of us just keeled over into untidy heaps, our arms, legs and bodies all mixed together. But the smell and heat, together with the moaning of some of the wounded, kept us from sleeping.

At seven o'clock the next morning the door was opened and for 10 minutes – under the watchful eyes of two paratroopers – we were allowed to wander into the small garden at the back of the building to relieve nature. Then we were made to fall in. The wounded were sent back to the hospital and the rest of us, with a minimum of ceremony, went to work. We were hungry, thirsty and very weary, but our Nazi masters couldn't be expected to be worried about that. We were only prisoners, and our price – 10 a penny.

9

Corpses and Graves

'Darky' Dear, who was one of the Squadron cooks, and myself were escorted by a paratrooper a little distance up the road to a house which had been turned into a German hospital. In a shed attached to the house was the dead body of a paratrooper and our task was to bury it.

'If we've got to do any burying, I think they should have let us bury our own dead first,' Darky said as we entered the shed.

'If you mean the man who died last night, I think the MO will want to see him first,' I replied.

I looked down at the paratrooper. He was a huge man and appeared to have bled to death from a gaping wound in the thigh – he was unbandaged.

I stooped and touched the body. 'He's still warm,' I said, giving an involuntary shudder.

'He's dead all right,' replied Darky. 'His neck's going stiff.' Again I shuddered. This was the first time I'd ever touched a dead body and I wasn't feeling very happy.

Darky took hold of him by the shoulders and I lifted him by the legs. We had hardly left the building when he slipped from my grasp. His clothing was slimy with blood and my hands were too sore to take much of a grip. Followed by our somewhat mystified escort, we went in search of something on which to carry the body. The best we could find was a deck chair.

We took the body into a small field at the back of the house. Another German guard was waiting for us and close by was a newly dug grave. We lowered the makeshift stretcher to the ground, and while the guard removed the identity disc from his dead comrade's neck and scratched the number on to the nearby wall, I cleaned the blood off my hands with a tuft of grass.

'Will he say a prayer or anything?' Darky asked.

I shrugged my shoulders. I doubted it.

No prayer was said – except perhaps by Darky or me. The guard finished his scratching, then, with a hearty heave, tipped the body into the grave. The grave was too short and too shallow for so large a body: it landed in a heap, an elbow and a knee protruding above the level of the ground. But the guard was quite up to the occasion, setting to work with the flat of his spade to hammer down the protruding parts. Then the three of us filled in the grave. The tip of the dead man's elbow refused to be buried and the guard had to use his spade again.

Almost before we had finished, another German appeared on the scene. He had a tommy-gun slung across his shoulder and in his hands he carried two entrenching tools and a short wooden stick. After a brief conversation with his comrade, he beckoned Darky and me to follow him.

'Now what are we in for?' Darky asked.

'Grave-digging,' I replied. Those entrenching tools told their own story.

Close to the hedge at the far side of the field, the German started to measure off a plot of ground three sticks long and one stick wide. Then he told us, in pidgin English, that the grave was for an '*Englander*', and that we were to dig it two sticks deep. We took off our tunics and set to work.

Removing the turf and the first few inches of soil was fairly easy work, even though neither of us was accustomed to handling an entrenching tool. The trouble started when we got about 6 inches down: the ground was almost solid chalk. We banged and chipped with all the energy we could muster, but our progress as very slow and the German started shouting at us. Still, all the shouting in the world wouldn't make us work any harder. What we needed were pick-axes or pneumatic drills.

I could feel the blood squelching between the wooden handle of the entrenching tool and my palms. 'What about a spell?' I said to Darky.

'You'll have Tarzan hitting you over the head if he sees you slacking,' he replied.

I looked at the German. His back was turned towards us, so I dropped the entrenching tool and sat down, panting. I had hardly settled down when I felt myself being whisked into the air and violently shaken by the shirt neckband.

'*Verflucht!*' roared the German. '*Verflucht!*' He shook me until my eyes felt as if they would leave their sockets. Then, with his free hand, he gave me a hard punch on the side of the head and dropped me back into the partly dug grave.

I landed in a heap, almost too dazed to think. I got slowly to my knees and felt around for the entrenching tool. I'll kill him for that, I told myself. I turned and looked up at him, the entrenching tool in my hand. 'I'm going to kill you, you bloody swine!' I whispered. Then I knew I couldn't kill him. He had unslung his tommy-gun and it was pointed at me.

In silence I carried on hacking and digging. For a time rage lent force to the blows I struck at the rock-like chalk, but as my blood cooled, so the strength behind the blows weakened. I still wanted to kill him, though – kill him quietly, when he wasn't looking, and drag him down into the grave we were digging, and pile all the chalk and soil on top of him.

Inch by inch we lowered the grave, until at last it reached the prescribed depth of two sticks. After throwing out the last of the chippings and dust, we helped each other out. Our clothes were almost white and were sodden with sweat. Weak and stiff, we were unable to straighten our backs.

The German told us to follow him and, picking up our tunics, we went back towards the house. But we didn't go inside; instead we crossed the road and went into a small corrugated-iron shed behind another wine parlour. Laid out on the rough earth floor were the bodies of about a dozen British soldiers, each in the attitude death had taken him. A paratrooper was busy with a Flit pump, trying to keep the flies away.

I turned to Darky. 'Can't we get out of here?' I asked. 'I'm going to be sick.'

He shook his head. 'I feel that way myself.'

Unwillingly, we stood and looked at the bodies. A few hours before, they had been alive. Now they were dead and indecent.

We heard voices behind us; three soldiers had followed us in. Now the paratrooper started bellowing. He detailed us to pick up the body nearest the door. I held back, unable to touch another corpse. Darky and the three soldiers raised the body, then left the shed. I followed like a lone mourner. Outside, I watched them cross the road and pass out of sight behind a house. Almost in a trance, I walked into the road. It was deserted. I suddenly wanted to run away. But where could I go? I turned left and started to walk. I found myself back at Doctor Cullen's makeshift hospital and went inside.

A mug of water was all I could be spared, but I was glad of the rest from grave-digging. However, within half an hour a party of prisoners arrived on the scene, among them poor 'Darky' Dear and some of the soldiers who had helped carry the dead. A solitary German was in charge and they were going in the direction of the landing ground. I was made to join them. What kind of work were we to be put to now?

Having crossed the bridge over the river, we turned right in the direction of our old camp. As we proceeded, we passed the body of an airman lying at the side of the track. He was on his back, his knees drawn up. He had ginger hair and his mouth was wide open showing his teeth. I recognized him as Freddie Betts, our ambulance driver. When we reached the stone building which had been the Regulating Office for the Fleet Air Arm we were halted. The building had been damaged and most of the tiles blown off its roof. The German guard spoke a little English, and told us to fall out but not to leave his sight.

We nodded our heads like sheep and smiled at his English.

He picked out two soldiers and told them to climb on to the 'house top'; the rest of us were to scout round and find some undamaged tiles. A nice quiet job, I thought to myself. He might very easily have sent Darky and me up on the roof, had his sense of humour run in that direction!

If there were any undamaged tiles, we failed to find them close to the building and the area of our search began to widen. Then I began to do a little scheming. The Orderly Room tent in which I had lived was near by. I might be able to do some good if I could reach it. Apart from destroying any papers that were there, I could retrieve bits of kit.

I had just started to work my way unobtrusively to the back of the building when another party of prisoners appeared on the scene. I returned to the building as quickly as I could, and began to poke about among the rubble. The new party numbered about eight and was told to help us search for tiles. After being warned that they would be shot if they tried to escape, they were told to fall out.

To my surprise, Lawrie and Dingle Bell were among them. After exchanging greetings, I told them of my intention to reach the tent. Lawrie wanted to come with me to rescue some of his kit, but I told him that it would be inviting trouble if two of us were seen there; much better if we went in turn.

Again I set off – to all intents quite aimlessly – in the direction of the tent. I was over half-way there when I heard a series of high-pitched whistles coming from overhead.

'Bombs! Run for it!' I heard someone shout.

I turned and ran for the building, but before I reached it the first bombs had exploded. I threw myself to the ground, clawing at the earth with my hands and feet in an effort to dig myself in. The ground all around me began to quake and erupt; the noise was deafening. I grew frightened, and angry. Frightened because I thought I would be killed; angry because I would be killed by British bombs! I continued to claw at the earth. If only I could get closer to it and surround myself with it, I would be safe. But the ground was too hard and my fingers made little impression on it. Then I tried to resign myself to the end. No one without shelter could hope to live through this for more than a few seconds.

Then suddenly the bombing stopped. It was all over and I was still alive! Getting to my feet, I shook myself. Yes, I was still in one piece and uninjured! I looked in the direction of the building. Smoke was coming from holes in the roof and the German was lying on the ground close to the wall. I walked over to him and saw that he was spattered with blood. Close by was Dingle Bell, dead or unconscious. As if from nowhere, Lawrie and the others suddenly appeared.

'Come and help me with Dingle,' I said to Lawrie. 'He's out cold.'

As I spoke, Dingle began to move. He slowly raised his head, and I saw that he had a wound in the neck.

'Is that what knocked you out?' I asked, drawing his tunic collar to one side.

He looked at me vacantly.

'He's not come round properly yet,' Lawrie said.

'Have you any more holes in you?' I asked, looking carefully over him.

'My back's hurting,' he said in a feeble voice.

'Can you stand up?'Lawrie asked him.

'My back's hurting,' he repeated.

'Better peel his tunic and shirt off,' Lawrie said.

Between us, we raised him into a sitting position, and then removed his tunic, shirt and vest.

'No wonder he's complaining about his back,' Lawrie remarked. 'Look!'

From the waist upwards, his back was pitted with small bomb splinters.

Half a dozen soldiers collected round us. 'Is he badly hurt?' one of them asked.

'No, I don't think so,' Lawrie told him. 'Mostly splinters. They must have dropped some APs.'

'What about his neck?' I asked. 'He's bleeding like a pig.'

'Another splinter, I expect,' he replied. 'Let's get his clothing on again.'

I turned to the soldier. 'Any of the others get hit?'

'Only the Jerry. He got blown off the roof.'

'Is he dead?'

He glanced across at the little crowd of prisoners who surrounded the German. 'I can't see properly. I think he is.'

While we were still struggling with Dingle's clothing, a party of Germans appeared. They glanced at Dingle, then went across to the other crowd.

'What're we going to do with him?' I asked Lawrie. 'Take him to hospital?'

'We might as well. He can't do any more work.'

We raised him to his feet, then set off for the road. Then we had another shock. Apparently bombs had been dropped among those working on the landing ground and long streams of wounded men were now limping or being carried to the First Aid Post.

By the bridge we were met by a party of paratroopers. They examined everyone roughly for wounds. Dingle was passed and Lawrie was allowed to accompany him, but I was sent back to work. About 10 minutes later I was back with Darky.

Another German was sent to carry on with the roof repairs. He spoke no English, but somehow he managed to make himself understood whenever he wanted anything done. We continued our half-hearted search for unbroken roof tiles.

I was at the back of the Fleet Air Arm Regulating Office and began moving slowly in the direction of the Orderly Room tent. I was still anxious to pay it a visit. When I was just past the Orderly Room tent I stopped and had a good look round. I wanted to make quite sure that I was unobserved. Everything was quiet and apart from the paratrooper's head, which kept bobbing up and down behind the pitch of the roof, there was no one to be seen. Or was there? Who was that close to the far wall of the Officers' Mess? It was someone crouching down on one knee – and he was wearing a British tin hat! I changed direction, walking slowly and very cautiously.

As I approached, I suddenly felt the blood drain from my face and I grew cold. It was Bill Williams! I stood there, looking at him, and the events of that fateful Tuesday morning flashed vividly into my mind. I saw him forcing his way along the trench, stumbling over arms and legs, and knocking the Aussie's rifle over. I saw the scuffle with Lofty Bond and I heard Lofty swear and say that he'd never make it. Then the chatter of the machine-gun and – silence. For Bill, it was eternal silence.

Slowly my feelings of horror were replaced by those of curiosity, but still I couldn't approach him. He had, quite literally, died as he had lived: at the moment of his death he had been down on one knee, peering round the corner of the Mess; in that attitude he had been killed.

Saddened, I turned and walked slowly away, wondering why no one had bothered to bury him. Near the entrance to the tent I could see the trestle table, loaded with papers and unopened mail. Beyond it was my camp bed, under which was an upturned bucket, sheltering a haversack containing my personal treasures. I had hoped that should the tent be burnt, the bucket would protect the haversack.

At last I was sufficiently close to be able to dart inside. I paused for a final look around. Yes, all clear; not a soul in sight. As I moved forward, I heard a rustling sound in the tent. I stopped. Then I heard a bark, and a moment later a dog appeared.

'You bloody piard!' I muttered aloud. 'What're you doing here?' The Greek dog, recently adopted as a mascot by the Squadron, was covered with mud and dust, and looked half-starved. It started barking again. I backed away, not anxious to be seen near the tent, but the dog continued to bark at me.

Someone started shouting, I turned and saw the German on the roof, standing and waving his arms about. Cursing the dog, I started to walk back to the Mess. The dog followed me, wagging its tail!

The German climbed down from the roof and began shouting again. What he was saying was pretty obvious: I was trying to escape and if he caught me again, I would be shot.

10

Salvage and Sabotage

I managed to get back to the First Aid Post, hopeful that Norman Darch could do something to ease the pain of my hands and arm. He cleaned them up, put some more ointment on them and bandaged me up. He could spare nothing more durable than crepe, as that was needed for the seriously wounded, who were still being brought in from the hills.

He had barely finished when there was a commotion out in the road. A German officer riding a bicycle was brandishing a revolver as he drove a party of POWs towards the landing ground. He wore a green uniform which he seemed to have long since grown out of. He was grossly overweight and had a neck which his tunic found hard to accommodate. His face was puce, his eyes protruding. I immediately knew who he was, as word of him had spread among all POWs in the area. His nickname was 'Bullneck',* and his job was to collect working parties of POWs to salvage crashed aircraft, fill in bomb craters, unload aircraft and do any of a dozen other tasks which might be deemed necessary.

When he saw me he dismounted, came over and let fly a string of German, poking his revolver in my ribs. '*Raus!*' he roared. '*Schnell!*' I joined the other unfortunates.

We jogged all the way to the landing ground, where he dismounted and, after dropping his bicycle into a shallow ditch at the side of the road, drove

---

* Oberstleutnant Snowadzki, the officer in charge of the Airfield Service Company.

us like sheep on to the landing ground. After our long run from the village, we were too exhausted to think clearly, but we guessed that our task was to rescue troops from burning aircraft.

Visibility was down to nil, but aircraft were still endeavouring to land, and some even to take off after unloading their human cargo. Within seconds of leaving the road, we were engulfed in a dense cloud of smoke made gritty with dust and sand stirred up by moving aircraft. We covered our faces with our arms, but even then we were nearly blinded. Breathing was no longer automatic – each breath was painful, as the dust and smoke burnt our throats and lungs – but the officer was impervious to conditions.

Somewhere ahead we could hear shouting. '*Heben*! *Heben*! – Heave! Heave!' The officer shepherded us in the direction of the voice. As we approached there was a sudden roar and an aircraft came tearing towards us out of the gloom. We dived out of the way and, as it passed, its slipstream nearly blew us all flat.

Three more cries of '*Schnell*!' brought us to the voice. Out of half-blinded eyes, I saw that its owner was a short, fat German. Like our shepherd, he was using his pistol to encourage his flock to '*Schnell*!', but they also had to '*Heben*!' They were dragging a troop carrier, minus its undercarriage, from a crater! So I was wrong about rescue work; we were to join a salvage squad.

Towropes had already been made fast to the wing trunks and, with about a dozen prisoners on each rope and another dozen on each wing, the plane was being jerked forward a few inches at a time. Animated by the bellowing of the German, we took up a position behind the wings and added what weight we could. Despite the heaving and shoving and a prodigious amount of swearing, the wretched plane seemed to be going deep into the sand instead of sliding along it. The German tried to spur us on to greater effort by threatening to shoot us, but we just hadn't any more strength. We continued to heave and shove, openly cursing the German for his stupidity. Surely he could devise some better means of moving 10 tons of aeroplane?

Someone suggested killing him and sneaking back to the village – the officer had left and he was quite alone – but before anything could happen, providence stepped in. Aircraft were landing and taking off in all directions, the pilots flying 'blind'. One of them flew straight into us and the whole tangle of wreckage went up in flames. The men on the towropes had seen it coming and yelled to us to scatter, so no one was hurt.

There was no question of trying to rescue anyone on board and, after collecting us all together, we were shepherded to another troop carrier about 50 yards away. It was a Ju 52 which had lost a wheel from its undercarriage and the whole machine was tipped up on one wing. After carrying out a brief survey, the German ordered about 20 of us to gather round the lower wing and lift. The rest were to climb on to the other wing and jump up and down, the idea being to see whether the aircraft could be made to balance on one wheel.

When we were all in position, the order was given to '*Heben!*' and '*Springen!* – Jump!' We heaved and jumped and the machine creaked and groaned, but nothing else happened. We tried again but with the same result. The German climbed up on the wing and saw that nearly everyone was close to the wing trunk instead of being up by the tip. Very angry, he waved his pistol about and drove everyone up the slippery metal surface until they were in danger of falling off. Again we heaved and jumped, and this time the aircraft began to tip over in the required direction. Perhaps the idea would work after all.

Out of the haze came another roar, and almost before anyone had time to move, another troop carrier ran into us. The result was something of a shambles. Those of us on the ground ran for our lives, but those on the wing tip were shot into the air and landed in a heap among the wreckage. We heard a lot of shouting and, as there was a risk of fire, went back to give what help we could. Men who were still conscious were either crawling or limping away as fast as they could. We hunted around in the murky gloom and found five bodies and a bloody shirt sleeve containing an arm. We carried the bodies well away from the wreckage, then examined them for signs of life. Amazingly, only one man was dead; the rest had broken arms, legs and ribs. But we found no one minus an arm!

The German decided to call off work and ordered us to the edge of the landing ground. We picked up the casualties, thankful to be getting away from the chaos. We'd almost reached the road when a shell from one of the Bofors landed just behind us. There were three more casualties to carry. Out of the kindness of his heart, the German allowed the wounded men to be taken back to the village.

For a while we hung around close to the road. Smoke and fumes continued to drift towards us, and we were all coughing and spluttering.

'What a bastard!' wheezed a soldier standing close to me. I nodded, not daring to open my mouth. 'A real bastard!' he said. Then he started to cough violently. I moved closer to him and thumped his back.

'For Christ's sake!' he gasped, so I stopped. Then I got a lungful of burning sulphurous fumes and started to cough with equal violence. He seized me by the arm and, both coughing, we staggered along the road.

'The village . . .' he wheezed between coughs. 'Let's . . . the village.'

We were coughing so violently that we lost all sense of direction and staggered from one side of the road to the other. All the way to the bridge we coughed and gasped. When we finally reached it, we were so exhausted that we collapsed on to the grass verge. But we had left the smoke and fumes behind and were breathing sweet, pure air again. After a time we recovered sufficiently to sit up. I glanced at the soldier. His eyes were red and inflamed and looked as if they were about to pop out of their sockets; his face was nearly purple.

'What about a drink?' he asked at last. 'Think we can make the river?'

'We can try.'

With an effort we managed to get to our feet. Paratroopers were passing up and down the road, but none of them took much notice of us.

'Better hold on to each other,' he said, taking my arm. As we lurched slowly along, he glanced at my face. 'You look bloody awful!' he said. 'How d'you feel?'

'Bloody awful!' I replied.

We made our way in easy stages down to the river. The water looked cool and inviting, and we lay down on our bellies and sucked it in by the mouthful.

'This is even better than beer,' said the soldier, shaking the water from his hair. We both continued sucking it up greedily.

The next time I looked at him, I saw that he was removing his boots and socks. 'I think I'll wash my feet,' he said.

I half smiled. Why the sudden urge for cleanliness, I wondered.

'I've not finished drinking yet,' I told him. Turning over, I drank a lot more of the river. It was icy cold but made me feel clean inside.

The soldier was paddling about, so, removing my shoes and socks, I did the same. We splashed about, pulling faces because the water was so cold, but we enjoyed it.

Then I found myself getting even more dirt-conscious than the soldier. 'What about washing our socks?' I suggested. 'D'you think we'll have time?'

'Why not?' he replied. 'They can't shoot us for getting clean.'

We set to work trying to get the filth out of our socks – and how filthy they were! I'd just finished one of them when there was a strange whistle over-head, immediately followed by a terrific explosion in the middle of the river. We both threw ourselves flat in the water and stayed there until all the stones and spray had finished raining down.

'That bloody Bofors,' grumbled the soldier. 'They couldn't hit a hayrick at 50 yards!'

I stood up, water dripping from every inch of clothing. 'I'm getting out of this,' I told him. 'If we don't get hit, we'll get drowned.'

Collecting my shoes and socks, I made for dry land. Then I stripped off and wrung out my clothes. One packet of cigarettes was still in good con-dition. The soldier replaced his boots and socks, then clattered across the stones and came and sat down next to me.

'Got a match?' I asked him.

He looked at the packet of cigarettes and shook his head. 'Where did you get those?' he asked in surprise.

'They came all the way from England,' I told him. 'Where can we get a light?'

'Tap a Jerry.'

I pulled on my trousers. They felt cold and clammy. 'Like to try?' I asked.

'Sure. Give's a fag.'

I opened the packet and handed him two cigarettes. 'The Jerry might want one,' I said.

He scrambled to his feet. 'He won't bloody well get one,' he said, handing me one back.

'Well, keep it,' I told him. 'It'll do for later.'

I watched him make his way slowly along the river bank to the bridge. Then he sat down on the parapet to wait for a German to come along. It was just his luck that that awful officer on his bicycle should come scorching across the bridge, driving another herd of prisoners towards the landing ground. The soldier stayed where he was instead of hiding. The officer yelled at him and brandished his revolver. That was the last I saw of him – a weary figure, trotting painfully along at the tail-end of the party.

11
The Bungalow – Knickers – Chicken Stew

After crossing the river I dressed again, then set off for the village. To avoid being shanghaied into another working party, I assumed a bad limp every time I approached any Germans. I got a few quizzical looks, but no one spoke to me. As I tramped wearily along, I began to realize how weak I was. I'd not eaten for over 72 hours, and I was so unsteady on my feet that I was constantly tripping and falling down. Then I discovered that I was talking to myself. At first I thought the voice came from someone behind me, but each time I turned round the road was empty.

'You're imagining things!' I said aloud after turning for about the third time.

'It might be someone hiding behind the hedge,' said a little voice.

'You know quite well it isn't. It's you – you're talking to yourself.'

'No I'm not. I haven't reached that state yet.'

I tripped and fell into the road again.

'What you need is a decent meal and a good sleep. That'd put you right.'

I grunted. A good meal! Was there any food left in the world? I doubted it.

'Well, why don't you make a break for it?' asked the little voice. 'This is a heaven-sent opportunity.'

'They'll shoot you if you get caught,' said a voice behind me.

I turned to see who it was and, as I did so, I tripped and fell again. Picking myself up with a curse, I continued on my way to the village.

There were times in my more normal moments when I began to feel somewhat guilty about my almost passive attitude towards the Germans.

There was no doubt that I was scared of them, and had reached the stage when I did just as they told me, even when it was something my conscience forbade, such as handling ammunition for them. I think there were many factors which affected me. To start with, I was a good deal older than most of the men I knew, who for the most part were single and in their early twenties, whereas I was married and in my thirties. Also, in pre-war days I had had some contact with decent Germans who were trying to escape from Germany. They had had a sorry tale to tell about conditions in their homeland, about the brutality of a large section of the German population, particularly the Brown Shirts and the military in general. As they would think nothing of murdering members of their own families, strangers, such as prisoners, meant nothing to them. My own attitude was that, being married and wishing to get back home in one piece, the less trouble I got involved in the more likely I was to attain my objective. If I wished to beat the Germans in any way, it would have to be by stealth and cunning. Outright boldness or disobedience would most likely result in my getting shot. So, the watchwords were cunning and stealth.

As I drew close to Dr Cullen's hospital, I saw that prisoners were collecting together in the roadway. I slowed down. If another working party was being formed, I would hide. Then someone shouted my name: 'Come on, Mike! We're off to find somewhere to live!' When I got a little closer, I saw that it was Darky Dear.

I formed up with the rest and two paratroopers counted us. We numbered about 30, mostly soldiers. After a slight delay, the order was given to march, and we set off through the village in the direction of the church.

'Where've you been since this morning?' Darky asked. 'Digging more graves?'

'Not bloody likely!' I replied, struggling to keep in step with the man in front of me. 'I did a spell of stretcher-carrying up in the hills, but this afternoon I've been helping to move wrecked kites off the landing ground.'

'I'd sooner dig graves, thank you,' he said. 'What's it like down there?'

'Bloody terrible,' I told him. 'Sand, dust, smoke and Jerry kites landing in heaps all over the place. It's like Dante's Inferno, but not quite so much flame.'

For a time we marched in silence. The man in front of me kept getting out of step and I was constantly tripping over his heels. At last I got mad and gave one of his heels a hard kick.

'Why the 'ell don't you keep in step?' he demanded, turning round and glaring at me.

'It's you who's out of step,' I snapped. I knew that I was inclined to roll about a bit, but the way he was marching made it impossible to avoid treading on his heels.

'You bloody Air Force,' he growled over his shoulder. 'No bloody kites, and now you can't even keep in step.'

83

'Why don't you wrap up?' Darky told him. 'You're always bitching about something.'

Then he turned to me and, for the soldier's benefit, said in a loud voice. 'He's been binding and bitching all day. I've threatened to pan him, and I will if he opens his trap again.' After that there was no more grumbling and the soldier contrived to keep in step, but it was a bad thing that we should start grumbling among ourselves.

Midway between the village and church we came to a small stone bungalow which stood in about an acre of ground. One of the guards held up his arm and we came to a halt.

'What's this?' asked Darky hopefully. 'Our new home?'

I shook my head. It was much more likely to have been commandeered as a home for paratroopers.

The guard opened the front door and peered inside. Then he turned and waved a hand at us. '*Kommen!*' he shouted. For a moment we all stood and gaped – we just didn't believe our ears – but then we all dashed wildly from the road, up the short garden path and in through the door.

There were only two rooms, both completely bare of furniture, and there was not even a fireplace or cooking stove. We divided ourselves between the two rooms, and each man set about choosing a patch on which to lie. It was barely five o'clock but we were quite ready to sleep. Then someone discovered a travelling trunk tucked away in a corner. In a twinkling a crowd had collected. With a loud guffaw, a woman's dress was thrown into the air. A dozen pairs of hands grabbed at it – at least it would serve as a pillow – but no one would forgo his claim and the dress was torn to shreds. Then followed a pair of high-heeled shoes, some stockings and a table-cloth. Everyone was laughing, and men from the next room came in to see what they could pick up. Out flew a pair of lace curtains, some more table linen and another dress – poor stuff for bedding. Apparently those nearest the trunk were hopeful of finding something more useful and were throwing the junk to the rest of us.

Finally the trunk was emptied and pushed to one side. All I had secured was a pair of ladies' plain white knickers! With an eye to the future, I had in mind using them as a spare pair of underpants. In the meantime, they would serve as a scarf when I was cold and a towel when I had the opportunity to wash.

We returned to our respective patches and made ourselves as comfortable as we could. Then we started talking about food. When were the Germans going to feed us? Was it really possible to eat stewed boots? How long could a man live without food? And what about the Geneva Convention? Gradually the chatter grew quieter and after a time stopped altogether. Just as the last of us was dozing off to sleep, the door opened and in clattered another dozen prisoners. In the reshuffle for sleeping space, I received a kick on the back of the head from an iron-shod army boot. I rolled over, then got to my feet – I couldn't get rid of the stars! While I was swearing and rubbing my head, the sea of bodies began to move towards me and, before I realized it, I had nowhere to lie down.

I did some more swearing and tried to chisel a new plot between two hefty soldiers, but it was no use; they seemed to have taken root and were immovable. I tried again between two smaller bodies, but they made such a row that I gave it up as a bad job. Treading carefully, I picked my way across to the trunk – my bed for the night!

When all was quiet again, I began thinking of escape. I considered my present position. In a bungalow, well back from the main village road, with not more than two German guards on duty, both at the front of the building. I would have difficulty reaching the window without causing a disturbance; bodies were strewn everywhere. The window was about 6 feet away from me and alongside it were two New Zealanders. There was no front window, only this one at the rear.

The guard on duty could occasionally be heard marching out by the front gate – but only one of them, though there had originally been two. I made up my mind to go out through the back window, then creep down to the bottom of the garden, which I had already judged to be about 100 yards long and 25 yards wide. When we had first occupied the bungalow, I had seen hens at the bottom of the garden, so the second guard might conceivably have broken into the henhouse for an illicit sleep. I must avoid that part of the garden.

My plan would be to leave the garden, then make my way in a straight line towards the sea, which I knew to be about 1 mile away if I steered myself in a direct line. All was very quiet, so I tied my shoes together by their laces, then felt about with my toes, trying to find a gap where I could place a foot. I soon found one, and in double quick time had planted both feet on the floor. So far, so good. I then had to pick out a space between two bodies where I could take my next step. I found a gap, but the body made a great noise when I moved a foot towards it. Apparently the owner had left a hand sticking out and I had trodden on it, hence the noise.

I apologized, then immediately took my next step, this time with no further trouble. Two more short steps and I was close to the window. I stopped to put my shoes in. Here one of the New Zealanders was either awake or, more probably, was a light sleeper. As I got close to him, he demanded to know what I was doing. I told him I intended making a break, would he help me with the window? In a trice he was on his feet, trying to open the window. It was jammed, but he managed to force it open.

Then I told him I was not too optimistic and would he be ready to let me back in if I had to return in a hurry. He promised that he would. I whispered my name and told him to let any RAF man he met know that I had made a break but that if he heard I had been killed by a guard, he was to report it to any senior NCO he could find.

With that, I put on my shoes and climbed out. I gave a tap on the pane to let the New Zealander know I was on my way and heard him close the window. As he did so, I suddenly began to feel lonely and wished I had chosen someone to come with me.

I listened carefully for a few seconds and heard the guard on duty at the front of the bungalow moving about, his equipment rattling noisily. But at least this told me in what direction he was moving; he seemed to be taking a T-shaped route, probably across half of the front of the bungalow, then walking up and down the main footpath leading to the door, then back and along the other half of the front of the bungalow. I decided that the noise he was making would drown any noise of mine, so I set off, trying to avoid any obstacles there might be.

When I was well down towards the bottom of the garden, I heard movement. Was it the other guard? I stopped and listened, then realized the noise must be made by more than one person, because it appeared to come from two directions at once. I moved carefully and slowly on my way, trying to identify the noise. Was it human or a domestic animal? By now I was growing quite frightened. The noise might well be from two guards prowling about, in which case they would probably be trigger-happy. I moved even more slowly, ready at a second's notice to change direction and head back to the bungalow. Then, as if to make sure I was properly frightened, I heard low, guttural voices, though what they were saying I had no idea.

I decided to return to the bungalow and call off my attempt, at least for the present. I hurried back towards the window. When I reached it, I knocked lightly and almost immediately it was opened.

'Thanks,' I said to the New Zealander. 'I think there are some Jerries about, I could hear them talking.'

I started to climb in through the window, when we both heard the guttural voices. One said to the other, 'Use your knuckle and break the sod's neck. Don't just pull it or you'll pull it's bloody head off!' The guttural voice was that of a Scotsman! So my fright had been caused by a couple of prisoners out raiding a henhouse. They were from the next room and had gone out through the window, the same as me. What a dreadful anticlimax!

The following morning the New Zealander told me he had heard that three prisoners from the next room had gone out but only two had returned; no one knew what had happened to the third man – he may have been attempting to escape.

I made my way back towards the basket, where I again curled up like a cat. After my heart had stopped running wild, I managed to get off to sleep.

When the guard came to open the door next morning, he thought we'd barricaded ourselves in. What with sleeping bodies resting against it, despite his heaving he managed to open it only a few inches. Then he poked his gun round the corner and started shouting. The sleeping bodies soon came to life and the door was pushed open. Somehow I had dozed off and managed to sleep right through the night, but now, as I uncurled myself, I felt like one huge and painful ache. I glanced down at my hands. They had begun to fester. With a sigh I closed my eyes.

Someone was talking to me and I looked up. It was Darky, asking for a cigarette. As I held out the battered packet, I noticed how ill and bedraggled he looked.

'Thanks', he said, taking one. Then he ambled off to get a light.

I blinked wearily. I'd have given all the cigarettes in the world for a cup of tea.

A soldier moved across from the doorway and came and sat on the trunk. 'Spare a fag?' he asked.

I fished out the packet again.

'If you hadn't flashed them I wouldn't have come on the scrounge,' he said, putting the cigarette between his lips.

I turned and looked at him. 'You don't have to apologize.'

'I'm not apologizing,' he replied quietly. 'I'm just tipping you off: don't flash that packet about or soon you'll have no fags left.'

I knew he was right, but I was past caring.

When Darky returned he looked almost cheerful. 'Come and sit out in the sun,' he said, offering me a light. 'It might cheer you up a bit.'

I followed him into the garden. For a time neither of us spoke, and thoughts of home began drifting through my mind. Was it fine in England? And what would my wife be doing? Would she know what had happened to me yet? Perhaps she had already received one of those frightening crimson-enveloped telegrams marked 'Priority', telling her 'We regret to inform you that ...' What did they regret informing her? That I was dead? Or only missing? How would she take it? I suppose she would just weep and weep. And when she could weep no longer, she would find that she didn't believe the telegram anyway!

'Do you think they'll give us any breakfast?' I asked.

'Yes,' he replied to my amazement. 'One of the blokes has been com-plaining to the Jerry guard that we've had nothing to eat for nearly four days. The guard didn't believe him at first, but he checked up with some of his mates, so they said they'd try and raise some grub for us this morning.'

A soldier standing close to us joined in the conversation. 'We'll get something all right!' he remarked sceptically. 'But it won't be conner – it'll be work!'

Darky's eyes flashed dangerously. 'You bloody misery,' he said angrily. 'If he says we'll get some grub, we'll get some grub.'

'We'll see,' said the soldier, taking a pull at his cigarette. Then he opened his tunic and deliberately took a hitch in his belt.

'That's my breakfast,' he said drily.

I glanced at Darky. 'You married?' I asked him.

He started. Evidently I'd broken his train of thought. 'What d'you think I

87

want a wife for?' he replied after a moment's pause. 'I've got enough worries without that.'

'Well, you look married,' I told him. 'Lots of wrinkles.'

He nipped the end off his cigarette and pocketed the stub. 'That's through cooking for you shower!'

Suddenly I was thirsty. Water – where could I get some water? I moved along to the crowd by the gate. Perhaps the guard would give me a drink from his bottle. I started to edge my way through the crowd, at first gently but, as resistance grew, roughly. At last I reached the guard. But he had no water-bottle. For a moment I stood and stared at him – it seemed impossible, no water-bottle, no water, nothing to drink! Then I cursed him to perdition.

Turning around, I started to push my way out of the crowd. If only Lofty were here, I'd soon get a drink, I told myself. Then I heard a sudden burst of tommy-gun fire, sharp, metallic and frightening. Like everyone else – including the guard – I threw myself to the ground.

For Christ's sake, what's happening?' someone asked in an agitated voice. Several heads bobbed up, including mine. I took a quick peep in the direction of the building, almost expecting to hear another volley, but instead I saw Darky and the soldier, pointing at us and laughing! Others saw them as well and, somewhat mystified, we began to get to our feet.

'What's happening?' I shouted. 'Someone being shot?'

'No,' replied Darky. 'The guard's out shooting our breakfast. Look!'

Sure enough, one of the guards had been out shooting and now he was walking towards us, carrying two dead chickens. Hopefully, we gave him a cheer. He responded with a smile and held up the birds for us all to see.

For a moment we watched the guard talking to his comrade and I wondered where the cooking would be done. Then, for no apparent reason, a doubt suddenly flickered into my mind. Were the chickens really for us, or were the Germans going to have them for their own breakfast? The sunshine seemed to fade and I felt disappointed and gloomy. No, they couldn't be for us, I told myself. Feed prisoners on chicken – never! In any case, what were two chickens between 40-odd men?

I felt a hand on my sleeve. 'Come along,' said Darky. 'There's a shed just round the corner, I guess that's where the cooking'll be done.'

Still downhearted, I went with him to the corner of the building. The guard on duty looked at us inquiringly, but Darky put on an authoritative air and, without a word being spoken, we passed him and made our way to the shed. The door was open, so we walked in. It was fitted out as a kitchen-cum-washhouse and seemed a clean and tidy little place. In one corner we espied a bricked-in copper; adjoining it was a somewhat primitive kitchen range. Darky made straight for the range and cast a professional eye over it, then he examined the copper.

'Not bad,' he said, replacing the copper lid. 'I could make a brew of tea in that, if we had some tea.'

Then he dragged open a drawer in a large table which stood close to the door.

'This might be useful,' he remarked, holding up a large carving knife.

'You better not let the Jerries see it,' I said. 'They might think you've got designs on their Nazi throats.'

With a short laugh, he pushed the knife to the back of the drawer. In a large cupboard standing against the wall, I found some chipped cups and saucers and a few large plates. Hanging on hooks close to the range were two cooking pans. All we needed was some food to cook.

'What can you do with two chickens?' I asked. 'There'll only be enough for half a dozen men.'

'Don't worry about that,' he said. 'We can set some of the lads to work digging up potatoes. There's plenty in the garden.' He rubbed his hands and smiled confidently. 'Spud and chicken stew. What more d'you want?'

I glanced through the doorway at the garden. 'What happens if the potatoes aren't ready for digging?'

'We'll eat the seeds.'

'Just like that!'

'Yes, just like that. You're too bloody particular, Mike.'

'Won't they be rotten?' I persisted. 'We'll all get the bellyache.'

He shrugged his shoulders impatiently. 'You can't be very hungry,' he said.

'I'd sooner have a decent cup of tea,' I told him. 'Your tea was always pretty good.'

'Liar!' he said with a smile. 'You were always complaining about it.'

'That was to keep you up to scratch.'

'What a bloody sauce you've got!'

'But it worked!' I squatted on the edge of the table. 'What's happened to the rest of the chickens?' I asked. 'There must have been at least a dozen when we came yesterday.'

'I expect the Jerries swiped them,' he said. His tone was strangely unconvincing.

'Pretty mean, leaving us only two,' I remarked.

He gave me a crafty look. 'They didn't swipe them all – only what was left of them.'

'Evidently he knew about the chicken-stealers – possibly even suspected me of being one of them.

'What does raw chicken taste like?' I mused.

'Bloody stringy, I should think,' he replied. 'Have you got one tucked away somewhere?'

'No,' I said, shaking my head. 'I was too slow.'

I had gnawing pains inside me. I could have eaten both chickens myself and was getting impatient about this meal we had been promised.

'Can't we start digging potatoes?' I asked.

He turned and gave me a withering look. 'And lose our jobs as cooks?'

I grunted. I suppose he was right. I licked my lips; they were dry and cracked. Getting up from the table, I took another look around. Perhaps there was some water in the shed. But there was none; neither was there any in the 'copper'. With a sigh, I joined Darky at the doorway.

'I'm starving,' I told him. 'I'm caving in.'

'It's punishment for turning down good food when it was offered to you,' he said lightly.

I suddenly felt rattled. 'For Pete's sake, stop rubbing it in,' I snapped. 'Have you never turned down a meal?'

He smiled apologetically.

'Sorry, Mike. I didn't know you felt like that.'

The minutes passed and my impatience increased.'I suppose they've not started cooking somewhere else?' I said. 'The Jerry's a hell of a long time coming.'

'There's no fireplace in the bungalow,' he said. 'Where else could they cook?'

'An open fire?' I suggested.

'Not if they intend feeding us all. They'll have to make a stew. Where'd they get a cooking pot?'

While we were still talking, the guard suddenly came round the corner of the building. To our relief, he was still carrying the two chickens.

'And about time,' Darky remarked, backing further into the shed.

The German appeared surprised at seeing us and for a moment halted at the doorway. Then he came inside and began shouting at us. I couldn't make out what he was saying, but he seemed very angry. Suddenly his attitude underwent a complete change and he held up the two birds.

'*Essen*!' he said proudly. '*Prima essen*!' Then he threw them on the table.

'What's he trying to tell us?' Darky asked, scratching his head.

' "*Essen*" is food – it's one of the few words I know,' I told him.

'I suppose he means it's for us?'

I shrugged my shoulders. I didn't know. He might have been telling us we were to cook the chickens for himself and his comrades, or he might not have even mentioned cooking.

Suddenly it dawned on the German that we had not understood him, and it was his turn to do some head-scratching. Then Darky took the initiative. He stretched out a hand and grabbed one of the chickens. Holding the bird close to his mouth, he went through the motions of eating it, at the same time pointing in the direction of the rest of the prisoners at the front of the building. The German's eyes lit up. Yes, that was what he had meant – cook the chickens for the prisoners.

I gave a sigh of relief. Food at last, I thought, and perhaps a drink – yes, a drink. I needed one more than ever. As the thoughts passed through my mind, I saw that the guard had a water-bottle. My eyes opened wide – water! He was talking to Darky again, but before I could speak he turned and pointed to the doorway. I thought he was telling us to leave, so I took a pace forward.

'Water?' I said, touching the water-bottle. 'Have you any water?'

He looked at me suspiciously and frowned. '*Vater – was ist lose?*'

'Water – w-a-t-e-r!' I repeated. Couldn't the dimwit understand? I opened my mouth. 'I want a drink,' I said, pointing to my dried-up tongue and again at his water bottle.

'*Ach! So! Wasser!*' he said, at last understanding what I meant. He glanced quickly around the shed and pointed to an iron pail. I needed no second invitation. I grabbed it and, with a hopeful look, walked towards the door.

'OK?' I said, nodding in the direction of the well at the bottom of the garden.

He beamed. 'OK!' he repeated, pronouncing the letters in true American style – some of his education had obviously been acquired from American films. He followed me down the garden path, and when we reached the well he worked the small windlass while I held the bucket under the pipe. 'OK?' he asked when the bucket was filled.

'OK,' I replied. We appeared to have found a common language at last.

Putting the bucket on the ground, I got down on my knees. This was the moment I had been waiting for ever since I awoke that morning. Dipping my face into the water, I sucked and sucked until my belly was blown out like balloon.

After topping up the bucket, we set off back to the shed. I'd lost the painful void under my belt and no longer felt like a wild animal. Life was almost good again. I pointed to the potatoes.

'*Essen!*' I said in my best German. '*Gut essen!*'

The guard nodded his head, then stopped and pulled up one of the plants. Clinging to its roots were a few pea-size potatoes.

'*Nicht gut!*' he said, shaking out the soil.

I put the bucket down and rummaged in the newly made hole. I found some more equally small potatoes, together with the seed, a black, leathery-looking object.

The guard wrinkled his nose. '*Nicht gut!*' he repeated.

You wouldn't say that if you were as hungry as we are, I thought. Anyway, we've got to have something to go with the chickens, and small as they are, they're edible. I collected a handful, then got to my feet.

'*Gut essen!*' I said, popping one into my mouth to convince him.

'OK,' he replied, nodding his head and smiling. '*Komm.*'

When we got back to the shed, Darky was sitting on an upturned box, plucking the first of the chickens.

91

'I think he's going to let us have some of the spuds,' I told him. 'They're no bigger than peas, and we'll have to dig up half the garden.'

He glanced at the bucket. 'Pour me out a drink,' he said. 'While you've been out enjoying yourself, I've got two eggs.'

'Two eggs!' I said. 'I don't believe you!'

His hand stole to the bottom of the feather-covered box. 'Here!'

Sure enough, there were two eggs, one with a deep-brown shell, the other white and shell-less.

'Where did you get them?' I asked.

'It's a secret. I'll tell you when the Jerry's gone.'

'Don't give me that bull,' I said.'Where did you get them?'

'I've told you, it's a secret.'

'Well, what are you going to do with them?'

'They're going into the stew,' he replied without hesitation.

'But can't we . . .?'

'No, we can't,' he interrupted. 'They're going into the stew.'

I shrugged my shoulders, then got him a drink of water. Bloody fool, I thought. We won't even know they're in the stew.

The guard started talking again, but when he remembered that we couldn't understand him, he pointed to the small pile of potatoes I had put on the table, and said 'OK?' Then he marched out of the shed.

'I suppose that means he's gone to get some of the lads spud-picking,' Darky said. Feathers were flying in all directions and the chicken was beginning to look pathetically small.

'What about the fire?' I asked.

'You can get it ready. There's some logs in the corner.'

'Shall I light it?'

'No, not yet. And we'll need another couple of buckets of water.'

I opened the fire door and found the grate clean. There was no paper in the shed, so with the aid of the large carving knife, I shaved chips off one of the logs.

'We've no matches,' I said when the fire was laid.

'The Jerry'll be back soon. Here, come and watch this.'

I walked over to him. He was squeezing the tail end of the second hen and grunting.

'Here it comes,' he mused. 'Cluck, cluck, cluck!' The out came an egg, shell-less but unbroken. He held it in the palm of his hand for me to see.

'Well, I'll be damned,' I remarked in amazement. 'You ought to have been a midwife.'

He smiled and slipped the egg into the bottom of the box. 'I don't think this one will lay two eggs like her sister did,' he said. He started to squeeze and massage, but nothing happened.

I walked to the doorway for some fresh air. It was clever but rather revolting. About a dozen prisoners were now in the garden and, using the heels of their boots, loosening the earth round the potato plants.

'The spud-pickers are at work,' I told Darky. 'I reckon that Jerry's on our side.' I felt in my pocket for a cigarette. 'Fag?' I asked, walking across to him.

'Thanks. Put it behind my ear. I can't smoke till I've finished this.'

'It's to suck, not smoke. We haven't a light.'

Then the guard returned. '*Was! Nicht essen?*' he remarked, sniffing the air.

'More water,' I said. Picking up the bucket, I carried it to the copper.

'Is this thing clean?' I asked Darky.

'Yes, I've dusted it out.'

I emptied the bucket. 'OK?' I said to the guard.

'OK,' he replied. Then we went to the well and got some more water. When we returned, he helped me to get the fire going.

'Shall I give the Jerry a cigarette?' I asked Darky. 'He's being very matey.'

'You hang on to your cigarettes,' he replied. 'The Jerry can always get some more; you can't.'

Almost as if he knew what had been decided, the guard gave us each a quick and unfriendly glance. Then he left the shed.

'D'you think he understands English?' I asked Darky.

'He understands "cigarette"!'

'I hope we haven't upset him. He's been quite helpful.'

'Sod him!'

When the chickens were cleaned and drawn, Darky carved them into small pieces and dropped them into the copper. Then he added some salt which he had found in the cupboard, after which he settled down to keeping the fire roaring.

Presently the potato-pickers began to bring in the fruits of their labour. They dumped the midget potatoes into the bucket, now half-filled with water. After scouring them, I ladled them into the copper.

'How long will it be before we eat?' one of the soldiers asked.

'Not for another hour,' Darky told him. 'And we want a lot more spuds yet.'

The soldier scowled. 'What about you coming and lifting a few?'

Darky got to his feet. 'I'm the cook,' he said. 'I'm a Service cook, understand?'

The soldier gave a sarcastic grunt and left the shed.

'Surly bastard!' I remarked.

Darky smiled, then sat down again. 'We'd be just as surly if he were the cook.'

I went and sat on the edge of the table. The stew was beginning to give off an appetizing smell and I was wondering how much, or how little, each of us would get when it was finished.

Darky moved restlessly on his seat, then got up and went across to the cupboard. 'My kingdom for a few onions,' he said, almost to himself. For a time he poked about among the crockery, then slammed the cupboard door. 'Not a bloody thing.'

'Not even any herbs?' I asked.

'Not a bloody thing – not even a bit of garlic.' His eyes roamed impatiently around the walls of the shed. 'I can't understand there being no garlic. The Greek peasants have it with every meal.'

'I don't think I like it,' I told him. 'It makes your breath stink.'

'Never mind the stink,' he replied. 'It would give a bit of flavour to the stew. It'll be pretty flat as it is.'

Then, for no apparent reason, he looked up at the rafters. I followed the direction of his eyes.

'Do you see what I see?' he asked in an almost excited whisper.

'I do,' I replied. 'Bloody garlic!'

He dragged the table into the middle of the shed, then climbed on to it.

'Reach me the knife,' he said. He cut a handful of garlic from the stem and handed them down to me.

'Stinking stuff,' I grumbled. 'It'll ruin the stew.'

'Bull!' he snapped as he jumped lightly to the floor. 'It's full of vitamins.'

'The troops'll create hell,' I told him. 'Onions, yes; garlic, no. It's bloody wop food!'

He pushed the table up against the wall, then took the garlic from my hand. 'Stew – garlic!' he said, holding it up in front of my nose. 'And that's final.'

At last the stew was ready and it smelt delicious. Each of the few spoonfuls I tasted during the final stages of its cooking made my mouth water and the garlic had definitely improved it.

'You can empty the cupboard of all the crocks,' Darky told me. 'Plates, cups, jugs – everything that'll hold stew.'

The sound of clattering crockery was a signal that the meal was ready and a crowd soon collected at the doorway. Everyone was talking and joking. We were to get some much-needed food at last, and the thought made us all happy.

Darky was busy ladling out the stew with a small saucepan. 'What about finding out exactly how many there are?' he said, glancing at the mob by the door.

'I'll line them up and count 'em,' I said, moving to the doorway.

'Come on, blokes,' I shouted. 'Line up. I want to count you.'

Obediently, they formed themselves into a long, winding queue. Then I went along and counted them. There were 32, so with Darky and me, 34.

'We'll have to take some back from each dish,' Darky said when I gave him the number. 'I'd only reckoned on there being about 30.'

I looked at the ration. It was anything but generous – about a quarter of a pint of liquid, four or five tiny potatoes, and perhaps a scrap of chicken flesh or a bone. The meal was a disappointment. By the time the men got it, it was cold, and for some unaccountable reason, the coldness made the garlic flavour too strong, and no one liked it. But worst of all, Darky misjudged the number, and he and I had to share one ration between us!

When everyone had drifted away, we each smoked a cigarette, then we scraped out the copper with our fingers.

'You should have kept those eggs,' I told him reproachfully.

He suddenly looked startled. Then he began to laugh. 'I forgot to put the bloody things in.' His face clouded over, and I could see that his conscience was beginning to cause him trouble.

I smiled. To me, this was indeed good news. 'Bloody good show,' I said, rubbing my hands together. 'We deserve something for going without our full ration.'

He shook his head. 'I feel peeved about it,' he said miserably. 'I really meant them to go in.'

I nodded. I knew that all right.

'What shall we do with them?' he asked. 'Keep them for the next meal?'

'What next meal?' I asked. 'You know very well we might be miles away the next time we eat.'

He gave a deep sigh – he was obviously worried. I gave him a slap on the back.

'Leave it to me,' I said. 'I'll do the necessary.'

Later on, I cooked the eggs and we ate them. But Darky's share nearly choked him.

12
Church is a Good Place for You!

During the morning the guards told those of us who wished to see the doctor for medical attention to fall in. Then one of them marched us down to see Dr Cullen. There were about a dozen of us and I was the only airman. Outside the First Aid Post I met Bunny Austin. I hadn't seen him since the night of the 'Black Hole', and because of his wounds I thought he might have been moved to a proper hospital.

'I've got something for you, Mike,' he said when he saw me. He went back inside the hospital and a moment later reappeared carrying a greatcoat. 'Here you are,' he said, handing it to me.

Somewhat puzzled, I took it from him. A glance at the name printed on the inside told me it was my own.

'I managed to get back into the tent for a couple of minutes,' he told me. 'I got my own as well.'

'Thanks,' I said, feeling in the pockets. In one of them was a towel, in the other a piece of soap and my gloves.

'The soap and towel were on the table. I thought you might be glad of them.

'I certainly am,' I told him.

He turned towards the First Aid Post. 'We better not stand about out here or we'll be getting picked up by the Jerries.'

'I've come to see if Dr Cullen can do something with my hands and arm,' I told him. 'Everything is festering, and gives me hell at night.'

I noticed that the other members of the sick party had disappeared.

'Have you seen anything of any other members of the Squadron?' I asked. He hadn't, but guessed they were working on the landing ground.

Suddenly a short distance up the road we could see – and hear – a party of prisoners being driven by that awful officer on his bicycle. As usual he was threatening them with his revolver. I darted into the hospital, hoping to see Dr Cullen before the officer arrived, but I was unlucky. It seemed that the hospital was on the officer's calling list, because he halted the party and went inside. The doctor was not to be seen, but Norman Darch appeared.

'How're the hands?' he asked, ignoring the German officer.

'Not so good,' I said, holding them out.

'I think I better try cleaning them up a bit,' he said. 'How about the arm?'

'It's a bit stiff.'

He got a bowl of water and, after removing the crepe bandage, bathed my arm and tied it up with a strip of clean cloth – apparently they'd found some more table-cloths or sheets. Then he set to work on my hands. Most of the raw patches were festering, and so also were some of the blisters. By the time he'd finished with them they were more painful than ever, but at least they were clean.

'What about a *Verwundet* label?' I asked, contemplating my newly bandaged fists. 'Do I look bad enough?'

'Not for the Jerries,' he said with a smile. 'You've got to be nearly dead to satisfy them.'

He picked up the bowl of water. 'You better beat it now. You've had enough of my time. Come back tomorrow and I'll have another look at you.'

'Any chance of getting my old job back here?' I asked.

'Not a hope. The Jerries are marking time on us. They think we're sheltering scroungers, so we've got to be very careful.'

I glanced round the room, which was still crowded with wounded. Going outside, I looked up and down the road. There were plenty of prisoners about, and Germans, most of whom were heading for the landing ground. Then I saw the well, and the thought of water made me thirsty again, so I decided I'd better fill up while I had the chance.

A small queue of Germans had formed up at the side of the well, and I tagged on the tail-end behind a tall paratrooper. He turned and frowned at me.

'*Englander?*' he asked.

'Yes,' I replied. '*Englander.*'

He surveyed my bandaged hands. 'Wounded?'

'No.' Then I changed my mind. He might chase me away if he knew I wasn't wounded.

'Yes – wounded,' I said, holding out my hands.

He ignored them and, after giving me a searching look, touched my torn sleeve.

'Wounded,' I repeated, as if sorry for myself.

He nodded sympathetically and a smile crept into his face. 'Wounded. That is bad!'

So he spoke English!

The queue shortened and we moved forward a few paces.

'You need drink water?' he asked.

'Yes. I'm thirsty.'

He glanced at my hands again. 'You have no cup?'

'No,' I answered. 'I'll drink out of the bucket.'

He shook his head. 'It is not permitted.'

I looked at him, putting as much disappointment into my expression as I could muster. It worked. He unhitched his water-bottle and unscrewed the cup.

'Use this. It is better.'

I took the aluminium cup. 'Thank you,' I said quietly.

We reached the well, and the paratrooper took the cup from my hand and filled it with water. 'Here,' he said, 'drink and I will get you some more.'

I emptied the cup and handed it back to him. He refilled it and I drank again. 'Thank you,' I said as I gave him back his cup. 'I feel better for that.'

He gave a friendly nod, and I suddenly felt that I would like to give him one of my precious cigarettes; he'd been kind to me, and there seemed to have been little kindness in life lately. Then I remembered he was a Nazi. Give a cigarette to a Nazi? But he'd lent his cup to an *'Englander'*. I looked up at him: tall, blond, blue-eyed, and German. A decent German, I thought, but I couldn't give him a cigarette. With a final nod, I turned and walked back towards the First Aid Post.

I saw the German officer and his press gang leave in the direction of the landing ground and breathed a sigh of relief – I'd avoided working on that accursed landing ground. When I met Norman Darch again he asked if I'd like a drink of tea. Naturally I said I would, so he took me into the back room and poured me out a cup. There was no milk or sugar, but it was very refreshing. Norman was quite busy but spared the time for a brief chat, telling me that Flying Officer Daston had been in for treatment. I had met him the previous day and he told me to warn any of the others who knew him to keep quiet about his identity: he was the Squadron Intelligence Officer. Norman also told me that the German Medical Officer had been to examine the British wounded and had arranged for some of them to be flown to hospital in Athens.

While we were talking there was a commotion at the front of the First Aid Post. Norman went to see what was amiss and I followed him. It was the German officer back again, this time busy collecting prisoners for work at the western end of the island, where more aircraft had come down. When he saw me, he told me to get outside and fall in with the other prisoners. As usual he had a number of paratroopers with him to round up any prisoners who appeared capable of walking, let alone working, and very soon our number was increased to about 20.

I fell in with the other unfortunates, a mixed bag that included some of the men who had been in the bungalow overnight.

They ought to have seen him approaching and made themselves scarce.

'What's up with your mitts?' asked the man next to me. He was still wheezing from his recent exertion.

I told him, adding that I had specially come to see the MO but that he didn't appear to be at the First Aid Post.

'You should refuse to work,' the man said. 'They wouldn't make me work if my hands were in bandages.'

I grunted. That's what he thought.

While we were waiting for the officer, a paratrooper came along the road in full battle dress, complete with tommy-gun and two belts of ammunition draped around his neck. As he passed, he glanced at us and saw the officer's bicycle propped against the wall. He walked across to it and, giving it as cursory examination, mounted and rode off in the direction of the landing ground.

'Now there'll be a bloody row,' commented the soldier next to me. 'Old Bullneck'll blame us.'

'Sod him,' said another soldier. 'It'll do him good to walk.'

Perhaps our apprehension was only subconscious, but just the same we began to fall in properly. The less Bullneck had to grumble about besides his bicycle the better.

Preceded by another half-dozen prisoners, he at last came out of the hospital. After giving us a curt glance, he turned to get his bicycle.

Now for it, I thought. This is where the trouble really starts. When he discovered that the bicycle wasn't where he'd parked it, he looked up and down the front of the building. When he realized it wasn't there, he turned and faced us, brandishing his revolver. Now he was going to blame us, as the soldier had predicted. He bellowed like a bull, and kept bellowing until I thought he would have a fit. None of us knew what he was saying, but we could guess.

'The man's a bloody maniac,' wheezed the soldier next to me. I agreed, but didn't waste breath saying so.

We jogged along, grumbling and moaning, and frequently barging drunkenly into each other. Bullneck was constantly at our heels, threatening us for not going faster, but we were all hungry and weak, and no amount of threatening could get us to increase our speed.

Our objective was a short strip of beach about 2 miles west of the village. We arrived there more dead than alive, but Bullneck seemed as fresh as a daisy. A Ju 52 had landed in the sea a few yards from the shore and we had to drag it out. Bullneck led the way. Splashing through the water, he scrambled on board in search of a rope. This he soon found, and began making it fast to the undercarriage.

'What is this bloody bloke?' asked the soldier next to me as we waited for further orders. 'A garbage collector?'

'Something like that,' I answered, peeling off my shoes and socks as a precaution against having them ruined.

I took the towel, soap and gloves out of my greatcoat pocket to make room for my shoes, and as I did so three boxes of matches fell out of the towel on to the ground. I hastily picked them up, casting a furtive glance at the soldier to make sure that he'd not seen them. Then I turned my back on him and, after making sure that each box was full, tucked them safely into a tunic pocket.

Matches! I was elated – and surprised to find they could affect my morale so greatly. They gave me a strange feeling of security, and superiority: with the means of making fire, I felt that I was no longer the destitute prisoner the Germans wanted me to be. Fire meant warmth and comfort, hot food and cigarettes. I was civilized again; I could make fire! Bless you, Bunny Austin.

We were organized into three parties, one to handle the rope, and two to heave on the wings. I was too late to find a place on the rope, but I had a light heart. We waded out to the aircraft, the water coming up to our knees. Bullneck was still fiddling about with the towrope and seemed quite indifferent to the fact that every time he bent down, his revolver holster dipped out of sight beneath the surface of the sea. At last everything was ready and Bullneck began to roar again. '*Heben*! *Heben*!'

To our surprise, the machine began to move forward quite easily and in a very short time we had it towed right up on to the shore. Water was draining out of the cabin in cascades, but there seemed to be no structural damage.

Bullneck began to smile. Things had gone well and he was pleased. The towrope was unhitched and put back into the cabin, and while he looked about in the hope of finding more work for us to do, we put on our shoes and socks. There appeared to be no more stranded aircraft in the vicinity, so with a slight air of disappointment, he fell us in and we set off back towards the village. He must have been very pleased, because he didn't make us run.

We were well on our way to the bungalow where I'd spent the previous night, when I heard someone ask, 'Where's Bullneck?'

We automatically slowed down and all heads turned to look. But there were no signs of him.

'Didn't anyone see him go?' the man next to me asked.

'He was trailing a long way behind when I last looked round,' someone said.

'I suppose the blokes at the back haven't done him in?' a voice suggested hopefully.

'He'll be back, don't worry,' someone else said. 'I expect he's behind a hedge spying on us.'

'Well, let's keep moving,' I suggested. 'There's an empty bungalow a bit further down the road. Maybe we can keep out of sight for the rest of the day.'

As we approached the bungalow, we saw some Germans in the front garden. When we got within a few yards, one of them walked into the middle of the road and halted us.

'Are you prisoners?' he asked in good English.

Someone shouted 'Yes!' The rest of us gave sarcastic though perhaps inaudible answers.

'Well, you must give us all your pencils and matches,' we were told. 'If you don't hand them over when we come round, you will be searched.'

I had no pencil and I'd no intention of handing over my three boxes of matches, but I had better make a token payment. What should it be? Half a box? Yes, but no more. I pushed a box open in my pocket and spilled out half its contents. Then I closed the box and brought it out, ready to hand over.

One of the Germans came along the ranks. 'Pencils, matches, pencils, matches,' he intoned.

When he reached me I gave him the box and, after glancing at its contents, he slipped it into his pocket. If he'd been a really worthy member of the Master Race, he would have noticed that the striking strip was unused!

'What's all this in aid of?' the man next to me asked. 'Do they want to write home to their mamas, or what?'

'Don't you know that a pencil's a lethal weapon?' I said. 'You can poke a man's eyes out with it, stab him between the ribs, or stick it in his windpipe.'

'You're a pleasant sort of bloke,' he remarked, pulling a wry face. 'Where did you pick up all those ideas?'

'It's what the Jerries believe. They sometimes give us more credit than we deserve – especially for doing horrible things with pencils.'

For a moment he remained pensive, as if calculating the amount of courage it would take to use a pencil as a weapon. Then he shook his head. 'I don't think I could do anyone in with a pencil,' he said. 'I'd never be able to look at one again.'

When the Germans had finished their collection, they held a brief discussion and it became apparent that they still weren't satisfied with their haul. Three more Germans from the bungalow joined them and, after warning us that we'd be shot if we resisted, set to work searching us.

As a very special concession, I decided that I'd surrender a full box of matches. The remaining box I would somehow smuggle through the search. As for the odd matches, I would make sure they weren't found and immediately started flicking them, one at a time, into the hedge.

The English-speaking German approached. I tried to make up my mind whether to let him find the matches I'd decided to surrender or hand them to him. Perhaps he would get a greater kick out of finding them himself. So be it. I held the third box in the palm of my right hand and, as he reached me, I slowly raised both arms above my head – the meek prisoner.

His hands went into my greatcoat pocket, and out came the matches.

'*So!*' he exclaimed, almost triumphantly. '*So*, you hide matches.'

'I didn't know they were there,' I said blandly. 'I must have forgotten them.'

'You lie,' he said. 'All you English tell lies.' His face suddenly looked mean, and I thought he was going to hit me. But he didn't; neither did he search my other pockets. With a growl, he moved along to the next man.

When the search was finished, the Germans held another discussion. I hoped they were not considering carrying out a more thorough search. If they were, I wasn't sure that I could smuggle the matches through again. And if they were found, I would get more than just a hard look.

My thoughts were interrupted by the German who had taken my matches calling us to attention. After telling us that we would be shot if we tried to escape, we were told to march.

'Not a bad bit of palming,' whispered the soldier next to me.

I glanced at him suspiciously. He smiled and stuck his tongue out of the corner of his mouth. Then his hand stole into his tunic pocket. 'I did the same,' he confided. The corner of a box of matches peeped out from his huge fist as he withdrew it from his pocket.

When we reached the church, our solitary guard called us to a halt. The sound of his voice brought half a dozen paratroopers out. From their varying states of undress, they had obviously been washing, but they all brought their tommy-guns with them – they were to be our guards. A few words were exchanged, then we were told to re-form into a single line, facing the church.

'Get ready to do some more palming,' the soldier said as we shuffled into our new positions. 'I think the bastards're going to search us again.'

I began to feel rather scared and almost regretted having kept the matches. If they were discovered, I was in for a rough time. Four of the Germans took up positions behind us and, to let us know they were prepared for trouble, started rattling the bolts of their tommy-guns. My scaredness increased and I was feeling physically sick. Somehow I had an idea that this search was being organized specially to find my box of matches!

The soldier started to whistle quietly. I glanced at him. He winked, then focused his eyes on my pocket. Then I remembered. Damn it, I should already have had the matches hidden in my hand. How was I to get hold of them without arousing the suspicion of the guard behind me?

I looked along the line. The search had already begun. I tucked both hands into my pockets and, throwing back my head, gave a noisy yawn. When I withdrew my hands, one of them held the box of matches. Then I deliberately turned my head and looked at the guards. They were watching the search.

Again the soldier winked. 'Cheer up, you'll make it!' I gave him a weak smile. I wasn't too sure about that. My self-confidence seemed to be drying up.

The search drew closer and I found myself gripping the box of matches so tightly that it hurt my hand. I slackened off my grip, but a moment later I was clutching it as tightly as ever. I looked at the soldier. He appeared quite unperturbed. I glanced at his left hand. Did it hold a box of matches? It was half-clenched, but the thumb was sticking out. Perhaps it was in the other hand. That was the advantage of having fists as big as hams.

Before I quite realized what was happening, it was our turn. Two of the paratroopers moved along, one starting work on the soldier, the other on me. I had intended holding my hand above my head. Not only would it convince the Germans of my meekness but, what was more important, it would put the matches out of view. However, it was too late. He went through all my pockets, including those in my shirt. So nimble were his fingers that he discovered in a small field-dressing pocket the stub end of a cigarette which I knew nothing about. But he replaced everything that he found. When he had finished with me, he took a pace back and gave me a penetrating look. I tried to stare him out, but after a few seconds my eyes grew weak and I let them droop.

To him that was a sign of guilt. He almost dived at me. 'Take off your coat,' he snapped. 'You are hiding something.' He dragged at one of my sleeves and accidentally knocked the box of matches out of my hand.

I was frog-marched into the churchyard and, with the help of another German, stripped to the buff and given a real search. The linings of my sleeves were ripped open, the bandages on my arm and hands were untied, and they even looked between my toes to make sure that I wasn't hiding anything. When they'd finished, they told me to dress. While I was struggling into my trousers, the rest of the prisoners filed by on their way into the church. As the soldier passed, he treated me to another of his encouraging winks.

'Can I go now?' I asked when I was ready. I had the greatcoat slung over my arm, and the loose bandages were hanging out of a pocket.

The English-speaking guard nodded. 'Yes,' he said somewhat grimly. 'Church is a good place for you!'

13
Nemesis

We spent the next three days in the church. Since my first visit, it had been occupied by paratroopers and the concrete floor was now hidden from view by a colourful assortment of parachute canopies spread out carpet-fashion. At first we thought they had been laid out to air, but we soon learned the real reason. Soldiers no less than civilians like comfort. And prisoners, like soldiers, also like comfort. During the day, we piled the canopies together in one large heap and lounged on them. At night we each scooped enough of them together to form a mattress; with another as a covering, we were comfortable and warm.

Had we been provided with something to eat and drink, we might almost have enjoyed the sojourn. As it was, the guards begrudged us so much as a bucket of water and by the end of the first day, most of us would have preferred to have been out working. We would at least have been able to quench our thirst. To make matters worse, we were not allowed to smoke, and to ensure that we didn't break the order, one of the paratroopers was always on duty inside the church.

The guards were sullen and uncommunicative, and we got the impression that all was not going well with their comrades on the battle front. Periodically, columns of paratroopers passed along the road in front of the church, some going east, others going west. I learned from a recently captured New Zealander that several thousand Greek and Cretan soldiers were fighting a little battle of their own at the eastern end of the island, and that though they were completely hemmed in and could only retreat into the sea, they were fighting tooth and nail and causing the Germans no end of trouble.

During the second evening, I was standing by the open door when an exceptionally long column of paratroopers passed the church. They were singing lustily and were armed to the teeth.

'They're off to try and finish the Greeks,' my New Zealand friend remarked, tapping his empty pipe against his boot.

'How far away are they?' I asked. 'We never seem to hear any firing from that end of the island.'

'10 miles, I guess,' he drawled. 'They haven't any heavy guns, so we wouldn't hear much at this distance.'

The tail-end of the column had barely passed when we heard a droning in the sky. It seemed to be coming from the direction of the landing ground, and I assumed it was a German aircraft on patrol. Within a few seconds it sounded to be almost overhead, then it dived.

'It's one of ours,' shouted the New Zealander excitedly as it came into view. 'It's after that column of Jerries.'

There was a sustained burst of machine-gun fire as the aircraft swept along the road, and the paratroopers broke formation and ran in all directions. I backed behind the doorpost. When the firing ceased, I poked my head around the corner. Bodies lay all over the road, and not a few were spreadeagled and motionless against the hedge.

The aircraft flew on until it was almost out of sight, then turned and came back along the road, again firing its guns. When it had gone, the guards pushed us all inside and slammed the door on us.

'That was a shaky do!' I said to the New Zealander. 'I hope he doesn't come back and strafe the church.'

He sank himself into a mountain of parachute silk.

'He won't do that,' he said confidently. 'He was after those Heinies. Besides, these walls are nearly 2 feet thick.'

I glanced up at the walls and windows. The walls were thick enough, but I wasn't sure how they'd stand up to explosive bullets or cannon shells.

Presently we heard two lorries tearing along the road, one after the other, then the shriek of brakes as they came to a standstill.

'They've come for the bodies,' said the New Zealander somewhat callously.

I nodded. I could picture vividly what was happening out there on the road. The rescue teams, with cold-blooded efficiency, would examine all the casualties, prodding them and rolling them about, trying to locate their wounds, or ascertain if they were dead. Then they would hump the wounded to a lorry and, when it was filled, it would be driven at breakneck speed to the nearest makeshift hospital. Then they would come back and attend to the dead, who would be collected, blood and filth still oozing out of them, and laid out at the edge of the road, exposed to the flies. Later, a burial party – perhaps composed of prisoners – would come and perform the last rights, and in a few days' time the relatives of the dead would be informed. There would be tears and sadness and broken hearts, but the war would go on just the same. The blood and filth would continue to flow. War was crazy and horrifying and, above all, filthy and bloody.

Early the next day we were marched off. We had reached the bridge before I realized what was probably in store for us – more work on the landing ground. I glanced over the parapet. Perhaps I could jump into the river and escape. To my consternation, I saw that it had almost dried up.

Two Messerschmitts were circling around high overhead, and Ju 52s were landing and taking off almost every minute. The air was thick with dust and smoke, and visibility was down to 20 yards.

'Back to the old grind,' I said aloud. 'I was hoping we'd finished with all this.'

'It wouldn't be so bad if they gave us something to eat,' the man next to me said. 'I'm just about all in.'

We left the road and went on to the landing ground. Someone came riding towards us on a bicycle, but the air was so thick we couldn't make out much about him. It was Bullneck, of course. He jammed on the brakes, bringing his iron mount to a halt a short distance from us, then held up a hand for us to stop. The senior paratrooper rushed up to him and saluted.

'So he's got his bike back,' remarked the soldier. 'I wonder where he found it?'

A moment later, an order was roared out dismissing the guard, and once again we were Bullneck's slaves. With a wave of his hand and a '*Schnell*!', he set us off at the double towards the centre of the landing ground. But we didn't double very fast – it was more of a dog-trot. When he found that shouting was having little effect on us, he drew his revolver and threatened to shoot us. If he had meant to scare us, he more or less succeeded, but he didn't make us go any faster. We were too exhausted for that, but it perhaps prevented us from slowing down.

Through the dust and smoke, I saw the silhouette of a Ju 52. As we approached it, I tried to guess what our next job was going to be. I concentrated on the undercarriage. Was it intact? If not, that meant we would be employed dragging it away from the centre of the landing ground. But it was intact! Well, perhaps we would have to unload the machine. Or was I guessing wrong? Was our job to fill in bomb craters? There were plenty about.

I soon had the answer. We were steered directly to the Ju 52 and when we reached it, I saw that it was a freighter, loaded with ammunition.

'What the hell,' exclaimed the soldier. 'That's ammunition, isn't it?' Apparently he also had recognized the black metal containers which so closely resembled portable gramophones.

'It is,' I said. 'And I expect they'll have us unloading it.'

'But they can't make us handle ammunition,' he replied in horror.

'You mean they shouldn't,' I told him.

'What happens if we refuse?' he asked after a pause.

'You know just as well as I do. We'll be shot.'

The crew of the aircraft had already stacked a large number of the containers close to the fuselage door and were now waiting for us to start unloading them. Waving his revolver in the air, Bullneck made us form up in single file. As each man reached the door, he was given two of the containers to carry to the road.

'This isn't good enough,' said the soldier. 'I'm sure there's something in the Geneva Convention about POWs handling ammunition for the enemy.'

I shrugged my shoulders. There was very likely something about feeding prisoners too, but that hadn't prevented us from being starved.

'Can't we do something about it?' he asked plaintively.

I turned and looked at him. 'What *can* we do?' I asked. 'He's got a gun!'

'Can't we make a complaint?'

'Yes, if you can speak German, but it won't do you any good. You're dealing with Nazis now.'

He heaved a deep sigh, but said nothing.

Then Bullneck started roaring again. He and a member of the crew appeared to be having a fierce argument with a prisoner at the head of the queue.

'Bloody good show,' I heard someone say. 'It's about time these Jerries were told a thing or two.'

'What's it all about?' I asked.

'He's telling the Jerries they can't make us carry ammo,' he replied. 'He won't get away with it, but it's worth trying.'

Judging by the loudness of his voice, he certainly was trying. His only weakness appeared to be his limited knowledge of German – almost every other word he used was pidgin English.

'Who is he?' I asked. 'I don't remember his face.'

'He's a major,' someone else said. 'I think his name's Bernard Kay. Anti Aircraft mob. He's a proper sod when he gets worked up. I've heard him go for the Jerries before.'

He was certainly no respecter of Germans, or of revolvers pointed at his face. He just stood there, arguing and laying down the law. It was the pilot of the aircraft who finally beat him, and that on a purely technical point. Under the Geneva Convention, he agreed, POWs were not allowed to handle ammunition, but we were not POWs – we wouldn't be that until we were officially registered – we were only prisoners.*

Knowing exactly how we all felt about handling ammunition and not wishing anything unfortunate to happen, the major walked the length of the queue and explained the position to us.

---

* The Comité International de la Croix Rouge has now stated that this is not the case and that the German argument was completely wrong.

'You must decide yourselves what you're going to do,' he told us. 'But what the Jerry says seems to be the law.'

We still felt like refusing, but the sight of Bullneck's revolver made us realize what would happen if we did. I collected my two containers, each weighing about 40 lb, and staggered off, muttering and cursing about the weight and about handling ammunition for the Nazis. Then I made up my mind to try and escape. It was the only thing to do if I didn't wish to carry ammunition. But where was I going to escape to? As I trundled along with my load, I looked across to the hills. They seemed so near, yet were so far away. But every pace I took was in the right direction; it was just a matter of taking sufficient paces!

Long before I reached the road, I was passing prisoners who had already dumped their loads and were now returning for more. As we passed, there was the usual good-natured banter, and one of them, seeing my bandaged hands, offered to help me. I declined – with thanks ...

The ammunition was being dumped in a small wood, and as I crossed the road, I passed a group of German soldiers. They were in green uniforms and wore ski caps with metal eidelweiss badges – the insignia of Alpine troops. When they recognized my uniform, they jeered at me, and one of them picked up a stone and threw it at my head. It missed me and I quickened my pace to get out of range.

Dumping my containers among the trees, I glanced around. There was no one in sight, but I could hear the Alpine troops baiting other prisoners. This was my chance. Treading as lightly as possible, I hurried off through the wood in the direction of the distant hills. I had covered only a few yards when I heard voices ahead of me. I stopped and listened but could see no one. The voices drew nearer and I knew they were not English. I doubled back a short distance, then struck out at right angles to my original course. If I kept going I would eventually come to the cart track which ran through the camp. Then I heard more voices, so I altered my direction well to the right. I stumbled on and before I quite realized it, I was out of the trees and back on the road.

A German soldier, standing with his back to me, was only a few yards away. I was about to cut back into the trees when he turned and saw me. With a 'Hallo!' he pointed his gun to the landing ground. I shrugged my shoulders. I was tired and weary, and didn't feel up to arguing with a man holding a gun. I walked slowly back on to the landing ground.

I could see groups of prisoners clustering around several aircraft. Which one should I join? The one nearest to the road – that seemed common sense. It turned out to be more than that – the aircraft was filled with loaves of bread!

I started to elbow my way through the crowd to the door in the fuselage and in doing so gave someone a hard crack on the shin. 'Sorry,' I said, quite insincerely.

'All right, hungry guts!'

I recognized the voice and turned. It was Lawrie. 'What are you doing here?' I asked, pausing in my scramble to get near the bread.

'What would you think?' he asked with a smile.

I grinned at him. 'I'm not the only hungry guts, then?'

There was a scuffle at the back of the crowd. It was a German with a load of sacks. He told us, in broken English, to fill them with bread, then take them to the roadway, where they would be loaded into a lorry. The loaves were pushed out of the doorway and as many of us as could get near started filling the sacks. But we did more than that; we tore off chunks of bread and ate them as we worked, and we filled our pockets, and the more cautious stuffed chunks inside their shirts. Then we moved aside to let others do likewise. And how good the bread tasted, better than the finest cake.

Presently the German returned to see what progress we were making. When he saw what was happening, he brandished his revolver. Those who had eaten their fill didn't seem to mind whether or not he used it; the rest ignored him and went on eating and filling their pockets – and occasionally dropping a loaf into a sack. He fired a shot into the air, and a moment later I saw Bullneck pedalling furiously across the landing ground towards us.

'Go on, Lawrie,' I said. 'Let's get working.'

But Lawrie was looking into the sky. I followed the direction of his eyes, but could see nothing.

'What is it?' I asked. 'A kite?'

'One of ours, I think,' he replied. 'I can't see it yet, but I can hear it.'

Then Bullneck arrived. He started his familiar ranting and raving and completely drowned the faint sound of the aircraft. Prisoners reluctantly started to fill the sacks, but I stayed close to Lawrie on the outskirts of the crowd. I glanced around to see which would be the best direction in which to run. The road didn't appeal to me and the only other place was at the end of the landing ground, where we had pushed the empty petrol drums.

Then I heard Lawrie's voice. 'Run for it,' he shouted. 'It's one of ours.'

We all turned and streaked away from the aircraft as fast as we could. As we did so, a Hurricane flashed by low overhead, firing its guns. I had over 100 yards to cover and before I'd made half the distance, another Hurricane appeared on the scene. It was very low, coming straight at me from the direction of the road. Almost as if the pilot had singled me out for special treatment, he started firing cannon shells and tracer bullets at me. As I ran, I could see the curved track of the tracers as they streamed towards me, their colour fading and finally disappearing just before they reached me. I was so sure they were striking the earth just in front of my feet that I tried to jump over them.

As I neared the edge of the landing ground, I began to pray for the protection of those empty petrol drums. Not long before I'd been cursing them, but now they were my last hope. My prayer was answered. I reached the edge of the landing ground safely, then did a dive. I landed, spreadeagled, between two of them. My arms were nearly torn from their sockets, and the chunks of bread under my shirt were nearly driven through my ribs, but thanks to the greatcoat, I suffered no bodily harm from the jagged bullet holes in the drums.

The Hurricane passed overhead, still firing. A moment later it turned about and, as it again approached, I could hear the metallic crackle of its bullets hitting the drums. I pressed my head close to the ground and held my breath. Then I felt a sting on the left wrist and another on a finger of the right hand. Immediately my wrist began to feel warm and damp – blood. 'The awkward swine,' I muttered under my breath. 'Why the hell doesn't he go for the Jerries?' I drew my left hand towards me but couldn't see the size of the wound because of the blood. My finger was marked as if it had been seared by a hot poker.

I could still hear the Hurricane, but its guns were no longer firing. I raised my head and was in time to see the aircraft disappearing over the hills. There were no signs of the second aircraft. For a time I remained where I was – the Hurricanes might still return, and though the drums gave little real protection, they made me feel secure, chiefly because they were English drums!

A shadow flicked across the narrow patch of ground in front of me. A German dressed in flying kit was pointing a revolver at me.

'Are you a prisoner?' he asked. His English was faultless, but there was a strange note of bitterness in his voice.

I slowly turned and got to my knees. Then I heard a faint click as he released the safety catch on his revolver. My heart began to pound. By now I should have grown accustomed to having a revolver pointed at me, but somehow I was more scared than ever. I had a feeling that this particular German was nursing some secret grievance against the British.

'Yes,' I said. 'I'm a prisoner.'

We looked each other up and down. Through a gap in his unbuttoned flying jacket I saw that he was wearing a pilot's badge.

'Stand up!' he commanded.

I got to my feet. Apparently I was not to be shot while on my knees.

'Are you wounded?'

I held out my hands. Blood was still trickling slowly from the wound in my wrist.

'Yes. I was hit by . . .' Then I stopped. I felt that I couldn't possibly admit having been hit by a British bullet; it would be too humiliating. I glanced back at the drums. 'It was those – I tore my hands moving them off the landing ground.'

'When?' he snapped, not believing me.

'A couple of days ago. They're full of bullet holes.'

'Let me see.' He stepped forward and took hold of my left hand.

'This is a new wound!' he said, examining my wrist.

I withdrew my hand, wondering why he was so concerned at my injuries. 'I expect I tore it on a drum,' I said. 'I was in rather a hurry to shelter.'

He smiled and his face was more friendly.

'Where do you come from?' he asked after a pause.

'Greece,' I replied. There was no harm in telling him that now.

He lowered his revolver. 'No. Where is your home town? You're English, aren't you?'

For a moment I hesitated. What was his interest in knowing where I came from? Had he some special motive or was he merely trying to be friendly?

His smile disarmed me. 'Salisbury,' I replied at last. Then I was angry with myself. You fool! I thought. He might know that Salisbury's close to the Plain and start questioning you. You better start wriggling out of it, and quick.

'I've only lived there a short time,' I added hastily. 'I don't know it very well.' It sounded weak, but it was the best I could do.

'I know Salisbury,' he said with sudden interest. 'I know the Cathedral and the Castle.'

I raised my eyebrows and muttered, 'Oh.' Then I began to wonder if he'd been on a raid over England and perhaps used the Cathedral spire as a landmark.

'Before the war?' I asked innocently.

'Yes, before the war.' A far-away look came into his eyes. His revolver was now pointing towards the ground. He was good-looking without being particularly handsome, and when he allowed his mouth to take its natural shape, his face seemed kind and friendly. He had grey eyes and a nose which was slightly hooked. I could see sufficient of his hair to know that it was dark brown.

I gave a faint sigh and the sound brought his thoughts back to the present. Moving his feet uncomfortably, he shuffled backwards a few inches, then put his revolver away.

'Come,' he said. 'Your Hurricanes are on their way back to Egypt. You are safe for the present.'

I followed him on to the landing ground.

'Where were you working?'

'On that Ju 52 over there,' I replied.

He looked across at the Junkers, then surveyed the landing ground. Most of the prisoners were back at work.

'Come along,' he said, leading the way to a nearby aircraft. 'You can help me unload.'

We reached the door in the fuselage. Two of the crew were manoeuvring a small AA gun into position, ready for unloading. That's one thing I just won't do, I told myself, handle a gun for them.

He exchanged a few words with the other two, then turned to me. 'You see, we are preparing for your friends,' he said with a rather grim smile.

111

I glared at him, then looked at the gun. 'You don't expect me to handle that, do you?'

'It is in your own interest,' he said, still smiling. 'Your friends might kill you the next time.'

'What if they do?' I asked brazenly. 'You wouldn't shed any tears.'

'But think of your home. You would never see it again.' His voice was thick with sarcasm.

'Well, I'm not helping with that gun,' I said resolutely. 'You can shoot me if you like.'

His hand slipped down to his holster. 'I might have to.' The smile had left his face and, as he withdrew the revolver, I realized that he meant business.

Then I did a mental somersault. When a gun is stuck against your ribs, noble decisions seem to disappear and you do as you're told. Of course you feel miserable about your weakness, and once you've broken your resolution, you have an excuse for breaking it on future occasions, but at least it enables you to evaluate yourself. Either you have a noble soul or else you're too tenacious of life.

'Would you help if you were a prisoner?' I asked in a lame voice.

'I am not a prisoner, so I don't know,' he replied. He knew it was an unsatisfactory answer and his mouth curled at the corners, making him appear as he did when I'd first seen him. He moved closer to the door. 'Come here.'

I moved over to him. He accepted my obedience as capitulation and put his revolver back in its holster. 'Take hold of that end,' he ordered. 'It's heavy, so get a firm grip.'

To hell with you, I said under my breath. I took hold of the metal leg with one hand and the baseplate with the other. I'll drop it as soon as it's clear of the kite. I'll wreck the whole bloody gun!

'Lift!'

We all lifted together and got the gun to the edge of the fuselage.

'Keep it like that a minute.'

I strained at the weight. Then I tried to see what would happen if I let go, and lowered my end slightly. I soon found out: the gun would capsize and land on top of me!

The other two jumped and got into position. Then we all lifted together again and gently lowered the gun to the ground.

'Quite simple, you see,' he said. I didn't know whether he was referring to the unloading or to the ease with which he had made me help them.

Then we unloaded the gun trolley and, after jacking up the gun, the pilot wheeled it to the edge of the landing ground. When he returned, I helped them unload the containers of ammunition, then we moved them across to the gun, all ready for use.

'You can go and help unload that other Junkers,' he told me when we had finished. 'It's full of bread.' He pointed to an aircraft surrounded by prisoners less than a 100 yards away.

I turned and glared at him. You swine of a Nazi, I thought. I suppose that's your idea of a joke. With my sore hands tucked into my greatcoat pockets, I stalked off.

I stood on the outskirts of the crowd. Everyone was either munching bread or stowing it away in their pockets. I felt inside my shirt. The bread was broken into small pieces and crumbs had worked down under my belt, making my waist sore. I threw out the bits and, slackening off my belt, jumped up and down until the crumbs fell out of my trouser legs.

Loaded sacks began to appear. I walked across to one and helped myself to a loaf. Then I broke it in half and tucked it inside my shirt.

'Come on, RAF, give me a hand with this.' It was a Kiwi, dragging a sack of bread along the ground.

'Where to?' I asked. 'The road?'

'Yep, there's a lorry waiting for it.'

I got hold of the sack and in silence we set off across the sand. When we were half-way we stopped for a rest.

'I suppose we better not stop too long,' said Kiwi, wiping the sweat from his face on his sleeve and looking up at the sky. 'Those Hurrybusses might be back any minute.'

I glanced up at the cotton-wool clouds and wondered whether any of our machines were lurking behind them. By dodging from cloud to cloud they could quite easily get over the landing ground without being seen and there was no German patrol in sight.

We set off again, all the time keeping our ears cocked for the sound of aircraft. The blood from my wrist was running in a long snaky stream down my hand and dripping from my fingers.

'Got a field-dressing on you?' I asked. 'I stopped a splinter and I'm still bleeding.'

'Sorry, RAF,' he replied. Then he slowed down. 'Where were you hit? In the arm?'

'No, the wrist.'

'You can have a bit of my shirt if you like. It's fairly clean.'

I smiled and started to drag the sack again. 'It's not as bad as all that,' I said. 'I expect it'll dry up presently.'

For a time we walked in silence. My finger was hurting so I snatched a lick at it. It tasted burnt and I had to spit to get rid of the taste.

'That's the lorry,' Kiwi said when we reached the road. As we drew closer I recognized it. It was an RAF vehicle. The last time I had seen it, it had contained the burnt body of a Rhodesian pilot who had been shot down in flames, and now it was being used as a bread van!

We got rid of the sack of bread and walked slowly back across the road. A motor-cycle combination came tearing along from the direction of the village, and I stopped to watch it go by. In the sidecar, standing on its hind legs, was the dog which had once been the Squadron mascot. He was as filthy as ever, but seemed happy with his new masters. I felt as if a member of the Squadron had gone over to the enemy.

I turned and walked after Kiwi. The last of the bread had been loaded into sacks and was now on its way to the lorry. Those of us with nothing to do were standing idly around the aircraft munching or talking. Suddenly everything went quiet and all eyes turned skywards. Was it a German on patrol or was it . . .

'It's one of ours!' shouted a voice.

'It's a Hurricane!' shouted the man next to me. 'Scatter.'

I didn't wait to see what it was. I just turned and ran as fast as I could in the direction of the drums.

As I approached the edge of the landing ground, someone shouted 'There's a shelter over here.' I changed course and a moment later fell headlong into a very deep slit-trench. Almost before I'd reached safety, a gun started firing.

'That's not a kite firing,' a soldier in the trench said.

'It's a cannon,' I replied shortly. 'Keep your head down.'

'Like hell it is,' he snapped back. 'It's ack-ack!'

There was a lot more firing, and this time it was mixed up with the roar of aircraft. Suddenly there was a sound like thunder, and I closed my eyes and stopped breathing. That's either a bomb or a kite crashing, I told myself, and it's pretty close at that.

Everything went quiet so I opened my eyes. A German was crouching on the floor next to me and he looked even more scared than I felt.

'All clear,' said a soldier, getting to his feet. 'Let's get out of this stink pit.'

I followed him out of the trench and kept in his wake as he sauntered along the edge of the landing ground towards the road.

'Was it a bomb or a kite crashing?' I asked.

'A bomb, I think,' he replied. I hoped he was right. It would be terrible if a shell from the gun I'd handled had brought down a Hurricane; it would almost be my fault!

We came to the gun. Three bodies lay close to it, one of them the German pilot.

14

'That Bloody Churchill's Airman!'

At the end of the day we returned to the little whitewashed church. There were about 35 of us and we arrived feeling very thirsty and weary. The parachute canopies were still spread out invitingly on the floor, but somehow we ached too much to be able to get comfortable.

'I feel about all in,' I said to Lawrie.

Propped up against the wall next to me, he half opened his eyes and sighed. 'Got any fags?' he asked.

I felt in my pocket and brought out the packet. 'Since when have *you* been smoking?'

'I don't want one,' he said wearily. 'I thought you might feel better if you had one.'

For a moment I toyed with the idea. Then I realized that one puff would just about make me sick. I was already feeling queasy. 'No,' I said, slipping the packet back into my pocket. 'I don't feel too good.'

He looked at his watch, then began winding it. 'Dare we go to sleep?' he asked without looking up.

I glanced around the church. Everyone was lying or sitting down, but no one appeared to be sleeping.

'Why not?' I asked. 'I expect we're here for the night.'

He wriggled away from the wall and stretched to his full length.

I unbuttoned my shirt and took out the two halves of a loaf. 'How much bread have you?' I asked.

He moved about uncomfortably, then, drawing up one of his feet, began removing a boot. 'A few odd bits.'

'You can have some of this if you're hungry.'

He pulled a sour face. 'I don't want any more. The last lot made me feel sick.'

I pushed the bundle into the sleeve of my greatcoat. 'That's how I feel.'

'I'm tired,' he said with a yawn. 'As tired as death.'

'I'm going to sleep,' I told him. 'I'm fed up with being awake.'

Using the rolled-up greatcoat as a pillow and pulling a heap of parachute canopy over me, I turned over. 'Good-night,' I said.

'It's hardly night yet. It's not even dark.'

I buried my head under the silk. 'Don't spoil the illusion,' I mumbled. 'I want to get away.'

Without even being asked, the German guard supplied us with two buckets of water for breakfast. Those of us who had bread shared it with those who had none, so when we left the church soon after eight o'clock no one was really starving. But it was not a very appetizing breakfast.

Out on the roadway we fell in in fives. Then we were counted. To show their disapproval of this continual counting, some Australians just behind me began to baa-baa-baa like sheep. The guards got mad with them and when the Aussies wouldn't stop their clowning, they set about them with the butts of their rifles and tommy-guns. The Aussies just laughed and swore – they thought it a huge joke – but the guards were really rattled.

We were marched west down to the strip of beach where, a couple of days earlier, Bullneck had made a party of us tow a Ju 52 out of the water. The whole area was now littered with aircraft, many of them complete wrecks. Prisoners were already busy unloading some of them, and there was a constant stream of men staggering across to the road with metal ammunition boxes.

We were shepherded across to a Junkers, and four men were detailed to climb inside and hand out the cases of ammunition. There was keen competition for this job, as it was considered the easiest, and despite the guard's protests about a dozen of us got on board. But in the end the guard forcibly ejected all except the fortunate four.

To ensure that there was no idling, we were formed into parties of three, each accompanied by a guard. In my party were Jake Edwards and Lawrie. Our guard was a nasty little Hun with very big ears, and almost before we had got hold of our boxes he was ranting and raving at us, and shouting 'Schnell!' Lawrie led the way, followed by Jake. Big Ears and myself were at the rear. At almost every step he was cursing me for not going quicker. Then Jake tripped and fell. Big Ears was on him like a hawk, dragging him to his feet and pounding him in the face with his clenched fists.

Then it was my turn to trip and fall. After being pulled roughly to my feet, he set to work dragging off my greatcoat, his idea being that I could work better without it. When he realized that it wouldn't come off without being unbuttoned, he tried to rip the buttons off. As a measure of self-protection, I hastily unbuttoned the coat and removed it. He took it from me and flung it as far away as he could. With it went my gloves, towel and the soap.

Dividing the beach from the road was a narrow but very deep ditch. Under ordinary circumstances it would have been quite easy to jump across, but loaded with two heavy boxes of ammunition this called for a considerable amount of strength and a good deal of skill. Lawrie got across safely and continued on his way to the road, but Jake was not so fortunate. He missed his footing, tried to save himself, then slipped and rolled to the bottom, his two boxes landing on top of him. With a mad shout, Big Ears jumped down into the ditch and began kicking him in the ribs and telling him to get up.

For a moment I just stood and stared. I knew the German was a nasty little swine, but I hardly expected him to use his feet. At each kick Jake grunted loudly, or gasped, depending on where the boot landed. Why doesn't he get up? I asked myself. He'll be kicked to death. Then I realized that perhaps he'd hurt himself when he'd fallen and was unable to get up. Something had to be done. Shouting at the Hun would do no good; it was no use trying to stop him by force – he still had his tommy-gun. Perhaps if I got down into the ditch and tried to help Jake to his feet ... Yes, that was it. But first I had better jump across with my own two boxes of ammunition. I walked back a few paces, then balancing the boxes carefully, started to run. One ... two ... three ... four ... up ... over. Damn it, I wasn't over. I was slipping, slipping, and then I fell in a heap at the bottom of the ditch. As I came to rest, an ammunition box caught me a hard whack on the side of the head. I was left with just sufficient sense to roll myself into a protective ball. Then I waited for what seemed an eternity for the kicking to start. It didn't. Peering over my folded arms, I saw that the German was still busy with Jake. My wits returned and, quickly scrambling to my feet, I seized one of the boxes and tried to throw it out of the ditch. I was too weak. In almost a frenzy, I started to climb out, dragging the box behind me. Then I slipped and fell back in. When I got to my feet, I saw that Jake had managed to get up and, with a box in each hand, was trying to scramble up the steep, slippery wall.

Again I tried to crawl out, dragging the box behind me. Half-way up I slipped and fell to the bottom again. When I got to my feet, the German moved towards we and indicated that I was to pick up both boxes. Evidently he thought I intended abandoning one of them. I knew that it was useless trying to get out with both of them, but just the same I took a box in each hand and started up the wall. By leaning forward until my chest was scraping against the earth, I found that I could work my way upwards, inches at a time. I was getting on quite well when I heard a clatter. Half turning my head, I saw that Jake was in a heap at the bottom of the ditch. He looked up at me.

'Give me a hand,' he gasped. 'I can't make it.'

For a moment I hesitated. If I kept going I might be able to get my own boxes out, then I could go back and help him. But if I went back now, I felt I'd never get my own or his out.

'Just a minute,' I said. 'I want to get my own out first.'

A look of anguish came into his face and I knew that he thought I was deserting him. But I just couldn't go back now. I struggled upwards a few more inches, my arms feeling as if they were being dragged out of their sockets. Then I heard the German shouting again. Glancing back into the ditch, I saw that Jake was in a heap on the ground with the German standing over him. I'd almost made up my mind to go back when Lawrie appeared. He took the situation in at a glance and, stretching down, took both my boxes. Then he scrambled down into the ditch.

'Come on, Jake,' I heard him say as he pushed the German to one side. 'Let me give you a lift.' He helped him to his feet. 'Never mind the ammunition. You climb out.'

Jake struggled painfully out of the ditch and, after heaving up the two boxes, Lawrie followed him. Then the three of us carried the boxes to the road, the German walking close behind.

Another batch of prisoners arrived to help with the unloading, and instead of having only three of us to guard, the German found himself with about 15. The new arrivals were all soldiers, mostly Australian. Before we'd made one round trip to the road, they were plotting how to dispose of the guard's body when they'd finished tearing him to pieces.

At this stage, Lawrie and Jake quietly disappeared, having attached themselves to a party whose guard was a little more humane. I made up my mind to join them at the first opportunity. I didn't relish being mixed up with the killing of a German guard.

The next trip to the road was almost my last. I fell into the ditch at almost the exact spot where Jake had gone in and the German jumped down after me. He started kicking and harassing me until I was so dizzy that I didn't know what I was doing. Every time I tried to get to my feet, his boot seemed to reach my ribs or legs, and down I went again. At first I took it very meekly, but then he caught me a blow on my sore arm, and I began to swear at the top of my voice.

I heard a gruff, 'What's up, cobber? This bloody Heinie annoying you?'

It was a burly Australian, standing on the edge of the ditch.

'Yes,' I shouted angrily. 'The bastard's been using his boots on me.'

The German backed away from me and pointed his gun at the Aussie. Then he beckoned me to get to my feet.

'Reach me the boxes,' the Aussie said, ignoring the guard. He stooped down and a large hairy paw was lowered into the ditch. I struggled to my feet, then handed him the first of the cases. It was whisked upwards, then the paw descended for the second one.

'I can see we'll have to fix this little bastard,' he said, glaring at the guard. 'He's lived too long.'

I agreed.

He helped me carry the boxes to the road, then we fell in with the rest of the party and marched back towards the Junkers. I was aching in every bone, and my hands were sore and burning. I've got to get away from this, I told myself. The next time I fall in, he'll kill me. I glanced around the beach. At least a dozen aircraft were being unloaded. Wasn't there one with a light cargo? Bread, for example. And one where the guard wasn't such a thug? But the streams of prisoners humping black metal cases told me what the cargoes were.

We passed within 30 yards of a Junkers. Two figures were squatting under the tail wing, apparently carrying out repairs. I wondered what its cargo was. If it was bread, I wouldn't mind helping to unload it – I was feeling hungry.

Suddenly I heard a shout. 'Come here, that bloody Churchill's airman!' In surprise I glanced around. The owner of the voice was obviously a German, but what kind of German?

'Come here, that bloody Churchill's airman!' This time the voice was louder and held an air of authority.

I looked towards the Junkers. The voice seemed to come from one of the figures under the tail plane.

'Yes, you. You know who I mean. The man in blue. Come here!'

With a strange sense of guilt, I glanced furtively at the uniforms of the other men in the party. I was the only one in blue.

Filled with foreboding, I left the ranks and walked slowly in the direction of the Junkers. I hoped the guard would call me back – there was something about that English-speaking voice I didn't like – but to my disappointment he seemed to have no objection to my going.

I came to a halt just short of the Junkers' huge corrugated tail plane. The two men, whom I assumed to be members of its crew, were sitting tailor-like beside the wheel, and both were smoking.

'Why didn't you come when I called you the first time?' snapped the nearest German.

I looked down at him, feeling rather helpless. I wanted to tell him that I hadn't known it was me he wanted but though my mouth opened and closed, I couldn't get a word out.

'Well!' he inquired, dousing his cigarette in the sand. 'Can't you speak?'

For a moment I continued to look at him, at his cold, blue eyes, his thin, cruel lips. He looked refined and crafty, and reminded me of a snake. Suddenly he lunged forward and his right hand shot up towards my throat. 'You insolent swine!' he snarled, as he grabbed my shirt. Then he threw himself backwards, dragging me with him.

I was jerked off my balance and as I fell forward my head hit the trailing edge of the wing. I felt something crack, and for a moment my whole head seemed to be filled with a blinding light. As I sank to my knees, everything went dark. For a few seconds there was no pain; I was just dazed. Subconsciously I was wondering whether I was going to flake out. Then it began to get light again, and I half opened my eyes. Through a slight haze I could see the German looking at me. With a trembling hand I felt my forehead. It was wet. Then my head began to throb and my eyes to fill with tears. Rummaging inside my shirt, I brought out the bloomers; they were filled with bits of broken bread. As I shook them, I saw the German snigger.

'Does it hurt?' he asked in a silky voice.

Ignoring him, I traced out the wound with my fingers. I could feel what seemed like a 2-inch gash in the already swollen skin, and the edges were torn and slimy. I pressed lightly against it with the bloomers, then wiped away the blood I could feel trickling down each side of my nose.

'Feel all right now?' he asked.

'Yes. Can I go?'

He rolled to his knees and faced me. 'No, you can't,' he replied, almost fiercely. 'You're an airman, so you should know something about tail wheels.'

'I don't know anything about German tail wheels,' I answered quietly.

'Well, now you are going to learn,' he said.

He turned and grasped the axle of the tail wheel. 'This has come out of its bearings and I want it put back,' he said, giving it a violent shake.

The second German crawled round to the other side of the aircraft.

'Get hold of this and push,' I was told.

I got hold and pushed.

'Harder. You're not trying!'

I closed my eyes and pushed harder, my head throbbing as if it would burst. The whole machine started to shake, then something made a loud click.

'Fine. That's done it,' I heard him say.

I opened my eyes and looked at him. He was examining the wheel. Then he turned to me.

'You can go now,' he said casually.

I got slowly to my feet.

'Just a minute. Have a cigarette.'

I looked around. He was holding out a packet of Gold Flake. For a moment our eyes met.

'I don't smoke,' I lied. Then I walked away.

15

Sabotage

Tired and weary after a long day spent unloading and carrying ammunition, we were fallen in and marched back in the direction of the little whitewashed church. The sun was already low and the cool air made our sweat-soaked clothes feel cold and clammy. There was little talking as we marched wearily along. We had finished work for the day, but we knew that once we reached the church we would be locked in for the night with little hope of either food or drink. But the thought of sleep was itself satisfying: for a few hours we would be unconscious to all the wretchedness which seemed to be filling our lives.

'Where d'you reckon we'll be sleeping tonight?' drawled the familiar voice of the man next to me. I glanced up at him. He was carrying his tunic, and the grimy, knotted handkerchief round his neck made him look like a navvy.

'The church, I expect,' I answered briefly. The Aussie cleared his throat and spat. 'If you mean that little whitewashed place up the road, it was full of Krauts when I passed it this morning.'

'I slept there last night,' I told him. Then I suddenly began to wonder whether they were taking us back to the 'Black Hole', and an involuntary shudder ran up my spine. I glanced along the column. There were at least 70 of us; surely they couldn't pack us all into that tiny room?

The head of the column approached the church and my heart began to beat faster. But no order was given to halt, and we continued along the road. So we *were* being taken to the 'Black Hole'. Thoughts of that ghastly night came tumbling into my mind, and once again I was cooped up with the dying and wounded, and with hardly enough air to keep from stifling.

I glanced at the hedges on either side of the road. Could I make a break for it? I'd do almost anything rather than go back there. But there were guards spread out on either side of us – at least 20 of them. It would be suicide to try and get away at present. Couldn't I ask to go to Dr Cullen's hospital? My head needed attention – they could see that themselves! And the wound on my wrist was festering. Besides, my hands were getting worse and if something wasn't done very soon I had visions of them turning gangrenous. That decided me: I would ask to go to the hospital.

As we approached the village, I began reciting what I was going to say to the guard. I had to have it all off pat – there must be no scope for misunderstanding or arguing. I had a fractured skull and was liable to go mad at any moment! My hands were infected and might be contagious! I had to appear wild-eyed and slightly demented, but I mustn't overdo it; otherwise they might think a bullet the safest treatment.

I was still practising my wild-eyed look when we passed the 'Black Hole'. Where the hell are we going? I asked myself. After 3 miles or so I received an answer. We passed the landing ground and followed the road almost to the next village. Then we were shooed into a large and rather beautiful church.

The last time we entered a little whitewashed church, we just bowled in as if it were any army hut. This new church was different. We walked in quietly and with some reverence, and when we were inside, we spoke in whispers and tried to behave with decorum. There was no furniture; nor were there any parachute canopies to be used as mattresses or blankets. There was just a large expanse of concrete floor. But for the comfort of our souls, there were religious pictures and tapestries on the walls, and on the lectern a very beautiful Bible.

Out in the courtyard prisoners had formed up into a queue and two men were serving out cans of water from a well. I joined the queue, then, after drinking all I could hold, went back inside the church. It was getting dark, so I choose my plot of floor and lay down. Every bone in my body began to ache. I hadn't imagined that concrete could be so hard. I rolled over on to my side, but that seemed just as bad, so I continued the roll and came to rest on my stomach and chest. I didn't ache quite so much, but soon my neck began to hurt from being twisted. I tied my shoes together to use as a pillow, but each time I breathed the leather squeaked. I turned my head so that my ear was not resting on the shoe, and in doing so gave my forehead a blow which made the wound start bleeding again. I was exasperated and felt like pitching the shoes away from me. Instead, I propped myself up against a pillar and began to recount all my troubles and woes. Fortunately, before I was able to get too deeply engrossed, another batch of prisoners entered the church, and the next half-hour was spent defending myself against hobnailed boots and people who made darkness their excuse for encroaching on other people's bed space. At last things began to quieten down and, still propped against the pillar, I dozed off.

Early next morning, the guards drove us out on to the road, where we were to be inspected by a German officer. Apparently some of us had complained we were unfit for work and he was coming to see exactly how bad we were. Of course, the inspection was a farce. If we could stand on our feet we were considered fit. As the guards made everyone stand properly to attention, no one was excused. When the officer had gone, we were counted, then marched off in the direction of the landing ground.

Next to me was a very small soldier with a bandaged neck. He was having difficulty in keeping up and periodically had to run a few steps to keep in line. Each time he did this he had to hold on to his RAF glengarry cap to prevent it from falling off.

'That was a bit of a sell,' he remarked as we marched along. 'I was hoping I'd be able to get out of doing any more work.'

'Trust them to slip a fast one across us,' I said. I glanced at the filthy bandage round his neck. 'What happened to you? Stop a bullet?'

'A bit of hand grenade,' he replied. 'It caught me right behind the ear-'ole.'

'Does it hurt?'

'It did at first, but it's all right now, except when I move my head about. What happened to your head?'

'A Jerry bashed it against the wing of a kite.'

'Accidentally?' he asked, again hopping back into line.

'No. He was mad with me.'

'Oh! What'd you said to him?'

'Nothing. That was the trouble. If I had said something, he maybe wouldn't have bashed me.'

'Dumb insolence,' he said with a smile. 'Do they have that in the Jerry army?'

I grunted.

'What d'you think they'll have us doing today?' he asked after a pause.

'Unloading kites,' I replied briefly.

He did another short sprint and got back into line. 'I'd sooner fill in bomb craters,' he said. 'If one of ours comes over, you can always lob back into the crater and shelter.'

I grunted again. I had unpleasant recollections of 'one of ours'! It may have been unpatriotic, but I wished they'd find some target other than the landing ground. For a time we marched in silence. In the distance I could see the snow-capped mountains glittering in the morning sun. They looked remote and safe, and I wondered how many Cretans were hiding in them. If I could escape, I would make in that direction, I decided. And if I found that we'd lost the island – and I was quite sure we eventually would – I would wait for things to quieten down, they try and get a boat and make for Egypt. As the thought developed, I tried to remember the geographical layout of the eastern Mediterranean. How close was I to friendly territory? Due south I could picture Derna – the nearest bit of North Africa to Crete. And somewhere to the east was Cyprus. But because it was an island, it would be difficult to find without a compass. To the west lay Italy. No use going in that direction! Egypt was the place, and as long as I kept going south I was bound to hit it. But I would have to be careful; if I drifted too far westwards, I would end up behind Rommel's front line! Then I began to wonder in whose hands Derna was. Up to a couple of weeks ago it had been in ours. The best thing would be to aim for Alexandria, then if I drifted it wouldn't matter.

As I turned the matter over in my mind, I began to realize how difficult getting round to the south of the island was going to be. No matter whether I sailed east or west, I would have to pass through a narrow channel, and all approaches were sure to be guarded. But couldn't I cross the island on foot and get a boat somewhere on the south coast? I asked myself. It would save that dangerous trip through one of the channels. But would there be any boats to be had? I knew little of the geography of the island and felt rather doubtful. Somehow I'd always imagined the south coast to be desolate and practically uninhabited.

The little soldier was puffing and blowing harder than ever. Perspiration was streaming from his brow and running down into the patches of mousy hair on his cheeks. How like an ape he was, I thought. Then my hand stole up to my own face and felt the week's growth. Perhaps I also looked like an ape!

At last we reached the landing ground. Aircraft were parked at random all over its surface, and on the northern perimeter were assembled the wrecks of nearly 100 planes – casualties of one week's fighting. The guards divided us into parties of about 20, then set us to work filling in bomb and shell craters. There were no shovels or spades, and we had to scrap the sand and earth into the holes with our bare hands – at least, that was the theory. As I couldn't use my hands, I used my feet, and the idea spread. Before very long, other ideas also spread . . .

The figure of a nearby soldier attracted my attention. He was wearing an army greatcoat despite the heat of the day, with the collar turned up around his ears. He also wore gloves and had a cap comforter on his head. Suddenly he turned and faced me. 'You bloody airforce are more bother than you're worth,' he grumbled in a thick voice.

I stopped work and looked at him more closely. Strands of matted hair were poking from beneath his cap comforter, his face was yellow and pockmarked and he had a very sour expression. He was a sick man, I decided, and he was hungry, but there was no reason why he should vent his spleen on me.

'What's the matter?' I asked. 'Don't you like the colour of our eyes?'

He screwed up his mouth. 'If you'd been 'ere when you was wanted, we wouldn't 'ave been prisoners,' he growled.

'Anything else?' I asked.

'Yes, now you come over and drop your bloody bombs and hit nothing.' His hand indicated the crater we were filling. 'This 'ere's a bit of your bomb aiming!'

'And that's a bit more,' I said, pointing to the wrecks on the far side of the landing ground. 'Just count them!'

He shot a hasty glance in the direction I was pointing, then with a grunt moved away from me. I drew a deep breath. I was glad it hadn't developed into an argument, because I doubted whether a single one of the wrecks could be placed to the credit of the RAF. But it showed me just how low our stock had slumped in the eyes of the Army.

When we'd finished filling in the crater, we were moved to another and even larger hole. Close to it was a burnt-out aircraft. It was impossible to tell what kind it had been, because most of it had been reduced to a large silvery pool of metal. All that remained of its original shape was part of the under-carriage, a broken wing and a tangle of stranded wires. We dragged what was left of the machine into the hole, then began scooping in the sand. It was like burying the remains of some half-cremated prehistoric reptile through whose veins had passed quicksilver instead of blood.

Three more filled-in craters brought us to another burnt-out aircraft. This time there was sufficient of the machine left for us to be able to identify it as a Ju 52. We poked among the wreckage in search of treasure – a filled water-bottle, oddments of food or even a first-aid box. I found a German water-bottle. It was rather battered but still contained half a pint of lime juice. I shared the drink with the little soldier. When we'd finished, I gave him the bottle and kept the cup (which I still possess).

At noon the various working parties were allowed to go back to the road for a rest. We were all tired and hungry, but there was no food for us.

The little soldier and I sat together on the edge of the road.

'Where did they nab you?' he asked, removing his glengarry and using it to wipe the sweat from his face. 'I'd have thought all you RAF people would have got away.'

'We didn't have any kites,' I told him.

'What happened to them?'

'Withdrawn to Egypt, like most of the ack-ack batteries,' I said with some bitterness.

For a time we sat in silence. Nearly all the others were lying down on their bellies, their hands clasped over the back of their heads as protection against the burning sun. I began to think about escaping again. If I'd been a 100 yards further along, I could have sneaked across into the trees. As it was, our guards were near and German soldiers were coming and going all the time.

'You didn't tell me where you were caught,' the little soldier suddenly said. 'Were you on the drome?'

After I had told him, he gave me an account of his own capture. During the initial air raid, he and five other soldiers had taken shelter in a slit-trench on the side of a hill. They'd known nothing of the invasion until they suddenly saw a party of paratroopers coming down the hill. At first they'd not identified them as enemy – none of them had ever seen a paratrooper before – but when a hand grenade landed in the trench – fortunately it failed to explode – they guessed they were Germans and opened fire. Then the paratroopers rolled more hand grenades down the hill into the trench. The little soldier was the only one of the five to come out alive.

I doused my cigarette and put the stub end in a pocket. I'd never heard of hand grenades being used like that before, but trust the Jerries to know all the tricks of the trade.

A Kiwi sauntered across and sat down next to me. 'How'ya,' he said by way of greeting.

'How do,' I replied. Then I recognized him as the man who was constantly arguing with the guards in some strange, German-sounding English.

He rolled on his side and drew up his knees. 'You working on the craters?' he asked, sucking idly at a blade of grass.

I nodded.

He turned and glanced furtively round. 'This afternoon we do it differently,' he said quietly.

'How differently?' I asked, somewhat puzzled.

'We fill them in in such a way that they cave-in when a Jerry aeroplane runs across them.'

Inwardly I smiled. That was just how most of us had been filling in craters all the morning. I looked down at his grimy face. The dark beard that covered his cheeks gave him a strange and sinister appearance.

'How do we do it?' I asked playfully.

He cast another furtive glance around him, then scooped out a handful of earth. 'No more treading in,' he said, letting the loose earth trickle through his fingers. 'Just pile it back in the crater as loose as you can. And if we have to bury any wrecked Jerry kites, don't pack earth under them. Make the craters as hollow as you can.'

'What about the guards?' asked the little soldier, giving me a sly wink.

'Leave that to me,' said the Kiwi knowingly.

'Who gets shot when they find out?' I asked.

He turned and gave me an aggressive look. 'Whose side are you on?' he demanded, removing the grass from his mouth.

'Listen, Kiwi,' I said, wagging a finger in his face. 'Don't start trying to give me any of your old bull. I'm full out to wreck a few Jerry kites, but I've no intention of getting shot through being a bloody fool. So far we've managed very well without any cloak and dagger stuff, so don't start trying to introduce it now.'

He lowered his eyes, then dug up another fistful of earth. 'It's not cloak and dagger stuff,' he said resentfully. 'It was just an idea I had.'

I lay back and looked up at the sky. 'If you'd kept your eyes open this morning, you'd have seen that most of us were doing it the way you suggest,' I said.

He moved about uncomfortably but didn't speak.

'Where did they nab you?' the little soldier suddenly asked him with an air of innocence.

The Kiwi glared at him angrily. 'Trying to be clever?' he demanded.

'Don't be so bloody thin-skinned,' I said.

Then the guards came and ordered us all back on to the landing ground and we were re-formed into parties. As we ambled across to a nearby crater, the Kiwi sidled up to me.

'No ill feelings?' he said.

'Of course not,' I replied. 'But don't start anything with the Jerries. We can do all we want under their noses if we use a bit of intelligence.'

During the first hour we had little opportunity for 'rigging' any of the craters. We had two new guards who for a while supervised our work very closely, even helping us to stamp in the loose earth. Then, like their predecessors, they began to show signs of boredom. They just stood close by, talking together, smoking. And because they were on duty and not allowed to smoke, they were more concerned about catching the first glimpse of a superior than us and the thoroughness of our work.

Presently we came to a very large crater. It had been so well blasted that there was insufficient loose earth in the immediate vicinity to make it good. Under ordinary circumstances, a guard would have escorted a party of us to the far end of the landing ground, where we would have collected a few tons of stone with which to fill it in. But close by was a Ju 52, its undercarriage broken and both wings hanging down like the arms of a wilted scarecrow. It we could use it, it would save us hours of scraping and stone-carrying. And it would enable us to make a really good job of the crater! I went up to the Kiwi.

'Here's your chance to help the cause,' I said, pointing to the Junkers. 'We want that kite to fill in the hole. What about it?'

He looked at the wreck, then at me.

'OK,' he said. 'We'll have it.'

Without hesitation, he stalked across to the guards, and I wondered how far he'd get. Something seemed to tell me that he wouldn't be anxious to come back until he'd got the machine for us; after what I'd said to him, he'd feel he was on trial.

He started chattering to the Germans and pointed to the wrecked aircraft. I wished that I could hear what he was saying, but I felt that to go closer would be unfair to him. For a time the guards seemed to be listening quite patiently. Then one of them waved a hand in the direction of the crater, as if indicating that the Kiwi was to go back to work. There was some more arm-waving and chattering, and I almost expected him to be chased away at gunpoint, but instead all three of them suddenly marched off towards the Junkers. It looked as if Kiwi had won the first round.

Everyone seemed to have guessed what was afoot, and for a time we all stood idly around, awaiting the outcome of Kiwi's efforts. If he were successful, this crater, which was well out towards the centre of the landing ground, was going to give our Nazi masters a really big headache.

The little soldier edged over to me. 'D'you think he'll get it?' he asked.

I glanced across at the Junkers. It seemed badly damaged, but it might be repairable. 'It depends on how much those Jerries know about kites,' I said. 'If they think it's a bad enough wreck, and they can pluck up enough courage to do something off their own bat, they might let us have it.'

At the far end of the landing ground the engines of another Junkers started up. For a few moments they roared at almost full throttle, then the machine began to taxi out into the fairway, sending up clouds of dust.

'It's coming this way,' said the little soldier. 'I'm beating it towards the road. I've had my eyes filled once today.'

'And I'm coming with you,' I said.

When we were half-way to the road, the Junkers roared by, its tail already in the air. We both stopped and covered our faces. There was a sudden blast and I felt the sting of hot sand on the back of my head and neck. When the noise had died away, I turned and peered through half-closed eyes. The air was thick was dust, and neither the wrecked Junkers nor the guards were visible. I felt a strange fluttering in the stomach. It was the escape bug biting me again, and those snow-capped mountains were beckoning . . .

'What about beating it?' I said, turning to the little soldier. 'We can make for the trees on the other side of the road.'

He screwed up his face into a human question mark and let out an, 'Eh?'

I glanced back over the landing ground. Already the dust was beginning to settle and I could make out the hazy outline of the wrecked Junkers.

'Let's beat it,' I said. 'You don't want to be here for the rest of your life, do you?'

For a moment he looked petrified, then he recovered. 'Where to?' he asked in a thin voice.

'The trees on the other side of the road. They'll do for now.'

I took hold of his sleeve and together we hurried off across the landing ground. Our luck was in. When we reached the road there was not a German near enough to challenge us.

'Come on,' I said, glancing up and down. 'Let's nip across.' In a moment we were among the trees and their dark shadows.

'Now we can slow down a bit,' panted the little soldier as he came almost to a halt.

'No we can't,' I told him. 'We've got to keep going.' I grabbed him by the arm. 'We're going to make for the hills, non-stop. Then we're off to the mountains.'

He shook himself free. 'But can't we have a rest first?' he asked. 'I'm all in.'

'No,' I told him, again taking his arm. 'If we idle about, we'll get caught. We've got to keep moving.'

We hurried on our way. In the half-light, we kept stumbling over moss-covered tree roots, which protruded above the earth like giant's elbows.

'What'll happen when the Jerries find we've gone?' asked the little soldier somewhat fearfully. He was slowly getting his second wind and was no longer puffing and blowing quite so loudly.

'I don't suppose they'll even miss us,' I told him. But the question set me thinking. More than once we'd been told that if one man escaped, the whole party would be shot!

As we neared the edge of the wood, we slowed down. 'Keep your eyes open,' I whispered. 'We'll have to be very careful now.'

Almost before I'd spoken the last word, we found ourselves mixed up with a lot of sleeping German soldiers. Since my last visit, the area had apparently been turned into a sort of marshalling yard for troops, and this particular lot were having a quiet nap in the undergrowth beneath the shade of the trees.

For a few moments all hell broke loose. They must have thought a counter-invasion had started. But before any damage was done, a blustering *Unteroffizier* appeared on the scene and demanded in broken English to know who we were and where we'd come from. Then he asked where we were going. I told him what had, for myself, suddenly become the truth: that we were in search of a quiet spot whereon to relieve nature. He didn't believe me and, brandishing his revolver, marched us back through the woods and on to the landing ground. It was fortunate that Kiwi and the guards had returned from their inspection of the wrecked Junkers, otherwise the guards would have received more of his tongue than they did. As it was, he told them that we'd been trying to escape and that they were to shoot the next prisoners who started to wander off.

When the *Unteroffizier* had gone, I went across to the Kiwi, anxious to know what luck he'd had.

'Bright sort of sod you are,' he grumbled when I reached him. 'Here am I, trying to sweeten the bloody guards, and you go and muck everything up.'

'How come?' I asked with an air of innocence. I felt rather guilty, but I didn't intend him to know.

'You ought to know they're scared stiff of *Unteroffiziers*,' he growled Noisily he cleared his throat and spat. 'What've you been up to?'

I lowered my eyes. I felt too embarrassed to tell him. It had been such a feeble effort, anyway. But I had to say something. 'We were looking for a tree,' I said defiantly.

'A what?'

'A tree,' I repeated. 'We wanted a riddle.'

129

For a moment he stood and stared at me. Then he spat again. 'Am I supposed to believe that?' he demanded.

I shrugged my shoulder. 'Please yourself.'

'Well, I don't.'

I looked past him and saw the wrecked Junkers. Dare I ask him what luck he'd had? It would at least change the subject. 'Are they going to let us have the kite?' I asked casually.

He licked his cracked lips and glared at me angrily. 'No.'

'No!' I repeated with affected amazement. 'Well, what's all the fuss about?'

He clenched his fists and for a moment continued to glare at me. Then he turned and marched round to the other side of the crater.

'A bladder of wind,' said the little soldier.

I nodded, then smiled. It was a milder epithet than the one I had had in mind!

16
Bully Beef and Bombs

Such was the size of the crater that it took us the remainder of the day to fill it in. We made innumerable trips carrying huge chunks of stone, and we scraped and scoured the ground with our feet until our ankles developed an almost permanent twist. Now at last it was finished, its surface flush with the surrounding terrain. But what a trap it was going to be! Despite the amount of rock and earth we'd dumped into it, it was about as firm as a rotten pear. My only hope was that I wouldn't be anywhere near when an aircraft ran across it.

We fell in by the side of the road. Our day's work was only over because it was getting too dark for the guard to keep an eye on us. Soon we were joined by the rest of the prisoners working on the landing ground, then we were all marched back in the direction of the church.

'What price glory?' remarked the little soldier as he trotted along next to me. 'I've worked a darn sight harder for the Jerries than I ever worked for our own people.'

That same thought had occurred to me more than once, and I'd tried to excuse myself by saying that it was because we almost invariably had a gun pointed at us.

As we passed through the churchyard gates we broke formation, some to form a long queue at the well, others to go into the church to stake out claims to bed spaces before it got too dark. I joined the water queue – my tongue was dry and as hard as leather. The little soldier left his water-bottle with me to fill, then went on inside the church.

I struggled with bandaged hands to extract the battered water-bottle cup from my pocket; the wire handles had somehow got caught up in the lining. While I was still trying to free it, someone shouted, 'Come and get it, boys. Bully and biscuits!' I looked towards the church doors. Standing there was a tall Australian, his face wreathed in a smile, and he was holding up a large service biscuit for us to see.

'Is it real?' an incredulous voice asked.

We didn't wait for a reply. There was a sudden wild dash and in a moment we were jostling and almost fighting each other in our efforts to get through the doors. As we crowded inside, the subdued light reminded us that we were in a church, and once again we were quiet and orderly. I tagged on to the tail-end of a queue which already stretched from the altar to the door and along the length of one wall.

Where was the little soldier? I wondered, glancing around the church. I couldn't see him anywhere. By the altar several khaki figures appeared to be dipping their hands in and out of a large box; clearly they were giving something away to the men who passed in front of them.

'See anything?' the man next to me asked.

'They're handing something out,' I told him. 'I hope it's food.'

'Who's handing it out?' he asked after a pause. 'The Jerries?'

'No, our own people.' I got back into the queue. 'Where've all these chaps come from?' I asked, pointing at odd groups of figures lying about on the floor.

'Perhaps they've evacuated a hospital,' he suggested.

I looked at them more carefully and saw that they all seemed to be wearing bandages. Strangely, they were taking no interest in the queue or in events up at the altar.

'I think they must have had their rations,' I said. 'They're not taking much interest in things.'

'Well, perhaps they can tell us what we're going to get,' he replied. 'We'll ask the next lot we pass.'

As we got closer to the altar I could see exactly what was happening. Four soldiers were handing out large, square, service biscuits, one to each prisoner, and a cheery-faced padre, still wearing his dog-collar, was slapping a small cube of bully beef on to each biscuit as its owner passed him.

'It's food all right,' I said to the soldier. 'Bully and biscuits.'

He rubbed his hands together. 'This is going to be good,' he said with enthusiasm. 'It's the first meal I've had for over a week.'

We passed a small group of wounded men, propped up against one of the pillars. 'Better not get too het up about the grub,' one of them said. 'I expect they'll run out before you reach the head of the queue.'

'Don't take any notice of him,' I said to the soldier, seeing a look of disappointment spreading across his face. 'He's only kidding us.' But I was feeling a bit scared myself. What would happen if they did run out?

As we drew closer to the altar, I could see, despite the failing light, that the men at the box were now handing out broken biscuits instead of whole ones. Did that mean they were getting short? Close by were three other boxes, but because they were tipped on to their sides I guessed they were empty. Now there were only half a dozen ... five ... four men in front, and I felt all my muscles tense. How many biscuits were left? Three ... two. Suddenly I was on the verge of tears. Would there be any biscuits left for me? Please God, save me one, or at least a few small pieces ...

Almost before I realized it, one of the soldiers was putting two odd halves of a biscuit in my hand. 'There you are, RAF,' he said cheerfully. 'Don't go and make a pig of yourself.'

As I passed the padre, he gave me my ration of bully beef. 'Sorry it's so small,' he said with a smile.

I discovered why I had seen no one coming away from the altar. We were being crowded together at one side of the church until everyone had been served as a precaution against anyone queueing a second time.

Together the two halves of my biscuit made more than a whole one. I grunted with satisfaction, then started to eat. The bully beef was mottled with fat, and as I nibbled it my mouth began to water and my tongue to revert to its normal size. Then I nibbled at the biscuit, holding a hand under my chin to catch any falling crumbs. The beef had all gone by the time I'd finished the first half biscuit. Then I began to ponder whether I should save something for breakfast. I glanced around at the other prisoners. What an evil, ill-kempt bunch they looked; every one of them seemed capable of murder. I'd better eat the rest of the biscuit!

When I'd finished, I felt in a pocket for a cigarette, then shuffled round until I found someone with a light. It was then that I saw Darky Dear, propped up against a pillar, snoring like a drunken man. I took out another cigarette and stuck it in the corner of his mouth.

'Wake up, Darky, you noisy hog!' I said. 'You'll be bringing the roof down.'

He awoke with a start. After gazing at me blankly for a moment, he opened his mouth to yawn. The cigarette fell out and slid down behind his unbuttoned tunic.

'What's that?' he grumbled, searching in the folds of his shirt.

'A cigarette,' I told him. 'If you weren't so bad-mannered you wouldn't have lost it.'

He found the cigarette. 'My tongue tastes horrible,' he grumbled. 'Give me a light.'

For a time we sat quietly smoking. When everyone had received his rations, we were told we could move freely about the church again. I glanced around to see if there was any space alongside the walls, but in a matter of seconds every inch had been taken.

'I think we'll have to park ourselves here for the night,' I said, dousing the butt end of my cigarette.

133

He looked around. We were surrounded by sitting or recumbent bodies. 'Talk about sardines,' he said with a sigh.

'At least it'll be warm,' I told him, and got to my feet. 'I'm going outside before it's too late. You stay here until I come back. We better not go together.'

I picked my way carefully to the church door, all the time keeping an eye open for the little soldier. But I didn't see him, and he wasn't outside either. When I returned, Darky went. Then we took off our shoes and, using them as pillows, settled down for the night.

The explosion woke me so violently that I didn't realize that I had been asleep. One moment I was lost in oblivion, the next I was sitting up and feeling scared out of my wits. The earth-splitting crash was followed by the sound of breaking glass as the church windows fell in on top of us. Then my ears picked out the sound of aircraft. So it was an air raid!

'Are they ours?' I heard Darky whisper nervously.

'Of course they are,' I said, feeling about for bits of broken glass. 'Why the hell don't they leave us alone? We've got enough trouble without them adding to it.'

Everyone started to talk, and soon the red glow of cigarettes began to appear.

'You'd better get the glass out of your clothes,' I said. 'I'm putting what I find into my shoes until the morning.'

Then there were two more nerve-shattering explosions. The church rocked violently, and another shower of glass and some pieces of masonry descended upon us.

'This is bloody good,' I head a voice say. 'You're not even safe in a church now!'

I jumped to my feet and stood close to the pillar. If the roof were to collapse, I would be safer there. Several of the others had the same idea and for a time we remained clustered close together.

'D'you think the church has been hit?' I asked Darky.

'No,' he replied. 'We'd have heard some hollering if it had been. Someone would have been hurt.'

I could still hear the drone of aircraft engines, but they seemed much further away. What was their target? Troop concentrations? The landing ground? But why had they dropped their bombs so close to us? Was it just bad aiming, or did they think the Jerries were storing ammunition in the church?

The babble of voices slowly died down and soon Darky and I were the only two left standing by the pillar.

'We'd better get down or we'll be losing our bed spaces,' I said. Feeling around in the dark with my feet, I managed to find an empty patch of floor. Then I lowered myself until I was flat on my back. It was then that I remembered my shoes – where were they? Turning over on to my belly, I began feeling about for them.

'Who's that?' someone demanded gruffly as my fingers wandered over a whiskery face.

'Sorry,' I whispered. 'I'm trying to find my shoes.' There was a bad-tempered grunt and the owner of the face turned his body noisily on to its other side.

I continued groping about, but the only success I had was in disturbing nearly everyone in the immediate vicinity by poking them in the eyes or the nether regions. Then I thought of Darky. Would he know where they were?

'Are you there, Darky?' I asked softly.

'Yes, what d'you want?' The voice came from the other side of the pillar.

'Have you seen my shoes?' I asked.

'For Christ's sake, get your head down,' hissed Whiskery-face.

'But I've lost my shoes.'

'Sod your shoes,' he growled. 'Get your head down or I'll pan you!'

I tried to measure his size by the dark outline of his body, but all except his head and shoulders seemed lost in the blackness. Perhaps I'd better take his advice.

I turned over on to my back and cupped my hands together under my head. But I was terribly uncomfortable and knew that I'd never get to sleep in that attitude. I felt about until I found the bloomers. Rolling them into a ball, I placed them under my head, then closed my eyes. For a time I tried to stop thinking, but thoughts kept popping into my head. I tried counting imaginary sheep. There was a large flock in a pen and I let them out, one at a time. When I'd counted about 50, I saw that they'd all turned into prisoners, so I had to send them back into the pen and start counting again. Again I let them out and began counting, but by the time I'd counted another 50 they'd all turned into paratroopers!

I looked up at the opaque patches which were windows. Through one I could see a star. While I was still looking, there was a bright-yellow flash which lit up the sky. Then there was an explosion and another yellow flash. In a moment I was on my feet, and everyone around me began to move about and to talk.

'This is bloody good,' grumbled a voice I'd heard once before that night. Silently I quite agreed: it *was* bloody good!

I continued looking up at the windows. The sky was filled with yellow light, and the inside of the church was as bright as if the sun were shining into it.

'I reckon it's a petrol dump gone up,' someone nearby said. 'Look at the smoke.'

The heart of the fire appeared to be almost due west of us and, judging by the original explosion, about 3 miles away. And there, to my personal know-ledge, was a dump of 20,000 gallons of aviation fuel.

'Are these your shoes?' asked a voice close by. There was a clinking of broken glass as I took them from him.

'Thanks,' I said. 'Where were they?'

'Where you left them – under me bloody ear-'ole!'

Again we settled down. This time I got off to sleep without counting sheep, prisoners or paratroopers.

17
The Worm Turns

The next morning I was awakened by the cheerful cry of, 'Grub up. Come and get it!' Carrying my glass-filled shoes in one hand and the bloomers in the other, I hurried across and tagged on to the end of a long queue. Our ration was again one biscuit and a small cube of bully, After collecting my share, I returned to my space near the pillar. Those who were wounded had their rations taken to them by newly appointed 'cook's mates'. When everyone had been served, the padre called for silence. Then he made a little speech. The church, he told us, was for the present to be our home. The Germans had promised to let parties of men go out each day in search of food, and it depended on their success how much we got to eat. If any of us knew the whereabouts of any food dumps, we were to let him know so that they could be raided. He also asked that we played fair and didn't try to get more food than we were entitled to.

Then he spoke about the wounded. He had little in the way of medical supplies, but said that he'd try and get more from the Germans. In the meantime, if all those who were in urgent need of attention let him know, he would do his best for them. He also had a word to say about working parties. The Germans had ordered that every fit man should go out to work and were holding him personally responsible. He told us that he felt he was betwixt the devil and the deep sea: he couldn't possibly order us to work, but if we didn't go he was afraid the Germans would make everyone – wounded and unwounded – work. Then he told us his name – Padre Hurst – and ended by saying that if there was anything at all he could do to help us, individually or collectively, we had only to tell him. When he'd finished speaking, he sat down on a wooden box in front of the altar and one of the cook's mates gave him his breakfast – a biscuit and a cube of bully beef.

'He's a good little bloke,' remarked Darky, who was sitting next to me. 'Lots of guts.'

I nodded in agreement. I was greatly impressed by the fact that he hadn't accepted his breakfast until everyone else had been fed.

At nine o'clock the Germans came for us. They lined us up in fives, then counted. Satisfied with the number, they set us off towards the landing ground. As we marched along, I again looked across to the snow-capped mountains. They seemed to be beckoning, and offering me shelter from the Germans.

During the morning we were made to fill in craters which had been made by bombs dropped during the night. As the hours passed, the few airmen who were in my party grew more and more unpopular. It was as if we personally had made the holes. We tried to make amends by working harder than the soldiers, but it seemed to make no difference. They just couldn't forgive the Air Force for being absent when the Battle of Crete started.

Early in the afternoon, Junkers freight planes began to arrive and we were switched from filling in craters to unloading cargo. During the initial switch-over there was a certain amount of confusion. The working parties were redivided, but as there were then insufficient guards to look after us, we began milling about and swapping over into parties where our friends were. The guards shouted at us and threatened to use their guns, but before they were able to restore order, we were all suddenly enveloped in a dense cloud of dust and sand whipped up by an aircraft which had landed almost on top of us. On the spur of the moment I decided to exploit the situation. Without waiting to see whether I was being watched, I casually sauntered off towards the road.

Remembering my previous misfortune among the trees, I was determined this time to steer well clear of them, so aimed in the direction of some rough and hilly ground a little distance to the east. As I reached the road, a giant troop carrier roared by. When it was nearly over the village, it made a clumsy sort of turn and came back towards the landing ground. Then it stalled and made a perfect three-point landing almost opposite where I stood. It ran along the uneven surface for a short distance, swaying and bumping, and rapidly losing speed. Suddenly one of its huge wheels hit what must have been a 'rigged' crater. Everything then seemed to happen in slow motion: the machine swung round on the bogged wheel, which dug deeper and deeper into the ground; the port wing hit the earth, sending up a cascade of sand; then one of the slowly revolving propellers struck the ground and with a crackling of metal the engine stopped. When the air cleared I saw that the four-bladed propeller had been bent into an almost perfect replica of a swastika.

I gave a grunt of satisfaction and hoped that the crater was one that I'd helped to 'rig'. Then suddenly, deep down inside me, I began to feel a little afraid. If the Germans could trace the crash to sabotage, some of us were going to get the chop.

I head footsteps and, turning, saw two men coming towards me, one a paratrooper, the other a prisoner. It was too late to avoid them, so I hastily fished out a cigarette.

They came to a halt in front of me. 'Got a light?' I asked the soldier casually.

'Sorry. Better ask the Jerry.'

I looked at the German. His mouth was agape and he appeared to be about as intelligent as a sheep.

'Light?' I asked, holding out the cigarette.

He shook his head, then began chattering like an excited monkey. For a moment I listened, trying to guess the subject of his babble, but he had such a toneless voice, and his face was so devoid of expression, I just didn't know what he was trying to convey.

I turned to the solder. 'What's he nattering about?' I asked. But he didn't know either. Again I held out the cigarette and said, 'Light.'

He looked at me sullenly and shrugged his shoulders.

'He's bloody dim for a paratrooper,' I said to the soldier. Then I felt a large paw grab my sore arm. I winced and tried to shake myself free. '*Komm*!' said the German gruffly. I knew what that meant!

He marched me across to a Ju 52 parked quite close to the newly wrecked troop carrier and handed me over to a German in a flying jacket. Then he and the soldier went off in the direction of the road. Immediately I was set to work helping unload motor-cycle combinations from the aircraft. The man in the flying jacket supervised the unloading, which was being undertaken by two members of the crew and two other prisoners. The first cycle was manoeuvred along the fuselage until it was opposite the doorway. I stood by, rubbing my sore arm and wondering why the other two prisoners were so sullen.

'You're not here for the good of your health,' said the man in the flying jacket, suddenly peering round the corner of the door.

I looked up at him, surprised at his English and wondering why he hadn't disclosed that he spoke it when I'd been handed over to him. When he'd backed out of sight, I turned to one of the other prisoners, a thin, weary-looking soldier, wearing a greatcoat but no tunic. 'Did you know he spoke English?' I asked.

'Yes.'

'Well, you might have told me.'

'Why?'

'I might have said something I didn't want him to hear.'

'That's your bloody pigeon,' he said gruffly.

My bloody pigeon! That was a really friendly attitude to adopt. 'All right, pal,' I said icily. 'Now I know exactly where I stand.'

He sniffed and wiped his nose on his sleeve. 'Why should I help the bloody Air Force? They never helped me.'

'Say no more about it,' I said quietly.

The combination was turned and pushed towards us. I took hold of the back of the sidecar and began to pull.

'I'd sooner fill in bomb craters than unload kites for the Jerries,' remarked the other prisoner sourly.

'Never mind what you'd like to do,' said a voice. 'Pay attention to what you've *got* to do or you'll be having an accident.' Inwardly I crowed like a well-fed cockerel on a dung heap.

The two members of the crew slowly eased the machine out through the doorway. As it left the aircraft, the thin soldier and his mate took the weight of the motor cycle and I hung on to the sidecar. Being unaccustomed to handling such unwieldy things, I failed to get a very good grip, and as the full weight was thrown on to me, I began to realize that I wouldn't be able to support it without help. I was about to holler out when someone suddenly shouted, 'Here they are! Run for it!' Almost simultaneously I heard the roar of aircraft and the sound of firing.

My two companions needed no second warning. They just let go. Before I could get out of the way, I found myself laid out on the ground, the motor cycle on top of me. In a panic, I wriggled about trying to free myself – I could see the earth throwing up little spouts of sand and I knew that each one was caused by a bullet. Then I stopped wriggling. The whole of my body had suddenly started to hurt and I was sure that I'd been hit in at least a dozen places. I closed my eyes and ground my teeth. What was the matter with my back? And my right arm? And when I tried to move my legs, both knees felt as if they'd been crushed. I opened my eyes, but all I saw was a strange patchwork of dun-coloured shapes. Should I call for help? I wondered. But everyone had run away. Then I remembered that I hadn't seen the Germans get out of the aircraft. Perhaps they were dead. I turned my head and looked towards the Junkers. To my surprise the three Germans were standing in the doorway, but apparently they hadn't yet seen me.

Should I shout to them for help? For a moment I was tempted, but I decided against it. I was damned if I would lower my dignity to ask Nazi barbarians for help, and if I was going to die, I would die quietly and in the privacy of my own company. I made an effort to get rid of some of the weight which seemed to be squeezing the life out of me. I was on my left side and part of the motor cycle was resting on my right arm. As I turned my head I saw a pair of feet coming towards me.

'What's happened to you?' asked a familiar voice. As the feet came to a halt, I looked up and saw the German in the flying jacket.

'Better get this thing off me,' I said, ignoring his stupid question.

He called his crew, and when they arrived they lifted the machine up and dumped it to one side. I rolled on to my back and gave a sigh of relief.

'Can you get up?' asked the German.

For a moment I pondered the question. Should I try to get up without assistance, or should I make them help me? I didn't want their help if it meant asking for it. But if I could somehow contrive to demand it – well, that would be different. I wriggled about to see exactly how much I could move. I seemed to hurt all over, but I began to think that perhaps I wasn't going to die. And the more I moved, the more I was convinced that I'd no bullets in me.

Then the German in the flying jacket and one of his crew closed in on me, and before I could protest they'd lifted me up and stood me on my feet. For several moments I swayed to and fro like a punch-drunk boxer. I seemed to have lost control over my knees and hip joints. But as I slowly gained equilibrium, I began to feel really wild. By what rights had these Nazis laid their filthy hands on me? It was degrading, outrageous! I glared savagely at the German in the flying jacket. I wanted to tell him just what I thought of him, but I was too angry to speak. Mistaking my expression for one caused by physical pain, he gave me a sort of half-pity, half-favour smile. Well, I didn't want his pity or favour. I wanted nothing from him – except perhaps his guts served up on a dog plate, and that went for the rest of the Nazi fraternity. As for work, I'd done the last stroke I would ever do for them and that was final.

Thus resolved, I shuffled round until I was facing the road. I would leave the landing ground and I would never, under any circumstances, return to it. Then a sudden doubt assailed me. Could I leave it without help? I looked down at my legs. You've got to make it, I told myself, and you've got to make it on your two feet, not on your belly! I took a deep breath. Forget the pain, forget everything except that you've got to reach the road. Deep down inside me a little voice stirred. What about these Germans? it asked. To hell with them, I snapped, I'm not their slave any longer. I took another deep breath, then with all the dignity I could raise, hobbled off.

I'd gone only a few yards when I heard the German shout. 'Hi, where do you think you're going?'

'To the church,' I replied without turning. If he wanted to stop me, he'd better try. But he didn't.

I soon began to feel that I'd perhaps bitten off more than I could chew. It was at least 2 miles to the church, and already my knees were so painful that I had to keep stopping to rest them. When I reached the road, I sat down and rolled up my trousers. The skin on both kneecaps was torn and bruised, but I was sure that wasn't the limit of the damage. I put both legs together to see if there was any difference in the shape of the kneecaps. I could see none, so I pressed lightly on one of them and gently moved it. The amount it moved seemed to depend only on the amount of pain I could bear. To my inexperienced mind, it appeared that both caps had been torn from their moorings and were now kept in position only by skin.

I reached for a cigarette and as I did so, I was reminded by pain that my right arm had again been damaged. I peeled off my tunic. The skin on the whole length of my arm was turning an unhealthy green, and when I tried to bend my elbow I got a feeling of cramp in the wrist and hand. With difficulty I got into my tunic again.

Then I began to think about escaping again. I just had to get away from these ruffians. I looked up and down the road. No one was within worrying distance, and everyone on the landing ground seemed too busy to notice me. I staggered to my feet. Where should I go? I looked across to the distant mountains. Then I realized that in my present state I could never hope to reach them – I wasn't even sure that I could reach the church! With a sigh I again sat down at the edge of the road. I was aching from head to foot and feeling utterly dejected. I went through my pockets for a match, but found none. After a brief rest, I decided to push on to the church.

I tottered slowly and painfully along the road. My kneecaps no longer appeared to be serving any useful purpose, because at every step my legs seemed to fold forward like those of a rag doll. I strayed along the grass verge in search of a stick or branch of a tree on which to support myself, but found nothing suitable. I was afraid to wander from the road in case I fell and did myself more damage. Then suddenly I saw the smouldering end of a cigarette lying at my feet. Someone must have passed this way very recently, I thought. But they didn't pass me or I'd have seen them. For a moment I stood watching the smoke curling lazily upwards and changing colour from blue to grey. Then, realizing that at any moment the glow might die out, I stooped to pick up the cigarette. As I bent forward, my legs gave way and I fell into a heap in the roadway. For a moment I was blinded with pain. I was sure that this time I really had broken some bones. As the pain subsided, I eased myself up and looked around for the cigarette end. When I found it, it was out.

What kind of a star was I born under? I asked myself.

At last I reached the church. Several wounded prisoners were at the well. Seeing water being splashed about reminded me of my thirst. One of the men had just filled a bucket, so I brought out my mug and asked him to fill it for me. When I'd finished drinking, I went inside the church. Everything seemed dim and grey. Most of the wounded were asleep and it was very quiet. Slowly I made my way to the altar.

The padre and two soldiers were giving first aid to a man who appeared to have a broken leg. I stood and watched. From his haggard and unkempt appearance, I judged that the man had only recently been brought in, and that this was the first treatment he'd had. I edged closer to where he lay on the floor. He turned his head and looked up at me.

'Have *you* a fag?' he asked in a husky voice.

I nodded, and as I slipped a hand into my pocket the padre glanced across at me. 'I think he needs a cigarette more than medical treatment.' he said with a laugh.

'I haven't any matches,' I said as I offered the man a cigarette. I glanced around the church and saw that some of the wounded were smoking. I took out another cigarette. 'I'll be back in a minute.'

When I returned and offered him a light, his hand was too unsteady to take it, so I removed the cigarette from his hand and, after getting it burning, put it between his lips. He took a long pull, retained the smoke for a few seconds, then, drawing back his head, blew out a long stream of smoke. Then he looked back at me. 'This is the minute I've been waiting for for almost a week,' he said. Then he went on smoking, oblivious to the world.

I felt in my pocket. I had three cigarettes left. Should I offer them to the padre and the two soldiers? I didn't want to – there were absolutely no prospects of getting any more – but as the seconds passed I felt a sense of shame rising higher and higher inside me. It was made more acute by the knowledge that I was smoking inside a church and that the padre kept looking at me. I tried to master the impulse to give them away, to argue that they wouldn't expect me to hand round such treasures as cigarettes, but it was no use. Without being fully conscious of what I was doing, I had the three cigarettes in my hand and was offering them round.

The padre shook his head. 'No thanks,' he said quietly. 'I don't smoke.'

'Neither do I,' said one of the soldiers as I held out my hand.

The other soldier accepted one. 'I'll give you one back as soon as I can get some,' he said with an apologetic grin.

When they'd finished patching up the man with the broken leg, I asked if they could help me. After examining my knees and arm, they bandaged them up.

'I got all this through working for the Nazis,' I said. The padre sighed and nodded his head. 'But I'm doing no more work for them. They've had the last stroke out of me.'

Again he nodded. 'I don't think you could work for anyone in your present condition,' he said. 'With those knees I'll be surprised if you can even walk properly for a long time.' And he was right.

18
On the Move

The working party had been paraded, counted and marched off to the landing ground, and those of us who remained – the sick, lame and lazy, as we were labelled – were reclining in various attitudes of comfort, or discomfort, on the church floor.

I was numbered among those who enjoyed comfort – I was the proud possessor of a blanket. For three nights I had shared it with its former owner, a lanky Kiwi, and during the daytime I'd had its exclusive use while Kiwi was out working. But on the fourth night he had failed to return and I'd not seen him since. I had made inquiries about him, but no one had been able to give me any definite information. I was sorry he'd gone because he was such a cheery soul. Well, it was an ill wind that blew no one any good; it blew me a blanket.

The monotony of the days was broken only by mealtimes and the coming and going of working parties. The padre always managed to raise enough biscuits and bully beef to ensure us a morning and evening meal; and sometimes there was even sufficient for midday as well. And when the working parties returned at night, they could be quite sure of something to eat. But we were always hungry, and the main topic of conversation was not the war or being prisoners; it was always food. When we weren't talking about it, we were thinking about it; and when we were asleep, we were dreaming about it.

My hands were improving rapidly, and so also was my arm. But my knees were still causing me a lot of trouble and I had great difficulty in hobbling about. I managed to keep as clean as one can without soap, but I never felt really clean, chiefly because I hadn't shaved for nearly three weeks. The padre was constantly agitating for better washing facilities and for an improvement in sanitary arrangements, but all the Germans would do was to lend us two shovels with which to dig a latrine trench.

There seemed to be no one in the church whom I'd known in pre-prisoner days, and being in Air Force uniform made me anything but popular. Nevertheless, I had one staunch friend: the little soldier wearing the RAF glengarry cap whom I'd first met on the way to the landing ground. A few days after I'd returned to the church with my damaged knees, he'd come in with several other prisoners, ahead of the main working party. As he entered the church we saw each other, and he came running across to my bed space over by the north wall.

'Well, stranger,' I said, looking at him coldly. 'What's been happening to you?' I wasn't feeling too pleased with him for having run out on me.

'It wasn't my fault,' he said, guessing the reason for the chilly reception. 'They came and collected a party of us to go to the next village to act as batmen to some Jerry officers. I didn't get the chance to tell you.'

'When did they come for you?' I asked. 'I was in church all the time, and I didn't even see a Jerry enter the place.'

'It was while they were dishing out food. I was at the tail-end of the queue, and two Jerries came along and grabbed the last six of us.'

'All right,' I said rather sullenly, 'I'll believe you.'

'I don't think you do believe me,' he said in hurt tones.

'Of course I do,' I replied. 'But I was beginning to think you'd purposely given me the slip. The Air Force aren't very popular around here, you know.'

'I wouldn't give you the slip like that,' he said reproachfully.

'I know you wouldn't. Come and sit down.'

From that moment we became real pals. The first thing I did was to find a name for him. He confided that at home he'd always been called William, but he didn't like it, and for personal reasons I didn't wish to call him Bill. Because of his diminutive size I nicknamed him Chota*. In return he called me Mr Micky. At first I was rather amused, but very soon grew annoyed. It was almost as if he'd set out to make me feel as old as Methuselah. When I could stand it no longer, I turned on him. 'If you don't cut out the "Mr" I'll start calling you "Master Billy"!' I snapped. He looked at me with his large, blue, innocent eyes and blushed. 'I'm sorry,' he said miserably. Then I felt mad with myself.

The padre had managed to scrounge a quantity of blankets for issue to the wounded. Because of his neck wound – it was showing no signs of healing –

* An Indian word meaning 'small'.

Chota had been excused further work and had, of course, qualified for a blanket.

At night we used my blanket as a ground sheet and Chota's as a covering. During the daytime we rolled both blankets together into a sausage and used them as a seat.

Chota was sitting with his back resting against the church wall, looking at his bare feet, and I wondered what he was hatching out. 'There's a rumour that the Jerries are moving us today,' he suddenly said.

I shrugged my shoulders. We'd heard that rumour at least a dozen times before. 'Where are they moving us to this time?' I asked.

'A camp close to Canea.'

'What camp? There's only a hospital there.'

'Perhaps that's where they're moving us to. We're all on the sick list.'

I fidgeted about, trying to get comfortable. These rumours always seemed to upset me and make me restless. 'Sounds a lot of poppycock to me,' I told him.

'It might be true. They can't keep us here for ever.'

'Don't you believe it,' I told him. 'They're quite capable of keeping us here until we die of starvation. Then they'll turn us into soap.'

'Are your knees hurting again?' he asked.

'I'm hurting all over.'

As it happened, it wasn't a lot of poppycock. Early that afternoon the Germans gave us an hour's notice to get ready for the move. They offered to provide transport for those unable to do the walk, and Chota was anxious that I should make use of it. But I didn't trust the Jerries and insisted on walking. Of course, he thought I was being stupid, but I wouldn't change my mind. The Jerries were barbarians and the less I had to do with them, the better I should be pleased.

At two o'clock the guard opened the door and we trooped out through the churchyard. As we formed ourselves into a long column, we were surrounded by paratroopers armed with tommy-guns and hand grenades. They counted and re-counted us, and when they were satisfied that they knew exactly how many of us there were, they counted us again to make sure. Before we finally set off, we were told that anyone leaving the ranks for any reason would be shot, and that they intended shooting to kill!

I turned to Chota. 'You see what I mean when I say they're bloody barbarians! If my knees give out and I have to leave the ranks, I get shot!'

'You keep hold of me and you won't have to leave the ranks,' he told me, tightening his grip around my waist.

The padre was at the head of the column and it was he who set the pace – dead slow. At first the guards were impatient and tried to make us go faster, but when they saw that some of us were already finding it difficult to keep up, they stopped worrying us. After we'd covered about 1½ miles we were allowed to halt for a rest.

'That wasn't too bad,' remarked Chota as we sat down at the side of the road. 'If they let us amble along like that and give us a break now and again, we'll make it all right.'

Bringing out the bloomers, I wiped the dust and sweat from my face. 'I suppose we will,' I said. 'But we've a long way to go yet.' I held out the bloomers. 'D'you want to borrow these?' Without recognizing the garment, he mopped his face, then returned them to me.

After a time, we got on the move again. No attempt was made to make us fall in or march in formation. As long as we kept moving, the guards left us alone.

We had covered another mile and were feeling tired again. 'Look at that!' whispered Chota as we trudged slowly along the grass verge. He nodded in the direction of a pile of stones. There, laid out on his back, was a dead Maori soldier, and balanced on the stones was his rifle. For a moment we paused to gaze at the body, now dark and swollen. How long had it been dead, I wondered. And what was the Maori's name. Suddenly I felt tears welling up into my eyes. He looked so lonely and to leave him seemed like deserting someone in need of help.

'Come on,' said Chota quietly. 'We can't do anything.' We trudged slowly on our way.

We passed many more bodies, both British and German, before we were allowed another halt. Someone plodding along behind us was keeping the count. 'That makes 17 of ours and 23 of theirs,' he would say. And when another corpse was seen he would adjust his figures accordingly, quoting them boldly when the number of Germans exceeded the British, and almost whispering them when the figures were the other way round.

Two more rests and a great deal more sweat brought us to our destination. It was a camp of tents and small stone buildings hemmed in by miles of barbed wire. Until a few days ago it had been a hospital. Now it was to become a camp for prisoners. As we passed through the gates, we were formed into parties, and the senior prisoner was given instructions as to which tent was to be occupied. Chota and I were with a party of about 50 who were detailed to a marquee. It was at the far end of the camp and within ¼ mile of the shore.

Chota and I were the last to enter the tent and I expected to find all the best plots taken. To our surprise, however, we saw that there was a large empty space at the other end, so we went along and laid claim to a chunk of it.

'This is going to be good,' Chota remarked as he spread out our blankets. 'A nice bit of soft sand to bury your hips in.'

I rubbed my hands together. Yes, it was going to be good. We had lots of room, and being so far from the entrance it would be quiet. What was even more important was that it was a long way for the Germans to come if they wanted us.

Suddenly Chota started to sniff. 'It's a bit stinky in here,' he said, wrink-ling his nose. 'What about some fresh air?'

I limped across to the nearest panel of canvas and unhooked it. My eyes nearly popped out. A yard away was the tail-end of a 250-lb bomb sticking out of the ground, and close to it was a piece of wood bearing the inscription: UNEXPLODED BOMB.

19
Plans, Ants and Apricots

What little sleep I had that night was spoilt by nightmares. Chota and I had moved ourselves and our blankets down to where the rest of the party was camping in the tent, but we were still too close to the bomb for us to enjoy much peace of mind. We inquired about moving to another tent, and even offered to sleep out in the open, but the Germans ordered us back. The bomb was not likely to go off as long as we didn't tamper with it, we were told!

When it was dark, we curled up in our blankets and tried to sleep. At first it was too hot, then when we unfurled our blankets it was too cold. Next someone started to snore. Then a mosquito started to buzz around my head and I had to hide under the blanket to escape him. But at last I drifted off into unconsciousness – only to be awakened by an ominous ticking. I began to sweat and could feel my hair start to bristle. Then I realized that the ticking came from my watch. With a whispered curse, I removed it from my wrist and tucked it into a trousers pocket. Again I drifted off, and again I was awakened by a ticking. This time I was quite sure that it was the bomb. The tick was loud and clear, and seemed to be coming from the right direction. I decided to rouse everyone, beginning with Chota. It was as well I did start with him – it was his watch ticking!

None of us expected any breakfast, so we were quite surprised when word went round that we were to queue up outside the padre's tent for food, and that we were to take with us something to hold a hot drink. I had my tin mug, Chota his bully-beef tin, so off we went to join the queue, which already stretched half-way round the camp. Yard by yard we drew closer to the padre's tent, until at last we could see the head of the queue. Each man was

149

being given a whole packet of army biscuits and half a pint of something resembling tea minus milk.

'I hope they don't run out before we get ours,' said Chota, displaying some anxiety. He moved slightly away from the queue and I could see that he was counting the number of men in front of us.

'We'll be all right,' I said reassuringly. 'We're nearly there.' But I was just as anxious as Chota.

Soon we were at the head of the queue. 'You see, we've made it!' I said cheerfully. This time I smiled because I felt like smiling. And Chota smiled back as happily as if he'd been told he could have anything to eat he cared to choose. We each drew a packet of seven army biscuits, each biscuit measuring about 3 by 2 inches, and about a gill of tea. We thanked the cooks, and almost bowed to them as we passed.

'Straight on,' droned a voice. 'Keep straight on.'

We kept 'straight on' until we came to the barbed wire at the other end of the camp. By the time we sat down, we'd already made a good start on our breakfast.

'How many biscuits are you going to eat?' Chota asked, his jaws grinding and his eyes shining.

'Five. I'm saving two for later.'

I sipped the tea. It was nearly cold but tasted good.

'Aren't you going to flog any for fags?'

I turned and looked at him. The thought hadn't even entered my mind! 'What made you ask that?'

He didn't answer immediately – his mouth was too full of food. Presently he half turned his head. 'It's one way of getting a smoke,' he said.

I grunted. I could do with a smoke, but I wasn't sure that I'd part with food for cigarettes. In any case, no one seemed to have any cigarettes to swap. But it was an idea. Then I found that it was an idea I couldn't get rid of!

'I wish you hadn't mentioned cigarettes,' I said, chewing hard at my biscuits. 'I'd almost forgotten that I ever smoked.'

'You old liar,' he remarked, picking crumbs from the folds of his tunic and popping them into his mouth. 'You even talk about smoking in your sleep.'

'Nuts!' I said, starting on my fifth biscuit. 'From the way you talk anyone would think I was a drug addict.'

He turned his head stiffly and gazed at the two remaining biscuits in my lap. 'What're you saving them for?'

'Later on. Aren't you going to save any?'

'No.'

'You'll be hungry by midday.'

'I believe you're saving them to flog for cigarettes,' he said with a sly smile.

Grimly I started eating again. 'You've goaded me into this,' I said. 'If you'd kept your trap shut I might have shared them with you.'

'I'd sooner you ate them,' he said with a mocking simplicity.

When I'd finished both biscuits, I wiped out my mug with the bloomers, then put it back in my pocket.

'What *is* that piece of cloth?' he asked with unusual interest. 'You seem to use it for everything but a hat.'

I held out the bloomers for him to view. 'Loot! I pinched them from a poor, unsuspecting Cretan maiden.'

He took them from my hands and examined them.

'I'm going to use them as a spare pair of underpants,' I told him. 'They're just about my size.'

'Rather a comely type of Jane, I should imagine,' he said, turning up his nose. 'Who was she?'

'I haven't an idea,' I replied, taking them back from him. Then I told him where they came from.

After a time we drifted back in the direction of the tent. On the way we stopped to watch two Germans constructing a small barbed-wire enclosure. They had a large coil of wire and were walking round and round in circles, spiralling out the wire as they went.

'What's that for?' asked Chota.

'I don't know, unless it's an open-air dog kennel!'

'*Abreisen!*' snapped one of the Germans.

'What does he say?' asked Chota, taking a step backwards.

'*Abreisen!*' snapped the German again. '*Abreisen!*'

'We'd better beat it,' I said, eyeing the German suspiciously. 'He sounds as if he has a liver.'

'They always seem to have livers,' grumbled Chota as we ambled off.

'What are we going to do about that bomb?' I asked when we got back inside the tent. 'I don't feel like sleeping with it under my ear again tonight.'

Chota stood by the tent wall and peered outside. 'It's still there,' he said ruefully. 'And there's a bunch of Jerries coming towards the tent,' he added.

I slid down to my full length and dragged the blanket over me. 'Well, come and lie down and try to look ill,' I said shortly. 'I expect they're coming to collect a working party.'

He left the tent wall and, sitting down, began to unlace one of his boots.

'What are you doing?' I asked irritably.

He took the boot from his foot, then turned it upside down. 'It's full of sand,' he said.

'To hell with the sand,' I snapped. 'D'you want to dig that bloody bomb out?'

He shrugged his shoulders, then deliberately let the boot drop close to my head. I suddenly felt angry and wanted to swear at him. For a moment I glared at his baby-like face with its patches of half-grown whiskers, and at his sulky little mouth with biscuit crumbs wedged in the corners. Then I turned on to my side and pulled the blanket round my neck. To hell with him.

In the distance I heard the quiet voice of Flight Sergeant Green. 'They only want half a dozen of you,' he was saying. 'It's to move some tables and forms.' Then I heard the voices of the volunteers, and there were more than half a dozen.

Presently there was a movement behind me. 'How long are we staying here?' Chota asked in a peevish voice.

I feigned sleep. I felt too annoyed with him to speak. I heard him breathe heavily as he bent to lace up his boot. When he'd finished he stood up, paused, then walked away. I opened one eye, then the other. He was out of sight. I rolled over on to my back. What the hell's all this about, anyway? I asked myself; losing your temper like some half-grown schoolgirl – and for no reason at all! Then I felt humiliated. I rolled over on to my side feeling very miserable. This life was getting me down. Again I closed my eyes. How long had I been a prisoner? I tried to count the days. I'd been captured on a Tuesday. What day was this? I didn't know. I tried working out where I'd spent each night; that might help. I knew that I'd spent two or three nights in the little whitewashed church, and one night in the Black Hole of Calcutta. Then we'd been in the big church about 10 nights. That meant that I'd been a prisoner for at least two weeks. Two weeks! Two weeks without a decent wash or a shave! Two weeks without a decent meal. 'Two weeks of *this*,' I said aloud, opening my eyes. I sat up. I've got to get away from here or I'll go mad! I threw the blanket to one side and struggled to my feet. I'm going to escape – I'm going to get away from here if I have to swim away! I stooped to straighten out the blanket.

'You'd better let me do that. You'll be hurting your knees again.'

It was Chota. He picked up the blanket, shook it, then laid it out flat. As I watched him my mind became less turbulent. 'Anything happening out there?' I asked, trying to sound casual.

'They're forming tables and forms into a hollow square at this side of the tent,' he said shortly.

He followed me as I limped to the wall and unhooked the canvas. Tables and forms were laid out neatly, and a German was putting sheets of paper at intervals all the way round the table.

'What's all this for?' I asked, somewhat mystified. 'Are they starting a school or something?'

'Search me,' he replied. 'It's got everyone guessing.'

For a time I continued to peer through the opening. Then the German, who had just finished laying out the paper, saw me. He started to shout, so I withdrew my head and hooked up the canvas.

'There's something fishy going on here,' I remarked to Chota. 'I'm going to have another peep in a minute.'

Presently Flt. Sgt. Green shouted from the far end of the tent that the Germans had given orders that the tent walls were to be properly hooked up, and that no one was to look outside. That made us all really curious, and everyone in the tent immediately set about finding himself a chink to peer through.

Chota dropped to the floor and raised a small fold of canvas. 'I expect they're going to interrogate us,' he said, peeping outside.

I looked down at him. 'What makes you think that?' I asked nervously. At the mention of the word 'interrogate', I had a sudden fluttering of the heart. I'd not forgotten the charges that they'd levied at us when we'd first been captured, and the prospects of being quizzed by the Nazis sent cold shivers up and down my spine.

'It's just an idea of mine,' he said, withdrawing his head.

'Well, it's a shocking idea,' I told him.

He looked up at me. 'D'you know, when I was first caught, a great hulk of a paratrooper came up to me and, after waving his gun under my nose, demanded to know where the underground hangar was.'

'What did you tell him?' I asked. 'That we didn't have any planes to hide?'

He gave a nervous smile. 'As a matter of fact, I thought we really had a secret underground hangar. Lots of our people did.'

'Oh, no,' I said, surprised at his gullibility. 'Surely you didn't fall for that.'

The colour rose to his face. 'How d'you know there wasn't one?' he demanded angrily.

I unhooked a piece of canvas. 'Well, you can take it from me there wasn't,' I said flatly. 'We didn't have any planes to fly, let alone hide.'

'Here they come,' I head a nearby soldier say. 'It looks like a Lord Mayor's procession.'

I pulled down the canvas and peered outside. The procession was led by two paratroopers, each carrying a tommy-gun. Immediately behind them followed six German officers, looking very pompous and well fed. Then came two British and two Greek officers; they were neat and clean but looked very haggard. Following them were two more paratroopers, and between them were two civilian prisoners carrying shovels.

'What's all this in aid of?' asked Chota loudly.

'Shut up,' I snapped, stamping my feet. 'D'you want to get us all shot?'

I heard him grunt, then he began to swear. I let go of the canvas and looked down at him.

'What the hell's the matter with you?' I asked irritably. 'You're worse than a bloody two-year-old!'

'You trod on me,' he grumbled, rubbing the back of his right hand.

For a moment I felt deflated. 'Sorry,' I said.

I dragged on the canvas and peered outside again. Four of the German officers were seated at the centre table, and two were at one of the side tables. The British and Greek officers, with the armed paratroopers standing behind them, sat together at the other side of the table. And the prisoners carrying shovels, together with their escort, were vanishing from sight behind a nearby sandhill.

What *is* this all about? I asked myself. They can't be court martialling the British and Greek officers. They'd make them stand up if they were. Well, were they going to court martial one of their own men? No, they wouldn't have enemy officers present for that. But I was sure someone was about to be court martialled.

Suddenly one of the Germans at the centre table drew out his revolver and hammered the table top. The rest visibly stiffened, as if sitting to attention. He must be the president, I said aloud. And a particularly nasty-looking president he was. He had a fat, purplish face attached to an equally fat and purplish neck, his jaws were shapeless, and his eyes were wide apart like those of a pig. On top of his head was a high-topped peak cap with a pair of goggles strapped round the hatband. A typical Nazi, I thought.

The president shouted an order, and from around the corner of our end of the tent appeared two Cretan civilians escorted by two paratroopers. So, they were court martialling civilians!

I unfastened a second hook and rested my chin on the canvas to keep it down. A German officer at the side table started to read rapidly from a notebook. Was he the prosecutor? I wondered. Then the president said a few words, after which one of the Greek officers – an interpreter, I presumed – began to speak. He spoke quietly and quickly, as if he were in a hurry to finish an unpleasant task. The two civilians, one old, the other young, stood staring in blank bewilderment. They understood the charges against them, but what they obviously could not understand was why one of their own countrymen should be acting for the Germans against them. To their peasant minds, it was the Greek officer who was accusing them, not the Germans.

When the interpreter had finished, the elder of the civilians began to speak. He was tall and thin, and the skin on his face was like yellow parchment. As he spoke, he kept blinking, as if he had just come into the daylight from a dark room. I didn't know what crimes they were charged with, but the old man was obviously denying his guilt, and at frequent intervals held out his large, bony hands, as if appealing to the court to believe him. The interpreter asked him questions, then told the President what he'd said. As the president and prosecutor asked more questions, the poor old Cretan got flurried. That was the end of his case. The court then set to work on the young man, and when he also had grown too flurried to defend himself, the president told the escort to take them both away. Then the court began to consider its verdict.

Chota edged closer. 'What d'you think they're charged with?' he whispered. 'Sabotage?'

I shook my head. 'I don't know. I suppose it could be that. But they might have been caught popping off their long-barrel flintlocks at some poor unsuspecting Nazis.'

It took but a very few minutes for the court to reach a verdict, then the president shouted for the prisoners to be brought back. When they appeared round the corner of the tent, I saw that both had their hands tied behind them. The president sat very erect and glared across at the two peasants, then he began to speak. The unfortunate men looked first at the German, then at the interpreter – for the moment they didn't understand a word of what was being said. Very soon, though, they did. As the interpreter rose to his feet and began speaking, a look of horror crept into their faces. They had been found guilty! The President barked out a short sentence and for a moment the interpreter just stared at him. Then he shrugged and gave a deep sigh. Turning to the prisoners, he quietly repeated what the president had said. Their eyes opened wide and they both tried to move forward to the president. The escort jerked them roughly back. The old man began to speak, but the president hammered on the table with his clenched fists, then shouted for them to be taken away. The interpreter sat down, and we watched the prisoners being hustled away.

'See where they're taking them?' Chota said in an awed voice. They were going in the same direction as the paratroopers and the two men with shovels had gone before the court had opened.

With a heavy heart I watched them disappear behind the sandhill. Poor devils, I thought. They didn't have much of a trial. Then I heard two bursts of tommy-gun fire and closed my eyes. We walked slowly to the entrance.

'They were supposed to have been caught mutilating dead Germans,' I heard someone say. I suddenly felt sick.

'Let's get outside again,' I said. 'This tent gives me the willies.'

Flt. Sgt. Green, whom I'd been told was the most senior NCO prisoner, was on the other side of the marquee, and appeared to be busy writing notes. That reminded me: I'd had the idea of making a list of all those men of the Squadron whom I knew to be prisoners, and questioning them as to how they had been taken, and if they could tell me anything about any of those who might be missing. So I stopped and asked Flt. Sgt. Green whether he could make use of such a list if I were to compile it. The answer was yes. He could send it via the Germans to the Red Cross. He seemed so sure of this that I imagined he had already been in touch with the Germans on the matter.

So, I started on the list, beginning with my own little bunch of men, especially mentioning Bill Williams. Then I went round the marquee looking for men whom I knew belonged to the Squadron. One or two of them were very worried about being prisoners, telling me that they had surrendered as they had no firearms. I told them that I had been in very much the same position, and that the five bullets I had in my Colt revolver I had exchanged for 10 cigarettes each – the Armoury had told me they had no Colt ammunition. The men asked me if they would be in trouble with the Squadron for surrendering. I could only tell them not to worry; none of us had received instructions about what to do if we were surrounded and cut off from the main body of men.

One of the troubles was that none of them seemed to know that the Commanding Officer and most of the Air Crew had gone to Egypt to pick up replacement aircraft for those lost covering the evacuation of Greece. Strange to say, even I – the CO's confidential clerk – knew little of the change in command. The new CO was a young Flying Officer who had been taken off flying duties, and he had issued no orders since taking over the Squadron. On one important occasion when I had delivered to him a signal indirectly concerning me, he told me to ignore it, duly throwing it away!

I subsequently learned that my list had reached Geneva, and was passed on to the Air Ministry.

Someone had spread word that the sun's rays contained vitamins, and because our meagre rations were very deficient in these essentials, we were all advised to sunbathe daily. As we had nothing better to do, we stripped to the buff and for a time absorbed vitamins.

Everything seemed very quiet. The sounds of war had passed away like a violent tropical thunderstorm. The Germans were leaving us alone and hadn't even troubled to turn us out for a daily 'count'. This was good for our peace of mind, but we were all terribly hungry and our spirits were anything but high. I looked up at the sky. There wasn't a single cloud to break its blueness.

Heaven is up there, I told myself dreamily. And one of these days, that's where you're going to end – unless someone finds you out first!

Then I began to speculate about the war. Was it really over in Crete? I strained my ears to try and catch the sounds of firing but heard nothing. Suddenly I began to feel uncomfortably hot. If the war was over, who had won? If we had won, why were we still prisoners? It was a shocking and agonizing thought. I closed my eyes again. If the war in Crete was over and we had lost, what was going to happen to us? Would we be sent to Germany as slave labour? Or would they keep us here on Crete, to starve, rot and die? Then I began to think again of the snow-capped mountains I had seen when we were being marched from the church to the landing ground. That was where I would go – no Germany for me. But my knees? I couldn't escape until they were better. How long was that going to be? We might be moved before I was able to escape. Was there no other way? What about Derna, 400 miles across the sea? Could I not make a canoe? For a while I pondered the question.

'Are you awake?' I heard Chota ask quietly.

I turned my head. Of course I was awake. Did he expect me to be asleep at this time of the day? 'Yes,' I said. 'Why?'

'I thought you were dreaming!'

'Dreaming!' I raised myself on an elbow. 'What made you think that?'

'You were talking.'

'Rot. You're imagining things.'

'You were talking and swearing,' he said, 'rather like a schoolmaster scolding a boy.'

'Bull,' I said, lowering myself back to the ground. But I began to have doubts about myself. 'What was I saying?' I asked, trying not to appear too curious.

'Something about Derna. You sounded as if you were trying to make up your mind whether to swim there or go by P&O.'

I closed my eyes. Had I been thinking out loud again? 'What else did I say?' I asked.

'Something about a broken-down lorry. But it was the language that was so amusing.'

I wriggled into a sitting position. 'What a state to be in,' I remarked. After a pause, I added, 'As a matter of fact, I was trying to work out how I could get away from here.'

'To Derna.'

'Yes. It's the nearest bit of North Africa to us.'

'You can't swim that far,' he said with a laugh, 'or is that why you want a lorry?'

I traced out an imaginary island in the sand. 'I was thinking about a covered-in lorry. I want the metal framework and the awning. I reckon I could make a dinghy or canoe out of it.'

'You might as well get the engine,' he said with a chuckle.

'If you're in a frivolous mood, we better change the subject,' I snapped. 'I'm being quite serious.'

He shrugged his shoulders. 'All right, let's be serious.'

'Well, I want to make a dinghy or canoe. Have you any suggestions?'

'You'd be drowned before you'd gone 10 miles,' he said.

'Have you ever sailed in the Med?' I asked. 'At this time of year, it would be a piece of cake.'

For a moment he was lost in thought, then he looked up. 'Talking of cake,' he said, 'what about grub, and water?'

'Those are only two of the problems,' I replied. 'There are plenty of others which'll be much harder to solve.'

For a time neither of us spoke, and I sensed that he was mentally listing all the difficulties he could think of: map, compass, food, water, German aircraft, submarines, not to mention obtaining the material with which to make the canoe. But I was determined to have a try. I just had to get away.

'Will you go alone?' he suddenly asked.

I looked down at the sand and rubbed out the island. I wanted him to come with me, he must have known that. But could we make a canoe large

157

enough to hold two people? And would it be fair to ask him to come? I suppose the most important question was whether he would want to. If he did, we could get over the other difficulties.

'I'd like you to come with me,' I said. 'I'll need your help.' As I spoke, I suddenly realized how much I would need his help.

He looked up at me and wrinkled his nose. 'I'll be seasick,' he said with a smile. He's refusing, I told myself. If you press him, you'll both be hurt. I stifled a sigh and tried to smile. Then I suddenly began wondering what the real reason for his refusal was. Lack of faith in me? Too many difficulties to be overcome? The danger? As long as it wasn't lack of faith in me I didn't mind, but if it were that ...

He slowly got to his knees. 'I'll help you build the canoe,' he said with a smile. For a moment he continued to look down at me, and I half expected him to say that he'd changed his mind and that he'd now come, but instead he said, 'You'll never get enough stuff to build anything big enough for two. And there's food and water.'

I looked back at the rubbed-out island and suddenly felt very lonely. I no longer wanted to go through with the idea.

He pulled on his slacks. 'I could do with a drink,' he said cheerfully. 'Do you want one?'

I nodded. 'Yes, bring one back for me.'

He ambled off to get his bully-beef tin and my mug. I rolled over on to my back and folded my arms behind my head. I'd intended discussing the possibilities of building a canoe with him, but all I'd succeeded in doing was getting him to refuse to escape with me. I looked towards my toes, and the sight of my naked figure made me feel uncomfortable. Was it that clothes raised us from the level of ignorant savages to that of civilized beings? Yes, and it was clothes that gave us courage. I crawled into my shirt and trousers. No more sunbathing for me!

I glanced at my watch. We still had another hour to wait for our afternoon meal.

'What about a prowl round the camp?' Chota suggested. 'I'm bored stiff.'

'I'm too tired,' I said without even troubling to look at him, and we lapsed into silence.

The sun was now behind the tent and we were in the shade. A stray ant found his way on to my arm and began walking towards my elbow. His gait was awkward and sluggish, and I began to wonder if he was also feeling the effects of the Nazi invasion. What are you after? I asked, picking him up and putting him back on the sand. He ran round in a small circle as if frightened, then disappeared under my trouser leg. You're very persevering, I mused. Let's see where you're making for. He manoeuvred his way across the folds in the material, at times vanishing from sight, but he kept going until at last he was on the front of my shirt. Then he stopped for a rest. I leaned forward and blew at him. He hunched up his back but stayed where he was. Again I blew, this time much harder, but he hung on and refused to be moved. I waited and watched, but he seemed to have settled down for a nap. Poor little ant, I thought. If you feel anything like I do, I'm sorry for you.

Again I looked at my watch. Would the hour never go? With a sigh I closed my eyes. Then I began to think about the ant. Did he have any brothers or sisters? Perhaps he was a middle-aged ant and the father, or mother, of a family of little ants! Then I remembered that ants were supposed to be quite brainless and that they liked being regimented. That was just how the Germans were. I suddenly began to despise the ant. I leaned forward and had another look at him. He still appeared to be fast asleep. Well, asleep or not, he was going. I wanted nothing to do with Hitler's insect friends! I flexed a finger and with a flick propelled him into the air. Then I leaned back again and closed my eyes, and as I did so I suddenly began to wonder whether I was not going a little mad.

I started to doze, and had almost reached the stage where I was no longer conscious of having a body when I heard a voice. I tried to ignore it. I wanted to sleep. But the voice insisted on being heard. 'Wakee, wakee! Show a leg! The sun's scorching your bloody eyes out!' I knew the voice. Whose was it? I struggled back to consciousness, all the while trying to place the voice, and through bleary eyes I saw Lofty Bond.

For a moment I was too surprised to speak. Then my wits returned. 'Lofty,' I exclaimed, climbing awkwardly to my feet. 'Where on earth have you been?'

'All over the place,' he said, smiling broadly. 'Today I've been doing a bit of looting.' Then I saw that in one hand he carried a lady's straw hat and in the other a small sack. With a grin he put the hat on his head. 'Like it?'

'Like it?' I said. 'You look like a loose woman!'

Laughing, he threw the sack to the ground and sat down. 'What's been happening to you?' he asked, removing the hat.

I told him briefly the events of the last few days, then asked him about Lawrie and the others. 'Lawrie's all right,' he said. 'I saw him this morning, and he's had a shave.' Then he opened the neck of the sack and peered inside. 'Have one,' he said.

I bent down and put my hand inside the sack. 'What are they?'

'Dried apricots. They're bloody good.'

I took one, then he tipped the sack towards Chota. 'Have one. Take a handful. There's plenty.'

'They are good,' I said. 'But they're a bit sour.' I swallowed a chunk of the fruit. 'Where did you scrounge them?'

'I've been out with a working party into Canea,' he said. 'We've been cleaning up the place a bit. It's been bombed to hell. I scrounged the hat to keep the sun off my head.'

I looked at him. 'You'd better lose it,' I said. 'It makes you look like a clown.'

Ignoring my remarks, he dug into his pocket and brought out a packet of Woodbines. 'Cigarette?' he said. My eyes nearly popped out. Then I remembered that I'd not smoked for days. What would happen if I started again? Would it upset me, and would it start the craving all over again? But they looked so inviting that I took one. 'I got them from a Jerry,' he said, 'He'd looted the Naafi.' He held out a lighted match.

I got the cigarette going, then inhaled deeply. It made me feel so dizzy that I thought I was going to pass out. Then I regretted having taken the cigarette.

'You'd better have the rest of the packet,' he said. 'I've got some more.'

I hesitated. Then something impelled me to take them. 'Thanks,' I said. 'I'll be able to start smoking myself to death again.'

Within a few minutes of Lofty's arrival, half the inmates of the tent joined us. They'd heard that someone had come into the camp with food and had come to see what they could scrounge. But Lofty wasn't the only one with food. There were about 50 others who'd come into the camp carrying bags or parcels of food under their arms. Lofty handed out his fruit, someone else doled out sweet biscuits, and a New Zealander handed round a box of chocolates. The same thing was happening all over the camp, and by the time our regular evening meal was ready, most of us had already had some kind of a feed.

We spent the evening relating our experiences, and trying to guess the probable course of the war from the rumours Lofty had heard in Canea. When it began to get dark, Chota and I manipulated our blankets so that there was room for Lofty, and the three of us settled down for the night.

'There's an unexploded bomb just outside,' I told Lofty as he made himself comfortable.

He pulled the blanket further round his neck. 'Why worry about it?' he asked. 'If it goes off, you won't know!' Which was typical of his philosophy.

At first the buzz of conversation kept us from sleeping, but after a while things quietened down and we were able to doze off. I'm going to sleep well tonight, I told myself. I'm full of food and I've smoked four cigarettes.

I don't know how long I'd been asleep, but suddenly I found myself dragged back to consciousness by an awful pain in the stomach. I'd eaten rather too much fruit, but it would soon be digested and then the pain would go. I tried to keep asleep, but the pain grew so violent that I couldn't. I rubbed my stomach and tried not to make too much noise. Then I realized that Chota was missing. I felt around in the dark – perhaps he'd rolled off the blanket – but he wasn't there. I stood up, feeling sick and in great pain.

'That you, Mike?' I heard Lofty croak.

'Yes,' I whispered feebly. 'I've got awful bellyache.'

'So've I. I think I've got diarrhoea as well.' He threw the blanket back and stood up.

'Chota's missing,' I said. 'Maybe he's got it as well.'

'Do you feel diarrhoea-ish?' he asked.

'I think it's coming on,' I told him. 'But I want to be sick.'

Just then Chota returned.

'What's up,' I asked him. 'Got bellyache?'

'Yes,' he groaned. 'I think my inside's fallen out.'

'Come on,' said Lofty. 'I've got to get outside.'

I followed him to the entrance of the tent.

'Which way do we go?' he asked.

'To the left. There's a large patch of ground we use over by the shore.'

'I don't think I'm going to make it,' Lofty said.

At last we reached the patch of sandy waste. 'Thank Christ for that,' I heard Lofty exclaim as he stopped. For the sake of privacy I walked on a little further. Then I saw there were at least a dozen other men scattered around. Apparently we weren't the only ones with bellyache.

When I got back to the tent, I found Lofty had already returned, but Chota was missing again. I got down on the blanket.

'It's those bloody apricots,' Lofty grumbled.

'I suppose it is,' I agreed, 'but they tasted all right.'

'We ate too many of them.'

Some of the men further along the tent began to move restlessly. Then I heard whispering and two figures appeared in silhouette against the greyness of the canvas. More bellyache and diarrhoea, I thought. The figures vanished hastily through the entrance.

'I think I'll have to go outside again,' I heard Lofty say presently. 'Got any paper?'

'No, not a scrap.'

He groped around by the tent skirting. 'I'll have to use the lining of this,' he said as he ripped the material from the inside of the straw hat. Then he strode off into the darkness.

20
All in a Day

By morning it was obvious that nearly everyone in the tent had been affected. Weary bodies were strewn untidily all over the place, and odds and ends of kit and clothing littered the ground – the result of hasty searches for paper.

'I don't think it was the apricots at all,' Chota said. 'I believe the Jerries've deliberately poisoned the water.'

I shook my head. I was feeling equally bloody-minded, but I knew it wasn't that. 'It's not the water.' I told him. 'Everyone's had a drink, but not everyone has bellyache.'

Lofty returned from another visit to the waste ground. 'Half the camp's got it,' he said in a weary voice. 'There's dozens of 'em out there.'

My inside began burning again. 'I'll have to pay another visit,' I said, getting to my feet. 'This'll be my seventeenth!'

'Hell, d'you keep count?' he asked. With a grunt I left the tent. Until now, life had revolved around three elemental facts: food, sleep and cigarettes – in that order. Now I was having to take account of a fourth circumstance – defecation – and it gave promise of taking precedence over the other three.

When I returned, I collected my mug, then went and joined the short breakfast queue. No one could queue very long, but not many missed out on the meal.

Soon after we'd finished eating, word went round that the Germans wanted a working party for Canea.

'I wonder whether I dare volunteer?' Lofty said. He got stiffly to his feet, then drew in his belly until it was nearly flat. Then he let it go and gave a sigh.

'Well,' I said, 'how is it?'

'I don't think it's all gone yet. I think I'll stay put today.' He brought out a cigarette and lit it. 'What about a scrounge round the camp?' he suggested. 'We might find some paper.'

'All right,' I said, 'but we'd better not go too far . . .'

'I think I'll stay where I am,' Chota said. 'I'll have to go again in a minute.'

'I'll stay and keep you company if you like,' I said.

'You go and have your prowl,' he replied. 'You might find something more useful than paper.'

'Yes, we might find a battleship,' Lofty said as he set off towards the entrance. Had those two been talking?

We ambled slowly through the camp. Outside each tent we saw the faithful indulging in their daily sunbath. 'It'd do some of them good if they were to have proper baths,' Lofty remarked when I told him about the vitamins. From the appearance of some of the feet we saw, I agreed with him.

We left the main part of the camp and reached an area which we had been told was out of bounds to prisoners. However, as there were no guards, no noticeboards and no barbed wire, we just kept walking.

'Looks as if there's been a few bombs dropped around here,' Lofty said, pointing to a large, untidy patch of charred wreckage. 'I suppose that was a tent, once.'

A little further on we came to a partly burnt-out marquee. Half the roof had been destroyed and long lengths of torn wall canvas were flapping gently in the breeze.

'Let's have a look inside,' Lofty said, coming to a halt. We glanced around to make sure that no Germans were watching us, then darted inside. There was little of any value to be seen – a few items of torn clothing, two broken chairs and a badly charred table, on which was a dish full of surgical scissors. When the marquee had been set on fire by a bomb, apparently the heat had been so intense that it had affected the scissors: the plating had been burned off, and the metal was now the very pale blue that steel goes when cooling after being heated in a forge. I tried cutting hair from the back of my hand but the scissors had lost their edge. Still, I pocketed several of them in the hope they would eventually come in useful.

'Not much worth having in here,' Lofty said, mildly disappointed. He left my side and walked to the far end of the marquee. I strolled across to the chairs. Perhaps they were repairable. No: each had broken legs and was badly burnt.

Then I heard Lofty swear. 'The bastards,' he said with great vehemence, 'the lousy Nazi bastards!'

'What's the matter?' I asked, startled at his outburst.

He walked back towards the entrance. 'I thought I'd found myself a pair of civvy boots,' he said. Then he stopped.

'Well?' I asked. 'What happened?'

'One of them had a foot in it.'

'A foot?'

'Yes, a foot.'

I shuddered. No wonder he'd sworn. 'It might have been a German foot,' I suggested.

'What? A German wearing brown civvy boots? Not on your life. I'll bet it was one of our blokes.'

'Was the other boot there?'

'Yes.'

Giving way to what I knew to be unwholesome curiosity, I walked over to where he'd found the boots. One lay on its side, empty. The other was upright, and a bloody mess of blackness and bone was sticking out of it. With my foot I tipped the empty boot upright. They were not a pair!

I walked slowly back to Lofty. 'They don't match,' I said. 'You couldn't have worn them.'

He shrugged his shoulders. 'Let's get out of here.'

We retraced our steps. Neither of us any longer felt interested enough to continue our prowl, and for a time we walked in silence, even passing two unexploded bombs without making any comment.

Presently I saw what appeared to be a small mountain of refuse about 100 yards off our course. 'What's that?' I asked with a nod.

We slowed down. 'Let's go and see,' he said, speaking without much enthusiasm.

As we approached the mountain, I saw that it was composed of about 90 per cent paper and 10 per cent miscellaneous junk.

'We could have done with some of this last night,' said Lofty as we came to a halt.

'I'm going to take all I can carry,' I told him. 'There's enough paper here to last a lifetime.'

I poked about and sorted out as much thin paper as I could find. Then I began examining the pile more thoroughly. Almost the first thing I found was a large, rectangular can. Judging by its weight it was filled with something other than air. I examined its fours sides, its top and bottom, but it bore no label. With difficulty I prised off the lid. It contained a white, odourless powder.

'What d'you make of this?' I asked, strolling across to Lofty.

'What is it?' he asked, straightening up.

'That's what I'm asking you,' I said. 'It looks like french chalk.'

He dipped a finger into the tin and had a smell. Then he dipped in again and had a lick. 'I think it *is* french chalk,' he said, giving another sniff.

Wetting a finger, I dipped it into the powder. 'I hope it isn't poisonous,' I said. It seemed quite tasteless. I put the tin on the ground and looked down at it. If it was french chalk, what could it be used for? Curing bellyache? Possibly. That decided me: I would keep it.

Lofty found a bent fork which he immediately straightened, and a leather belt which he buckled round his tunic. Then we decided that we ought to be getting back to see how Chota was. 'We can try the chalk out on him if he's no better,' I suggested.

On our way we passed close by the main gate. 'The working party's coming back early,' I remarked, noticing a large number of men outside. We stopped and looked across at them.

'That's no working party,' said Lofty. 'There are too many of them.' Then I saw that the column stretched right back along the road and out of sight.

'Who are they?' I asked. 'I'm sure they don't belong to this camp.'

He shook his head. 'Search me. New prisoners I should think.'

We walked along a little further, then stopped again. I pointed to a small tree-strewn hill about ½ mile away. 'There's thousands of them. Can you see where the column ends?'

'Let's get closer to the wire,' he said. 'Perhaps we can find out who they are.' When we were within about 20 yards of the wire we halted. Then he cupped his hands and put them to his mouth. 'Where are you from?' he shouted. There was no reply, so he tried again. 'Hey! You! Where're you from?' This time he got an answer.

'From Sphakia. Got any grub?'

'Sphakia,' I heard Lofty repeat. 'Where the 'ell's that? I've never heard of it.'

'South of the island,' the voice said. 'We tried to get away before the capitulation, but they couldn't get us off.'

'*What* capitulation?' Lofty shouted back in a puzzled voice.

Three men by the wire suddenly drew closer together. Presumably it was one of them who was giving us the information. They held a brief discussion, then back came the voice, 'Haven't you heard? The island was surrendered to the Heinies on 1 June.'

'Hell's bells,' Lofty muttered to himself. 'That's pretty rich. Now what d'we do?'

'Ask him how many of them there are,' I said.

Again he cupped his hands. 'How many of you did they catch?' he shouted.

The three men again held a discussion, and presently the answer came. 'About 8,000 but we're not all here.' There was a brief pause, then, 'How many of you are there in this camp?'

'About 1,000,' Lofty replied. Then he turned to me. 'That's about right, isn't it?' I shrugged, not knowing whether it was 1,000 or 2,000.

Then the voice came back again. 'How're you off for grub?' To which Lofty replied, 'Bloody awful. The bastards're starving us.'

I glanced hastily around to see whether there were any Germans near us. Fortunately there weren't. 'We'd better get on our way,' I said. 'Come on.' With a sniff and a grin, he turned and joined me.

'I suppose capitulation does mean surrender,' he said as we walked along.

'I think so,' I replied. 'I expect they use the word because it doesn't sound as bad as "surrender".'

'Lot of bull,' he snorted, and I agreed. 'Another 8,000 in the bag,' he said after a brief pause. 'That's a hell of a lot.'

'They must have been surrounded,' I remarked.

'So they had to capitulate,' he said somewhat sourly.

I gave him a sidelong glance. 'Don't start throwing stones.'

'I'm not throwing stones,' he snapped. 'I was thinking of that shower at HQME. If they'd got properly organized, this wouldn't have happened.'

The tin of chalk was getting heavy, so I started carrying it in front of me with both hands.

'I agree with you about that,' I said. 'A bunch of deadbeats trying to run the war by remote control! It was the same at home until Churchill got in and cleared them out.'

'He ought to go to Egypt and have a good clear out there as well,' he said.

When we got back to the tent we found it crowded with new faces. In preparation for the new prisoners, the Germans had given orders that everyone already in the camp had to be packed into four large marquees, leaving the rest of the tents empty. We struggled along to our bed spaces.

'Thank goodness you've come back,' Chota said breathlessly. 'I've had a hell of a job keeping our plots intact.'

I glanced at our new neighbours. What a horrible scruffy bunch they were! Unshaven, unwashed, long-haired. Heaven preserve me from getting as bad as that.

I planted the tin of chalk close to the tent wall, then sat down next to Chota.

'What's in the tin?' he asked.

'French chalk. At least that's what it looks like.'

He raised his eyebrows. 'Oh. What're you going to do with it?'

'How's the old bellyache?' Lofty asked him in a silky voice. 'Got it under control yet?'

'I've been twice since you left,' he replied innocently. He leaned back against the tent wall. 'It's the paper business that's getting me down. I've even been using bully-beef-tin labels.'

'Quite a good idea,' approved Lofty, slumping down on the other side of him. He felt in his pocket and brought out a sheaf of paper. 'Here you are,' he said with a grin. 'Soft enough for a baby's bottom.'

'And here's some more,' I said, handing him my contribution.

Chota's eyes lit up. 'Where'd you get it?' he asked in surprise.

'From Uncle Adolf,' replied Lofty. 'And there's plenty more where that came from.'

Chota stuffed the paper into his pocket. 'How's your bellyache?' he asked, looking at us each in turn.

'Mine seems to be settling down a bit. I've not been for over an hour,' I told him.

'And so's mine,' said Lofty, leaning over and playfully patting the lid of the tin of chalk.

Suddenly Chota jumped to his feet. 'I think I'll have to pay another visit,' he said in a tone of alarm. 'It gives you no warning. You just have to run for it.'

'Well, thanks to Uncle Adolf you'll be able to enjoy this one,' I told him.

'And when you come back, we'll try out the french chalk,' Lofty said. But Chota was already on his way.

I looked up and down the crowded tent. Surely there was some face I knew among this great mob. Without a word to Lofty, I got to my feet and pushed my way out into the stream of human traffic. So many newcomers were taking up residence that there was no longer any room against the marquee walls. They were now forming themselves into two more rows down the centre. As there was a constant stream of men coming and going, and many of the occupants were milling about, it seemed hopeless trying to find a familiar face. However, once caught in the human stream, it was not easy to get out, and very soon I found myself at the entrance. By hanging on to a tent pole, I was saved from being carried right outside.

As I debated whether I should return to Lofty or let myself be pushed outside, I saw Lawrie. He was sitting in the very corner of the tent talking to Fred Greenhalgh, a mutual friend.

'Lawrie,' I shouted, letting go of the tent pole and forcing my way towards him. 'Lawrie.'

He looked up at me and stared hard. Apparently my hairy chops made it difficult for him to recognize me. Then his face broadened into a smile. 'Well, if it's not Mike,' he said. He jerked himself further into the corner. 'Come and sit down. Move over, Fred.'

He held out his hand, and I stooped forward and grasped it. Then I fell, rather than sat, down between them.

'What a crowd, and what a stink,' I said, still holding his hand. 'It reminds me of a circus.'

'Never mind the crowd,' he said, 'tell me how you are. Have they been treating you decently?'

I wrinkled my nose. 'They've been leaving us alone since we came here. But they don't give us much to eat.'

He shook his hand free and put it into his pocket. 'Are you really hungry?'

'Hungry,' I said. 'I'm starving. Look at this,' and I drew in my stomach until it was concave.

He brought his hand out of his pocket. 'Here, eat these,' he said, giving me a fistful of what appeared to be small dog biscuits.

'Thanks,' I said, popping one into my mouth. 'Where did you scrounge them?'

'A Jerry paratrooper gave me a bag of them.' He turned to Fred. 'D'you want a few more?'

Fred shook his head. 'Later, if I get really hungry. I don't like caraway seed.'

I was wondering what the flavour was, and now I knew. 'When did you get here?' I asked, still chewing.

'We both arrived a few days ago. We've been working in the German compound, on the other side of the camp.'

'Did you sleep there?'

'No. We were in the next tent to this one, but they kicked us out to make room for the new blokes.'

'It's a wonder we didn't meet before,' I said. 'I've been here since it was first occupied by prisoners.'

'We've only been sleeping here. They had us working by seven o'clock every morning, and we seldom got back before nine in the evening.'

'Did they feed you?'

'There was nothing organized, but a couple of paratroopers used to share their rations with us.

'What happened to all the food they captured from us?' I asked. 'There must have been tons of it.'

'It was all sabotaged. As soon as they landed they sent a squad of para-troopers to find the stores. They found thousands of tins of bully, sausages, milk and goodness knows what else, and they stuck a bayonet through every single tin. In a couple of days it was all rotten.'

'What a bloody stupid thing to do,' I remarked. 'Why didn't they collect it all and send it back to the Fatherland? They're supposed to be starving, aren't they?'

'Who told you that?' asked Fred. 'It's the occupied countries that are starving.'

Lawrie held up his hands. 'Let's not get political,' he said. 'We've got enough worries without bothering about all Europe.'

Fred got to his feet. 'I think I'll have to go out side again,' he said.

'Diarrhoea?' I asked.

He gave a sad little nod. 'Had it all last night.'

I felt in a pocket and brought out some paper. 'D'you want some of this?'

His face brightened. 'Thanks. I was wondering what I was going to use this time.'

'There's a mountain of it out there,' I said, nodding vaguely to the tent entrance. 'Lofty and I filled our pockets.'

The two of them exchanged glances, then Lawrie gave a short laugh. 'Fred used a £1 note this morning – the most expensive pennyworth he's ever had!'

'It was a 10s note,' corrected Fred. Then he left the tent.

'Have you had it yet?' I asked Lawrie.

'No. I've been lucky so far.'

'You've been lucky in more ways than one,' I remarked. 'Where did you scrounge the razor?' His face was pink and hairless.

'One of the paratroopers lent me his,' he replied. Then he smiled. 'It was rather funny. Before offering me the use of his razor, he told me – in a mixture of schoolboy English and German – that I looked like one of the Apostles. I asked him which one and he got rather embarrassed. I don't think he could remember the names of any of them.'

Still smiling, he turned and contemplated my ragged whiskers. 'I wonder which of the twelve he'd have thought you resembled?' he asked after a pause.

I ran a hand over my hairy face. It felt like a long-haired hearth rug.

'It wouldn't have been anyone out of the Bible,' I replied. 'He'd have decided that I was a Bolshie and shot me.'

21
Profitable Excursion

Soon after the new prisoners arrived in the camp, the Germans provided us with a small tent for use as a surgery. It was staffed by a recently captured British Medical Officer and half a dozen men from the Royal Army Medical Corps. As soon as the MO opened up shop, Chota and I went along to see him. As I expected, he took a very serious view of Chota's neck wound, which had by now become badly infected. He dressed the wound but said that he would try and arrange with the Germans for him to be sent to hospital. He had no facilities for treating anything except very ordinary complaints. In the meantime, Chota had to attend twice a day for treatment.

My injured arm and hands were almost healed, but my knees were still very painful. After bandaging them so that I had difficulty in bending them, he advised me to rest as much as possible. Apparently no permanent damage had been done, but it was likely to be some weeks before I would be able to walk properly.

Of course, we told him about our tummy trouble – nearly everyone in the came had been to see him about the same thing – but as the Germans gave him so little in the way of drugs, he was unable to do anything for us.

At about the time the MO arrived, we discovered that the padre was no longer with us. He just suddenly disappeared and it was only weeks later that we heard he'd been sent to Germany. The senior prisoner – other than the MO – was a British warrant officer, and he took over from where the padre had left off. Before he had gone, the padre had succeeded in getting the Germans to provide a lorry and each day a party of prisoners went out in it in search of food. Apparently there were a number of food dumps on the island which the Germans had not found, and the foraging party always contained men who knew their exact whereabouts. Each evening, when the lorry returned, it was invariably loaded down to its back axle, but we were still hungry, and it would have taken several lorry loads to keep so many mouths satisfied.

Chota and Lofty were asleep and as I was in a restless mood, I decided to go for a stroll round the camp. It was very hot, and I fashioned the precious bloomers into a sort of hat to protect my head from the burning sun. I left the tent and went in the direction of the waste-paper mountain. I needed some more paper and I might find something to read.

As I walked along, I noticed a small crowd of men in a circle a short distance from the camp boundary. Changing direction, I ambled across to see what was happening. My knees wouldn't bear the strain of standing on tiptoes, so I edged my way to the front of the crowd. Then I saw the cause of the attraction. The small barbed-wire enclosure Chota and I had seen being constructed a few days previously was in use. It contained a solitary prisoner – a British soldier.

'What's he in there for?' I asked the man in khaki next to me. 'Has he gone mad or something?'

'He tried to escape,' was the answer. 'He's there for three days with nothing to eat or drink.'

I looked through the barbed wire. The soldier, dressed only in shirt and shorts, was lying on the sand and trying to keep the scorching sun off his head and face with his hands. I glanced around the circle of sad, hairy faces. All eyes were staring pitifully at the unfortunate prisoner. Again I looked at him. What degradation, to be thrown into a wire cage like some wild animal.

'How long has he been here?' I asked.

'Don't know,' replied the man in khaki. 'All day, judging by the colour of him.'

I turned and pushed my way to the outside of the circle. More Nazi culture, I thought. There seemed no limit to their barbarity.

I continued my walk. To my surprise, the mountain of junk had diminished in size to that of a molehill and I nearly walked by without seeing it. I picked out as much of the paper as I considered usable, then decided to make a tour of the whole western area of the camp.

About a quarter of a mile away was a small olive grove, and with no definite plans in mind, I decided to make for it. After some time I came to a rather grand well, and almost at my feet was a slit-trench – a real Aladdin's cave. Inside there were two pairs of socks, a vest, some handkerchiefs, a shirt, a haversack, a pipe, a piece of soap and a safety razor – what treasures! I would be a millionaire among paupers!

And there was more. In another slit-trench I found a sleeping bag. At first

I was disappointed, but then, when I spread it out on the ground and carefully examined it, I suddenly saw a use for it. It was made of heavy waxed canvas, and measured about 6 feet by 2 feet. Two such sleeping bags would make a canoe!

Anxious to tell the others about my haul, I made my way back to the tent.

Chota was laid out on the ground, his head and shoulders covered with a blanket. I bent down and listened to his breathing. It was faint but regular.

'Are you asleep?' I asked.

He stirred restlessly.

'Chota, are you awake?'

He uncovered his head. 'What's up?' he asked wearily.

'I've had a find,' I told him, dumping the haversack and sleeping bag at his side.

He sat up stiffly. 'It's giving me hell,' he said, holding both hands to his neck. He looked pale and very drawn.

'What did the doctor say when you last saw him?' I asked, sitting down next to him.

'Oh, the usual. Said he was having difficulty with the Jerries about getting me into hospital. In any case, I don't want to go.'

'Well, if it's going on like this, the sooner you're in hospital the better,' I told him.

'Not a German hospital,' he remarked sourly. 'I've heard all about them.'

I moved the haversack along until it was between us, then unbuckled the tags. 'I've got a heap of useful stuff in here,' I said. 'Found it in an olive grove on the other side of the camp.'

'Did you find any paper?' he asked. 'Lofty's got bellyache again.'

'I met him on the way out. Hasn't he got any?'

'No, he's used it all. I gave him the last bit I had.'

I pulled out the towel, still comparatively clean. 'Now we can have a wash in comfort,' I said. 'I've even got some soap.' He took hold of the towel and held it to his nose. 'I expect it's a bit earthy,' I told him. 'It came out of a slit-trench.' I counted out the hankies, then gave him one. 'There's one each for Lofty and Lawrie as well.'

'Then he saw the vest. 'You'll look good in a clean vest,' he said. 'Now you'll be able to wear those fancy bloomers you carry around.'

I continued to pull stuff out of the haversack, and as each item was brought into the light of day he made some wisecrack about it.

'I don't think you neck's half as bad as you make out,' I told him. 'You're far too perky.'

'It really is bad,' he said. 'It's hurting like hell.'

I brought out the pipe and cigarette ends. 'A pity you don't smoke,' I said. 'It might ease the pain.'

'What're you going to do with the sleeping bag?' he asked.

'Sleep in the bloody thing. What would you do with it?'

With a grunt he dragged the bag towards him and felt the canvas. Then he partly opened it and stretched it to its full width.

'How long is it?' he asked.

'6 or 7 feet. Why?'

He slowly rolled it up again. 'Pity it's not a couple of feet longer.'

'A canoe, you mean?'

He nodded. 'It would be big enough for one.'

'That's the chief reason I brought it back with me,' I told him. 'I only want a bit more canvas to lengthen it, and some metal strips to make a frame.'

'So I was right,' he said with a smile.

'I'm still going to sleep in it.'

His smile developed into a laugh. 'And be seasick in it as well.'

Presently Lofty returned. 'Heard the news?' he asked, peeling off his tunic and sitting down.

'What news?'

'They're going to move us?'

'Going to move us? Where?' I asked in surprise.

'To an olive grove.'

From his description, it was the olive grove from which I had just returned.

'Where did you hear about it?' Chota asked him.

He shrugged his shoulders. 'Oh, outside,' he said with indifference.

'Out among the worm casts?'

His face slowly broke into a smile. 'That's a good one,' he said. 'Out among the worm casts. It's good enough for *Punch*!'

'When are we supposed to be going?' Chota asked.

'Tomorrow. At least, that's what they say.'

'You don't seem very worried,' I remarked. 'Don't you believe it?'

'Of course I don't. I never believe rumours.' Then he began to smile again. 'Out among the worm casts. Clever, that!'

22
Goodbye to Chota

At eight o'clock the following morning an *Unteroffizier* visited the tent. We were to move to an olive grove – *the* olive grove – at ten and would be searched as we entered our new abode.

'The grape vine seems to have functioned very efficiently,' I remarked to Lofty after we'd been given the news.

'It's the worm casts,' he replied, with an enigmatic grin.

'Meaning ...' I said, with a puzzled frown.

'Natural fertilizer. Pull your finger out!'

I smiled at him. That was typical of his humour.

'Do you think they'll give us tents to live in?' Chota suddenly asked.

'You've got some hopes,' Lofty said. 'They'll be wanting all the tents themselves.'

'There's no room for tents in the olive grove,' I told them. 'It's full of trees.'

'What happens if it rains?' asked Chota, looking rather worried.

Lofty sniffed hard. 'You'll get wet.'

Chota's face clouded over. 'There's no need to be nasty,' he said resentfully.

The Flight Sergeant appeared and told Chota he was wanted at the surgery. 'Better take all your belongings, if you've got any. I think they're flying you to hospital in Athens.'

'To Athens!' said Chota, with a look of amazement. 'Why Athens?'

'Because that's where the nearest hospital is,' the Flight Sergeant told him. Then he turned to Lofty. 'You'd better help him,' he said. 'Carry his kit for him.

Chota's expression was one of misery and indecision. It was obvious that he didn't wish to part company with us, but he knew that unless he received effective medical treatment soon, something serious was going to happen to his neck wound.

With a sigh, I sat down and dragged the haversack towards me. If Chota was going to hospital, he would need some extra kit. I picked out what I thought he would require most: two more hankies, the vest, soap and the towel. As I rolled everything into his blanket, I could feel hot tears at the back of my eyes. We'd grown very attached to each other, and now he was going. Of course, there was still Lofty and Lawrie – they were as steady and dependable as rock – but with Chota it was somehow different. I suppose the truth of the matter was that, because he was young and inexperienced, I felt I had a special responsibility towards him.

I climbed awkwardly to my feet. 'Here's your blanket,' I said, trying to keep my feelings under control. 'You'd better get going or they might change their minds.'

'You're in a hell of a hurry to get rid of him,' Lofty remarked, taking the blanket from my hand.

'I am,' I said with a forced laugh. 'I don't want to see him sent to an olive grove. He might revert to type and go back to living in the trees.'

Chota looked at me with reproachful eyes but said nothing.

'Well, what about coming across to the surgery with us?' Lofty said.

I shook my head. If we were to say goodbye, I wanted to get it over with right away.

'I haven't decided to go yet,' Chota said, suddenly ramming his hands into his pockets.

'For crying out loud,' exclaimed Lofty, exasperated, throwing the blanket roll to the ground. 'Have we to go over all that again?'

'You'd better go, Chota,' I said coaxingly. I stooped and picked up the blanket roll. 'It's the only way to get proper treatment for your neck.'

He gave a deep sigh. 'I don't suppose the treatment will be any better than what I get here.'

'Of course it will,' I said. 'They'll have doctors, nurses and proper medical equipment. Here, the MO hasn't even got any clean bandages.'

Lofty stamped his feet impatiently. 'Come on, no more bull,' he said. 'Get your goodbyes over and let's get going.'

I held out my hand. 'Cheerio, Chota.'

'Cheerio, Mike,' he said, taking hold of my hand. 'Take care of yourself. I expect we'll meet up again somewhere. England, I hope.'

'Germany, you mean,' put in Lofty.

Chota turned on him almost angrily. 'No, not Germany,' he snapped. 'I'm not going to rot in one of their stinking prison camps.'

'Well, you're about to start in that direction,' replied Lofty arrogantly.

'Take no notice of him,' I said, squeezing his hand tightly. 'And be quick and get your neck better.'

Lofty led the way, and I followed them to the tent entrance. After a final handshake and another 'Cheerio', I watched them disappear in the direction of the surgery.

For a while I stood outside the tent, lost in thought. Would we meet again? How pleasant it would be if, when the war was over, we could renew our friendship. How nice it would be to see him with his neck healed, dressed in clean clothes and with some happiness in his eyes instead of so much sadness. I began to reflect on what he'd said about not wishing to rot in a German prison camp. It had always seemed inevitable that, unless we escaped from Crete, we would end up there. Strange that whenever I had broached the subject of escape, he had shown so little interest. I had assumed that meant he was prepared to accept the inevitable, but now he said he wasn't going to Germany. What had he in mind?

I looked up at the cloudless sky and wondered what it was like in Germany. I felt lonely and depressed. Because I'd known the island when I was free, I felt that it could never hold the whole of me prisoner, but once I left it and reached Germany, I knew that every vestige of freedom would go.

I went back inside the tent and began getting my kit read for the move. The space where Chota had been seemed strangely empty, and to look at it gave me the melancholy idea that I was seeing an unkempt grave. 'I'm glad we're moving out of here,' I murmured.

'Going to miss your mate,' said the man whose bed space was next to Lofty's.

'Yes,' I replied, rolling up the blanket and packing it inside the sleeping bag. 'He was a good kid.'

I found room for the tin of powder in the haversack, and when everything was ready I stood up.

Glancing at my watch, I saw that we still had half an hour to wait before the move began. I was feeling nervous and fidgety, and needed something to keep me occupied. Then I thought of Lawrie. Why not move myself and my kit down to his end of the tent?

Just before ten o'clock, the order was given for us to start moving.

'Where do we parade?' asked Lawrie when we got outside.

'It doesn't look as if we do parade,' Fred told him. 'Everyone seems to be wandering off on his own.'

All around us men were streaming from their tents across the dusty sand in the direction of the olive grove. Some carried blankets or greatcoats, and a number also had haversacks, but the great majority had nothing at all to carry except the ragged clothes which draped their thin, half-starved bodies.

We hurried towards the gap in the barbed wire. The air was thick with dust thrown up by hundreds of tramping feet, and I began to cough.

'I'm all of a lather,' I panted. 'What's the hurry?'

'Yes, let's slow down a bit,' said Fred. 'We've got the rest of the war to get there in.'

'No we haven't,' argued Lawrie. 'Let's keep moving or all the best billets'll have gone.'

'What billets?' I asked, mopping my face.

'Well, trees, then. We want to get under a tree, and if we don't hurry they'll all be taken.'

We hurried on, and at last passed through the gap in the barbed wire.

'Is this the way you came on your looting expedition?' Fred asked.

'Yes. I thought the Jerries had set a trap. I was quite convinced they'd mined the ground, or hidden someone with a gun.'

'But nothing happened?'

'No. But I was scared.'

We reached the footpath and continued along it in silence until we got to the grove. It had been totally enclosed with barbed wire except for a small gateway, and here we had to form a queue, to be let in one at a time by two paratroopers who counted us as we passed.

'Well, we've made it,' remarked Fred, breathing heavily.

Lawrie shook his head. 'That's only the first stage,' he said. 'We've still to get our tree.'

The queue shortened, and one by one we passed the paratroopers. Almost before I was clear of them, I saw Lawrie running like a hare and making for the far end of the grove.

'He can still run pretty quickly,' I said to Fred, with a feeling of envy.

'He'll beat those others,' he replied, nodding in the direction of a score of soldiers obviously bent on the same mission.

'I think the main road runs past the far end of the grove,' I remarked. 'It should be good to be back within sight of some sort of civilization.'

Then I suddenly remembered that we hadn't been searched.

23
Banished to an Olive Grove

When we met up with Lawrie, we found that he'd laid claim to a large and very leafy olive tree. The trunk was about 18 inches in diameter, and its dense foliage provided a canopy which would have given shelter to at least a dozen men. It was situated at the far end of the grove, about 60 yards from the barbed-wire fence which ran parallel with the main road. The turf at its trunk would make an excellent place on which to camp.

'Well, what do you think of your new home?' asked Lawrie. He was seated under the tree, looking very pleased with himself.

'Pretty good,' I said. Dumping my kit on the ground, I sauntered around the tree two or three times and patted its well-gnarled trunk. It was a good, solid tree, and it seemed warm and friendly.

Lawrie scrambled to his feet. 'And now what about getting ourselves organized?' he asked. 'Where do you want to sleep? Here or at the back of the tree?' I glanced around to see what our neighbours were doing. Every tree in sight seemed to have been claimed, and blankets and oddments of clothing were already hanging out to air on the lower branches. The nearest tree was directly opposite us, about 15 yards away. Under it were four soldiers busily settling in. One of them, stripped to the waist, was hammering a nail into the tree trunk with the heel of a boot – an improvised coat-hook, I guessed. At this rate, the grove would soon resemble a large and very untidy gypsy encampment.

I rolled over and looked at the ground on the other side of the tree. 'This is the best side,' I said. 'It's much lighter and I expect it's drier.'

'All right,' said Lawrie. 'Where d'you want to park your bed?'

I felt the ground. It was tinder-dry and rather hard. 'I might as well stay where I am,' I told him. 'What about you and Fred?'

'This'll suit us,' he replied, stamping the turf lightly with his feet. Then he stooped and picked up his blanket. 'Fred and I'll share our blankets. You'll be all right in your sleeping bag.'

I stood up and surveyed the plot of ground which was to be my bed space. With my head close to the tree trunk, my feet would point almost due west. I spread out the sleeping bag and arranged the blanket inside it: it looked comfortable and inviting. Then I remembered Lofty. He had no blanket, and now that Chota was gone, there was only one blanket between us. I looked down at the sleeping bag. Could we both squeeze into it? No, that was out of the question – Lofty was far too big. Could I come to terms with Lawrie and Fred? At a pinch Lawrie and I could get into it, then Fred and Lofty could have the two blankets. That seemed the most sensible solution.

I looked up at Lawrie. Should I ask him now or wait until Lofty arrived? While I was still trying to make up my mind, he started speaking to Fred. 'I think I'll stroll down to the village pump,' he said. 'Are you coming?'

Fred got to his feet and stretched. 'I'm too tired really, but I've got a thirst on.'

'Come on,' said Lawrie encouragingly. 'The walk'll do you good.'

Lofty didn't join us until late in the afternoon. He'd seen Chota and a number of other sick and wounded men loaded into a lorry and driven off to the landing ground at Maleme. They'd been told that they were being taken by air to a hospital in Athens, and that when they were better they'd be sent to a camp in Germany. When Lofty had said goodbye to him, Chota was in tears. 'You ought to have come and seen the kid off,' he told me reproachfully. 'You were pretty bloody mean, considering how long you'd been together.'

I could feel Lawrie's and Fred's eyes on me, and felt rather ashamed. I should have gone with him, but it wasn't meanness that stopped me ...

Presently Lofty started opening a blanket roll. 'Chota told me to tell you the Jerries said there was no need for them to take blankets and clothing – the Jerries are going to rig them out when they get to Athens. He's sent everything back, but he said I could have his blanket.'

'I'd been wondering what we were going to do about a blanket for you,' Lawrie remarked.

I glanced miserably at the few odds and ends that I'd packed for him that morning, and wondered if the story about being rigged out by the Jerries was true. Perhaps he was annoyed with me and this was only an excuse for not accepting the things.

'Did any of the others take kit with them?' I asked.

'No, they were all travelling light.'

But somehow that didn't satisfy me; they might have had no kit. 'Was he mad with me for not seeing him off?' I asked.

For a moment he pondered the question. 'No, not exactly mad,' he said after a pause. 'But he would have liked you to be there. It's obvious, isn't it?'

I dragged the haversack towards me and packed away the things Lofty had brought back. I would decide what to do with them later. Then I fished out the pipe. Why not have a smoke? After shredding some of the butt ends and filling my pipe, I went in search of a light. When I returned, all three of them were asleep. I sat down against the tree and contemplated my surroundings.

Everywhere men in various stages of near-nakedness were busily settling in. Most seemed to have established themselves under trees. There was a constant babble of voices, and I was reminded of a crowd of noisy children on the seashore. Occasionally I heard the sound of hammering, or the breaking of branches as someone gathered material with which to make a cave-dweller's mattress. So this is how prisoners are treated, I mused. Just round them up, herd them into an olive grove and leave them to rot. I'd read of prisoners being locked up in castles and fortresses, and I'd heard how Hitler had imprisoned tens of thousands of unfortunates in concentration camps, but I'd never before heard of prisoners being banished 'to the woods' and left to dwell there like primitive cavemen.

I looked towards the opposite tree. There were now seven men where originally there had been four. One of them, a man as hairy, and naked, as an ape, was swinging from one of the lower branches. 'Don't pull any more down,' I heard one of his companions say irritably. 'There'll soon be no bloody shade left. But the hairy one continued his assault on the branch, jerking himself violently up and down in an effort to tear it from the trunk. Presently the branch broke, and the man fell with it to the ground. In a trice he was astride the branch and stripping it.

For a while I watched him, wondering what he had in mind. When the branch was stripped, he collected two other branches which had already been prepared and proceeded to fasten them together with a bootlace. The result was a framework resembling a small goalpost. Then he laid a rather dirty sheet across it and, with the help of one of the others, set to work erecting it. It was to be either a tent or an awning.

My pipe had stopped bubbling. After tapping out the dead embers, I put it back in my pocket and glanced at my three sleeping companions. Then I began to think of Chota, Where would he be by now? Would he have reached Athens? Perhaps he would already be tucked up in a nice, comfortable hospital bed.

I gave a sigh and glanced back at the sleeping figures. There were four of us, yet somehow I felt I was the odd man out. Lawrie and Fred had paired off – that was understandable, because they'd been together a long time. But Lofty? He seemed too independent to join up with anyone.

My eyes wandered down to the sleeping bag. What about that canoe I was going to make? I wouldn't need a partner if I escaped. The canvas was thick and tough, much better than a lot of canoes were made of. But the frame? Well, what about using wood? Those soldiers opposite had made a frame for their tent easily enough. But what about tools, and nails? And how about getting it down to the sea? There was barbed wire all round the olive grove, and, according to Lofty, guards as well. I moved uncomfortably. Now you're making excuses, I told myself. Are you sure the real difficulty isn't lack of courage?

Slowly I got to my feet. It's not a question of courage, I said, it's a question of common sense. But inside me I wasn't sure. Feeling lonely and depressed, I drifted off in the direction of the well. Perhaps I would see someone I knew.

As I passed each tree I slowed down, but all the faces I saw were strange to me, and somehow seemed unfriendly. The trench near the well where I had discovered the oddments of kit was now being used as a latrine, and close by someone had started a fire. I took out my pipe, and as I walked along I filled it with butt ends.

'D'you mind if I take a light?' I asked, picking up a smouldering faggot.

'Go ahead,' drawled one of the semi-naked soldiers who sat by the fire. He watched in silence while I got the pipe going. When it was burning I threw the faggot back on to the fire.

'Going to do some cooking?' I asked.

'What d'you think we're going to cook?' he asked in a surly voice. I looked at him in mild surprise. With a scowl he turned his head away. I glanced at his companions. They were all staring into the fire. What an unsociable bunch, I thought. Turning on my heel, I walked slowly away.

The well had become the centre of great activity in the grove. About a dozen men were up on the catwalk heaving at the capstan bars, and a continuous cascade of water was flowing from the pipe into the buckets, bottles, petrol tins and other receptacles held under it in turn by men in the long queue.

Close to the well were some large, flat slabs of stone, and on these a number of men were washing their clothes. Because they had neither soap nor scrubbing brushes, they were pounding the soggy garments against the slabs in the manner of dhobi wallahs. As they worked they sang, and I wondered what they found in life worth singing about. One of them started to sing 'Waltzing Matilda', and very soon everyone in the vicinity had abandoned their own songs and joined in – including me!

Slowly I made my way right round the grove. In the corner nearest the road, I came to a large bomb crater. Looking down into it, I wondered what size bomb it had taken to shift so much earth: there was room for at least two double-decker buses.

While I was still contemplating the hole, I heard someone shout. I glanced across to the far side of the crater and saw about a dozen men camping out against the barbed wire. I didn't recognize the voice, so I walked round the edge of the crater towards the wire. Then I saw that it was Flt. Sgt. Green, who had been in charge of the marquee.

'Hello,' I said in surprise. 'I thought you'd have got a tree.'

'We're quite happy where we are,' he said with a smile. 'Where're you camping?'

I nodded in the general direction of the tree. 'We've got a pretty good place,' I told him. 'There's just the four of us.'

'Aren't you afraid of the guards taking pot shots at you?' I asked.

'We've stopped worrying about the Germans,' he replied. 'They're not worth worrying about.'

I looked along the row of faces. There was only one that I didn't immediately recognize. It belonged to a middle-aged man who sat huddled in a greatcoat against one of the stakes supporting the barbed wire. He was smoking a pipe and eyeing me intently. I strolled across to him.

'Hello,' I said.

'You know me?' he asked, taking the pipe from his mouth and smiling.

'I know your voice,' I said, searching my memory. Then I remembered. It was Abe Zelbard, one of our Palestinians. 'It's your whiskers,' I said. 'What a difference they make to you.'

'But you also have whiskers!'

'Not as bad as yours,' I said, rubbing my cheeks.

'You look – how you say?– villainous!'

'Villainous,' I repeated. 'Do I look as bad as that?'

At that point two Germans come stalking towards us on the other side of the wire.

I watched them pass.

'Guards?' I asked.

Flt. Sgt. Green nodded. 'We're trying to buy food from one of them.'

'You're soon getting organized,' I remarked. 'I suppose that's the advantage of having someone with you who speaks their language.'

Abe was quite a linguist. He spoke, Arabic, Hebrew, Polish, German and passable English. He owned his own chocolate-manufacturing company in Tel Aviv and, as sales manager, travelled to almost every country on the Mediterranean coast.

In the distance someone blew a whistle.

'That means, "Come and get it",' said the Flight Sergeant, rising to his feet. Everyone began to bustle about.

'I'd better be getting back,' I said briefly. 'See you later,' and I set off for my own part of the grove.

Back at the tree I found Lawrie and Fred in a state of high excitement. They also had been for a stroll, and Lawrie had found a sleeping bag. It was almost identical in size and colour to mine but had the advantage of being lined with fleece.

'Where did you find it?' I asked, running my fingers over the soft lining.

He pointed vaguely behind the tree. 'In a slit-trench over the back,' he said.

'Over the back? Where?' I asked in a voice which must have betrayed my incredulity. It seemed unbelievable that anything so bulky as a sleeping bag could have remained undiscovered for so many hours after the grove was inhabited.

He straightened up and opened his mouth to speak. Then with a shrug he closed in and deliberately turned his back on me.

'He didn't tell you he had to hop over the wire to reach the trench,' said Fred quietly.

Lawrie turned round. 'You don't have to believe me,' he snapped. For the first time since I'd known him he was angry.

For a moment no one spoke, and I could feel my face getting hot with embarrassment. I'd not meant to imply disbelief; rather had I intended to question where he'd found it.

'Did you find anything else worth having?' I asked, hoping to break the tension.

As I spoke, I saw one of his hands slide into his tunic pocket. 'Yes,' he said. 'This. It's for you.' He brought out a dessert spoon.

I looked down at the spoon, glad that for a moment I could escape his unfriendly eyes.

'Here. Take it,' he said impatiently, pushing it into my hand. Then he turned to Fred. 'Let's get into the grub queue.'

24
Pots and Lice

'D'you think we could eat our boots if we stewed them?' Fred asked.

I gave a deep sigh. How many more times would I hear that same stupid question? 'You can eat anything you can get into your mouth and swallow,' I told him. 'Whether it fattens or kills you is another matter. Stewed boot would probably kill you.'

He turned his head slightly and looked at me. 'Why?'

'Because you haven't enough acid in your guts to digest it.' I yawned, then sighed. 'I'm even more bored than hungry,' I said. 'Let's change the subject.'

There was a sudden movement on the other side of the tree and Lofty sat up. 'And I'm more bored than hungry too,' he said gruffly.' Bored with hearing you pair of stupid clods talking so much tripe.' He got to his feet and, after shaking himself like a wet dog, strode off in the direction of the well.

Fred and I exchanged glances, then lapsed into silence. In the distance I saw Lawrie approaching. He was walking much quicker than usual.

'What d'you think?' he said when he reached us. 'The Jerries are sending a cartload of food into the camp.'

'Where did you hear that?' Fred asked in a disbelieving voice.

'A couple of Aussies told me,' he replied. 'They've just arrived, and say they saw the cart out by the gate.'

'Where did you meet them?' I inquired.

He crossed his arms and began scratching his back ribs. 'Down by the bushes.'

I turned to Fred and winked. 'I wonder what the origin of the song about the "Old Bull and Bush" is?'

For a moment Lawrie glared at me. 'Don't you believe me?' he asked angrily. I had visions of a rumpus, so decided to be very tactful.

'Of course I believe you,' I said soothingly. 'But it's those Aussies. Some of the things they say are just a lot of nonsense. They seem to like pulling our legs.'

I glanced at Fred, who wrinkled his nose and nodded as if to say, 'Between us we've upset him again.' Lawrie certainly was upset. Somehow he seemed to be so irritable and short-tempered these days, the slightest thing made him fly off the handle.

The minutes passed in silence, each of us waiting for the other to speak. I pulled out my pipe, meaning to have a smoke. The rustle must have misled Lawrie into thinking one of us was getting to his feet. He turned and saw that we were still seated. For a moment he hesitated. Would he come and sit down, or would he make some excuse and go for a walk? He chose the latter.

'See you later,' he said to Fred, then, without even a glance in my direction, stalked off.

'All because of a rumour,' I remarked, putting the pipe back in my pocket.

'Rumours, rumours, rumours,' said Fred in a tone of exasperation. 'They've caused us more headaches than anything the Jerries have done.'

Rumours had become the curse of our existence. Never an hour passed without some wonderful tale being circulated: we were about to be released from captivity; America had come into the war; we were to be moved to a luxury camp, and so on. Many of the stories could so easily have been true that when they were eventually proved false, morale often collapsed completely.

Presently the sound of cheering reached our ears.

'Now what's happening?' I asked, scrambling to my feet. Glancing around at the other trees, I saw that nearly everyone was standing up and looking in the direction of the well.

'It must be the food arriving,' said Fred as he joined me. 'Let's go and meet it.'

As we left the shade of the trees and joined the procession of men already moving in the same direction, I began to wonder whether perhaps Lawrie hadn't been right after all. We ambled along the new but well-worn path which stretched from our end of the grove to the well. Half-way along we saw a party of men coming towards us carrying an immense packing case. Following immediately behind was a large, cheering crowd.

'It *is* food,' I said excitedly. 'Just look at the size of that crate.'

We moved over to the edge of the path and came to a halt. Fred's eyes were shining with excitement. The men with the packing case passed slowly by. Then we saw another party of men coming along the path carrying an even larger case.

'For crying out loud,' I exclaimed. 'Are we seeing things?'

There was another mighty cheer and the procession came to a halt.

185

'They're going to open them,' Fred said. 'Come on, let's get closer.'

We set off towards the nearest crate, pushing and shouldering our way through the crowd. The men who had been doing the carrying were now leaning against the case, mopping their brows.

'It's going to be a sod to open,' one of them said. 'The lid looks as if it's been put on with 6-inch nails!'

'We'll open it all right,' said one of the others, pawing the case. 'We'll smash it open if we can't get the lid off.'

The onlookers began to get impatient. The men on the box looked around, then at each other. One by one they began examining the case. 'We want a crowbar,' one of them said.

'Anyone got a bayonet?' a voice asked.

'Or a decent jack-knife?'

A hefty Aussie behind me came forward. 'I've got a knife,' he said.

Then two others came to the front with knives, and work was started on raising the lid. One corner was soon lifted and jammed open with a stone. Then someone appeared with a long wooden stake.

'Now we should see some action,' Fred said.

We watched intently as the stake was forced into the opening. Then, as pressure was brought to bear on it, there was a loud ripping noise and the long nails began to drag. Tension was high. At any moment now we would know what the case contained. The nails creaked and squeaked, and slowly the lid was forced open. Suddenly it was off and lying on the ground, and everyone surged forward.

'Keep back, there,' someone shouted. 'We can't get the stuff out if you're going to crowd round like this.'

Those in front began to press backwards and gradually everyone was pushed away from the crate. Whatever the contents, they were hidden from sight by layer upon layer of waxed brown paper. As each sheet was removed and thrown to one side, a dozen pairs of hands grabbed at it greedily – paper was still in urgent demand!

'Why the hell are they so slow?' I said to Fred. 'Can't they take the paper off quicker than that?'

'At last there was a sudden hush. They'd come to the end of the packing paper. One by one the men who had been removing the lid looked into the crate, and we in the background stood on tiptoe in an effort to see what it contained. One of the men suddenly laughed, then turned and faced us.

'What's in it?' someone shouted.

The man turned and put his hand inside the crate. 'It's full of these,' he said, holding up an enamel chamber pot for us all to see.

Then pandemonium broke out. With angry yells and shouts, everyone surged forward, intent on looking inside the crate. Clearly many of them didn't believe that it contained no food. Those of us nearest the crate were almost swept off our feet in the rush.

'Tip it up,' someone near me shouted. 'There might be something under-neath all those bloody pots.' A score of hands grabbed the crate and turned it on its side, and its contents began to pour out with a clatter on to the ground, but it contained nothing but a few dozen – to quote service nomenclature – 'Pots, enamel, soldiers, for the use of'.

Back at the tree we met Lofty. He had been present at the opening of the other crate, which we already knew had contained only books.

'That's all I could get,' he said, pointing to two volumes which lay on top of Lawrie's sleeping bag. One was *Robinson Crusoe*, the other Oliver Wendell Holmes's *Autocrat of the Breakfast Table*.

'Quite a find,' I remarked. 'Have you read either of them?'

'What d'you take me for?' he asked. 'I read Westerns and murders.'

'Well, we might get a few tips out of *Robinson Crusoe*,' I suggested.

He grunted. 'The paper'll come in useful.'

Presently Lawrie rejoined us. He was no longer quite so sullen, but obviously he was still unhappy about something.

'Did you join the scrum when the cases were brought in?' Fred asked – not an altogether prudent question!

'What cases?' he asked innocently.

'One of pots, and one of paper to go with them,' Lofty told him with a chuckle.

Lawrie shrugged but didn't speak.

I looked across at Lofty, hoping that he wouldn't pursue the subject. I needn't have worried. He'd picked up one of the pots and was wearing it as a hat!

'That just about suits your type of beauty,' I remarked. He leaned forward and shook his head until the pot fell into his lap.

'Catch,' he said, throwing it across to me. 'You try it on. It might suit your type of beauty even better.'

I let the pot remain where it had fallen. Lawrie glanced down at Fred. He wasn't amused, that was quite obvious.

'Come for a walk,' he said. 'I can't talk in this atmosphere.'

Fred got slowly to his feet and, without another word, they left us.

I leaned back against the tree. 'What's the matter with Lawrie?' I asked, 'He's getting hellishly irritable.'

Lofty stretched his arms and yawned. 'He's lousy,' he replied.

'Oh, I don't know about being lousy,' I said, feeling that that was being rather too critical. 'But he's pretty trying at times.'

'Do you know what a louse is?' he asked rather pointedly.

I looked across at him. What a strange question to ask! 'I've never seen one,' I replied. 'But I've a good idea what they are and what they look like.'

'Well, that's what Lawrie's got – lice! And not just one. He's got hundreds of 'em.'

I shot up into a sitting position. 'He's got lice? Rot!'

'He's been scratching himself raw for the last couple of days. I'd have thought you'd have noticed it. Anyway, I expect that's what's made him so bloody irritable.'

I let out a whistle. 'But where's he caught them?' I asked. 'He can't have got them from us. We haven't got them.'

'How d'you know we haven't. Have you looked inside your pants or vest lately?' He had a sardonic gleam in his eyes.

I scratched the back of my head. 'Well, I'll be damned,' I exclaimed, ignoring his last remarks. 'I thought Lawrie was the cleanest man I'd ever met.'

He turned on to his side and, with a smile, asked, 'What are you scratching your head for? Feeling itchy?'

I stopped scratching. 'Of course not. I was trying to think.'

He started scratching his chest. 'I reckon I've got 'em as well.'

I looked away from him. Obviously he was trying to torment me, but out of the corner of my eye I saw him begin to examine the seams in the front of his shirt. Then my back started to itch, then my legs and my arms.

For a time neither of us spoke, and I tried not to give way to the urge to scratch. But it was no use. The itching got worse and no longer seemed imaginary, and I just had to do something about it.

'Damn and blast you,' I grumbled. 'I'm itching all over.'

'Cheer up,' he said with a laugh. 'Just take your clothes off and have a good look at the seams. That's where the lice hang out.'

'Well, if they're in the seams, how can they bite you? Are their heads on stilts?'

He stood up and peeled off his shirt and vest. 'I'm bloody sure I've got something,' he exclaimed in a suddenly sobered voice. Then he sat down and began to examine his clothes.

'I think I'll have a look as well,' I said, struggling out of my shirt. 'This itching seems more than imaginary.'

For the next five minutes I carefully investigated all the seams in my shirt, but found nothing creeping or crawling. 'There's nothing in that,' I said, pushing it to one side. Then I removed my vest and repeated the process. But again I drew a blank. 'I suppose you're not pulling my leg?' I said. 'I've not found anything yet.'

He glanced up. 'I'm dead bloody serious,' he said. 'Lawrie's got 'em, and if he's got 'em, I reckon we have.'

'Well, have you found anything?' I asked.

He shook his head and sniffed.

I crawled back into my shirt and vest, then slipped off my trousers and began to examine the leg seams. Then I had a shock. Under the folds of one of the seams, I saw a long line of minute kipper-like insects. I gasped and recoiled in horror. 'My God,' I murmured aloud. 'How long have I been carrying these things around on me?'

Lofty looked up. 'Found something?'

'My trousers are alive,' I said. 'Come and look.'

He peered across. 'Where'd you find them? In the seams?'

'Yes. There's hundreds of them, all in Indian file.'

He stood up and removed his trousers. 'Maybe I'll find some in mine,' he said, in what sounded almost like a hopeful voice, and sure enough he did.

'So we're not only bored stiff and starving,' I said mournfully. 'We're lousy as well!'

He gave a lively nod. 'Cheer up,' he said, 'at least it'll be something to occupy your mind.'

25
Nazi Culture

We were sprawled out under our tree. It was now late June and because the day had been hot and sultry, we were feeling too exhausted to do anything but lounge about, and grumble. The causes for our grumbling seemed to be rapidly increasing: many had lice; we all had diarrhoea; the well was drying up; our rations had been reduced; the weather was oppressively hot; and the guards were so trigger-happy that several men had been shot even though they had been well clear of the barbed wire.

'Just hark at those bloody cicadas,' growled Lofty, looking up into the branches of the tree. 'They're enough to drive you crazy.'

With a look of despair on his face, he got to his feet. 'If I'm here much longer, I'll go crackers,' he said. Then he began to take off his shirt – he had long since discarded his lice-ridden vest. I looked at his thin, whiskery face, and his bony body. He was one of the lean types, but now he was little more than a skeleton.

Since the day we had arrived in the olive grove, a truce had existed between the Germans and ourselves. No longer were we chased or chivvied, or made to stand for hours while they tried to count us. As long as we behaved ourselves and didn't try to escape, they left us in peace. So far there had been odd occasions when the truce was temporarily broken, but things had always been patched up within a few hours. Now, however, the truce had been broken and this time we seemed to have reached an impasse.

It all started when we were told that the Germans had given orders that we were to provide a working party of 200 men to go and clear up a badly bombed village. Ordinarily, there would have been no difficulty in collecting volunteers – such an outing might prove very rewarding – but someone hit on the idea of bartering labour for better rations. We were then being provided with two meals a day: for breakfast a couple of spoonfuls of porridge, one biscuit and a mug of milkless, unsweetened tea; for the afternoon meal, the same without the porridge. The bartering was an excellent idea, but the camp spokesman knew that unless he got an absolutely cast-iron agreement with the Germans, they would break their word.

With a show of great politeness, the Germans were told that as soon as they gave us proper rations we would muster the necessary men, but not before. Of course, they flatly refused. They were the masters and we would do as they ordered; 200 men were to be ready for work at eight o'clock the following morning, and if they weren't there, they would come and get them.

Promptly at eight o'clock the next morning, a large party of paratroopers appeared outside the grove gate. Apparently they'd come to collect the working party. Everyone who lived in the vicinity of the gate had moved overnight and the well, which was but a short distance from the gate, was completely deserted. Two of the paratroopers entered the grove and began shouting. Evidently they wished to speak to the senior prisoner. If there had been any cooperation with the guard on the gate, they'd have learned that the senior prisoner had gone 'sick'. They kept up the shouting for about 10 minutes, then, growing weary of being ignored, they left.

Then the rumours started to fly. First, the Germans had seized a young army private and unless we produced the working party by nine o'clock, he would be shot. Then, we weren't to be given another crumb of food until we did provide a working party. With the rumour came news that the young soldier had been returned to us – 'unshot'!

'Where did you hear it?' I asked Fred, who was the bearer of the story.

'Some chaps a few trees away told me,' he replied. 'They say they saw the Jerries bring the soldier back into the grove.'

'Well, if it's true it's all the more reason why we should start doing some cooking,' remarked Lofty.

'What about trying to make some kind of a glop out of that french chalk?' he suggested. 'We can try cooking it in one of the pots.'

'OK,' I replied. 'You know where it is.'

He reached and took the tin from my haversack.

'Hand that pot over and lend me your spoon,' he said.

'How much are you going to make?' I asked.

He scooped out a quantity of powder into the pot. 'We'll make enough for a couple of spoonfuls each. If it's any good we can make some more. Hand me the water-bottle.'

There was very little water in it. He began mixing the powder into a thin paste.

'Can you see anyone with a fire?' he asked.

'There's one over there,' said Lawrie, who'd been taking a passive interest in our activities. He pointed to a small log fire about three trees away.

'Good,' said Lofty, getting to his feet. He turned to me. 'Are you coming?' He was holding the pot by its handle and stirring the contents vigorously.

I stood up. 'Yes, I'll come with you. You'll need some moral support when those chaps see what you're cooking in.'

We walked slowly across to the fire. 'Mind if we do a spot of cooking?' Lofty asked.

The three men sitting together on the opposite side shook their heads in unison. No, they had no objections; doubtless they sensed they would receive suitable payment.

'A strange cooking pot,' one of them remarked solemnly.

Lofty grinned, then got down on his haunches by the fire and placed the pot close to the flames.

'What is it?' one of the others asked in a cultured voice. 'Some sort of porridge?'

Lofty began to stir the mixture. 'I'm not sure. It's something we found.'

The three men exchanged glances, then, without further comment, concentrated their attention on the pot. It was obvious from their expressions that they didn't believe him. They thought this was the beginning of our excuse for not giving them any. Presently a bubbling sound began to issue from the pot.

'How's it going?' I asked.

'It's beginning to look like billposter's paste,' he said, ladling out a spoonful and letting it flop back into the pot.

I leaned over. 'Are you stirring it properly?'

'Of course I am,' he snapped, peeved that I should doubt his culinary capabilities. 'What we want is more water.'

I hurried back to the tree.

'How's the meal getting on?' Lawrie asked flippantly. 'Nearly ready yet?'

Briefly I told him what was happening, then, after filling the water-bottle at the well, hurried back to Lofty.

'Tip the lot in,' he said, holding out the pot. 'It's gone nearly solid.'

'Have you tasted it yet?' I asked, sitting down next to him.

'I tried a bit on my finger. It tasted like what it looks – billposter's paste.'

The man with the cultured voice got up, then came round and peered into the pot.

'May I taste it?' he asked politely.

Lofty glanced up at him, then removed the pot from the fire. 'Stick your finger in,' he said, holding up the steaming mess.

The man frowned. He was obviously not accustomed to sticking his finger into pots of food, either hot or cold. Still, with a shrug he mastered his aversion and, after wiping his hands on the seat of his trousers, stuck a finger in.

'I would say that it is custard,' he announced gravely.

'Custard's yellow,' I reminded him. 'This is bluey white.'

'It may have gone stale,' he said, and with a shrug returned to his seat.

'Any more water?' Lofty asked. 'It's still pretty thick.'

I turned the bottle upside down. 'It's empty. Shall I try to get some more?'

He drew out a spoonful of the mixture. 'What d'you think? Is it too thick?'

'Lend me the spoon,' I said, taking it from his hand. I dipped it into the pot and stirred. 'It's not too bad. It's about the same as porridge.'

He removed the pot from the fire, then stood up. 'Well, let's call it done.'

I rubbed my hands together. 'I reckon it'll taste all right. Come on, let's get back to the tree.'

For a moment he hesitated. 'What about these blokes?' he asked in a low voice. 'Should we give them some?'

I looked across at the three mute figures. It might almost have been a winter's evening, judging from the way they were huddled together. Lofty turned and faced them. 'You got a bowl or something?' he asked.

I watched their faces, expecting to see them brighten. The man with the cultured voice raised his hand. 'No, no,' he said with a pained frown. 'That's quite all right.' His companions just shook their heads and continued to look glum. A shadow of a smile crossed the face of the man with the cultured voice. 'Thank you for the offer,' he said politely, 'but we'd rather not.'

Inwardly I began to smile. Was it that they didn't relish eating food which, apart from its doubtful origin, had been cooked in a chamber pot?

Back at the tree Lofty doled it out. 'And don't blame me if it makes you sick,' he said as he noisily scraped out the pot. But it didn't make us sick. On the contrary, it tasted very pleasant, and had it been sweetened it could easily have passed as hot blancmange. Using my fingers, I removed the last trace of food from my mug. Unfortunately it was getting late or I would have suggested to Lofty that we cooked some more.

Lawrie returned from the latrine. 'I feel bloody awful,' he remarked as he slumped down on his sleeping bag. 'I've just been turned inside out.'

I looked at him. Even in the failing light I could see that his face had lost all its colour. Then I noticed that he was trembling from head to foot.

'Diarrhoea again?' I asked.

'Yes. And that new abort, or whatever the Jerries call it, is a blooming death trap.'

'What's it like?'

He turned and tried to make himself more comfortable. 'It's a long, deep trench. They've stuck a trestle at each end to support a long pole. You have to balance on the pole when you're operating – you're in midair over the trench. But it's getting on and off the pole that's the trouble. With your trousers at half-mast, you need to be a contortionist and a trapeze artist rolled into one.'

193

'Sounds bloody grim to me,' remarked Lofty with a shudder. 'Do we *have* to use it? Can't we still go behind the bushes?'

'No,' Lawrie replied. 'They've put them out of bounds. Wired off the whole area. But in any case, we couldn't have gone on like that much longer. It was getting pretty poisonous.'

I reached for Lawrie's mug. 'That stuff turned out all right,' I said, handing it to him. 'Here. Try it. It's got cold, but it may settle your guts.'

He took the mug with trembling hands, then smelled its contents.

'It's all right,' Lofty told him. 'You don't have to smell it. Just get it down inside you.'

With a weary sigh, I got to my feet. Soon it would be time to turn in, but before doing so I would have to pay a visit to the 'abort'. I'd better go while there was still some light; if I had to go during the night, I might get lost – or worse!

I walked slowly through the grove in the direction of the bushes. It was here, according to Lawrie, that I should bear left, then 'follow my nose'. I reached the newly erected wire which enclosed the bushes, turned left, then began to memorize the exact route by noting the sizes of the various trees I passed.

And so I came to the abort. It was everything Lawrie had told us, and more. He hadn't mentioned the 6-foot pole resting ominously against one of the trestles which was to be used to fish out anyone unfortunate enough to fall into the trench; nor the facts that the abort was visible from the main road, which was only 20 yards on the other side of the barbed wire, and that the German guards found the sight of a dozen men, all perched in a row with their trousers down, so interesting that they just stood there gaping, instead of patrolling the approaches to the grove.

The next morning the sun forgot to shine, leaving the sky heavy and over-cast. As usual I made my breakfast last as long as possible, then, having queued at the well until I could get water to fill one of the pots and my bottle, I returned to the tree for my morning wash. Using a handkerchief as a face flannel, I had a complete wash down. When I'd finished, I packed away my kit and ambled down to the barbed wire close to the road.

Everything on the other side was very peaceful – just a lot of trees, and half a dozen guards wearing British topees and having a quiet smoke. For a time I hung about, listening to snatches of conversation from other prome-naders; for the most part they were talking about food. Then I met Abe Zelbard.

'Hello Meekie,' he said. 'You walk alone?'

I nodded. 'Yes, just walking alone, and admiring the scenery.'

He took his pipe from his mouth. 'May I walk with you?'

'Of course.'

We began strolling up and down, all the time keeping an eye on the road over the other side of the wire. Suddenly Abe stopped.

'You no smoke, Meekie,' he said in a surprised voice.

'No,' I said. 'I've got a pipe but no tobacco.'

He brought out a well-worn pouch. 'Here,' he said, handing it to me. 'It is very strong tobacco, but it is better than nothing.'

I filled my pipe, then he lent me his lighter.

'You're doing well,' I remarked. 'How did you get this past the Jerries?'

'It can be done,' he said with a little chuckle.

After getting my pipe going, I gave him back his lighter.

'How're you getting on at your end of the grove?' I asked.

He hunched his shoulders. 'So, so. We manage. But the food! Soon we get very thin.'

'Soon,' I said. 'We've all *got* thin. I think these bloody Nazis are trying to starve us to death.' I glanced at my watch. 'I've never known time to drag so much. All we seem to do is count the minutes between each meal, such as it is. And each minute seems as long as an hour.'

Abe took his pipe from his mouth and looked at me. 'Are you hungry, Meekie?'

'I'm starving,' I told him with emphasis. 'If I press hard enough on my belly, I can feel my backbone.'

He smiled rather sadly. 'That is bad, very bad. But what can we do about it? Everyone is the same.'

My pipe went out and I asked him for his lighter. Then I began to wonder where he'd got his tobacco, and what about the food he'd hoped to get from the Germans. What was he using for money? I got the pipe going again. 'This is quite good tobacco,' I said casually. 'Where did you get it?'

He took his pipe from his mouth and looked into the smouldering bowl. 'Not bad,' he said. 'I got it from the Jerries.' Then he returned the pipe to his mouth.

'That's the best of being able to speak German,' I remarked.

He gave me a sidelong glance. 'I had to pay for it,' he said. 'They give nothing for nothing.'

'I don't suppose they do,' I said with a smile. 'But what do you use for money?'

He raised his left arm and bared his wrist. 'My watch.'

'Your watch! You mean you sold it to them?'

He nodded. 'It was a good watch,' he said sadly. 'I had it for many years. Now it is gone.'

Again my pipe went out. 'What did they give you for it?' I asked. 'Tobacco?'

'Cigarettes and tobacco. The tobacco I keep, the cigarettes I pay for extra food.'

So that was how it was done! I held out my wrist and showed him my watch. I wasn't anxious to sell it, but I was getting terribly hungry.

'How much would I get for this?' I asked.

'You want to sell?'

'If I could get a lot of cigarettes I would.'

He took hold of my wrist and looked closely at the watch. 'What make is it?'

I told him. 'I don't know how much it cost. It was a present.'

'It is bad to sell a present,' he said reproachfully. Then he looked up at me. 'Was it from your wife?'

'How do you know I'm married?' I asked.

He removed his pipe and tapped the side of his head with its stem. 'I know you, Meekie,' he said with a smile. 'I know all about you.'

I frowned. 'You know all about me,' I said. 'That sounds as if I had a murky past.'

He gave a short laugh. 'No, no. I mean nothing bad. But I know you are married.'

I grunted. 'Well, it's not from her,' I said, still dissatisfied with his explanation. 'It was from a friend.'

He sucked his pipe, then blew out a cloud of smoke. 'What would the friend say?'

'Never mind the friend,' I said, somewhat irritated by his interest. 'How many cigarettes would it bring?'

He hunched his shoulders. 'It is difficult to say – 30, 40, 50. Who knows? It is for the Jerries to decide.'

'Well, I'm not letting it go for nothing,' I told him. '50 cigarettes isn't enough. I want at least 200.'

'200!' he exclaimed with a pained smile, then he laid a hand on my arm. 'Try not to sell the watch, Meekie. It would be bad.'

'I don't think I will if I'm not going to get a decent price for it.'

He let go of my arm and for a moment we looked at each other. Then I suddenly realized that he thought I was lying to him – that the watch *was* a present from my wife. I smiled at him. I'm beginning to like you, Abe, I thought. As for the watch, well, unless I get really pushed ...

During the afternoon, three more crates were brought into the grove. No wild rumour preceded their arrival. They were just carried in through the gate and dumped on the ground. Almost before news of their arrival had circulated, they were opened and their contents – 1-gallon water cans – were ready for distribution.

When I reached them, I was surprised to find only about a dozen men there. Either news of the windfall had not yet got around or, more probably, the heat of the day had sapped nearly everyone's energy. I looked inside each crate. Cans had been taken from two of them, but the third was still full. I helped myself to six of the cans – all that I could reasonably carry – and, after making sure they were sound, rushed back to the tree.

'How's this for a find?' I said to Lofty, proudly parking them in a row at his feet, and metaphorically wagging my tail.

'Crikey,' he exclaimed, his eyes opening wide. He leaned forward and grabbed the nearest of them. 'Where did these come from?'

'There's three crates of them down by the gate, and no queue.'

He unscrewed the filler cap. 'Something must have gone wrong with the grapevine,' he said, holding his nose to the bung.

'Where're Lawrie and Fred?' I asked.

'Somewhere sculling around. Why?'

'Well, I reckon we could do with some more,' I replied. 'I want at least four myself.' If I ever succeeded in making a canoe, I would need as much water as I could carry.

He screwed back the filler cap. 'I'll come with you,' he said.

'Come on, then. You can carry the cans. I want to get some wood.'

When we reached the crates, we sorted out four more cans, then I asked him to help me with the wood. It took us half an hour and cost us some blood and broken fingernails, but when we'd finished I had four planks, each about 5 feet long and varying in width between 6 and 12 inches, and some lengths of batten. Lofty wasn't satisfied. We could do with some firewood, so we set to work and broke up one of the other crates. After struggling back to the tree, I laid the planks flat under my sleeping bag, then put the nails we had saved inside my haversack. I would decide later how best I could use them.

Shortly afterwards, Lofty had to visit the abort. When he returned, he was laughing to himself and seemed highly amused. 'You never saw the bloody likes of it,' he said, flopping down on to his blanket like a great bear and covering his face with his hands. I walked round to the front of the tree.

Lawrie had returned. 'Well, tell us all about it,' he said. 'Has someone fallen into the abort?'

Lofty uncovered his face and sat up. 'You know the main road runs close to the barbed wire down by the abort? Well, just before I got there, a party of women had come up the road, all loaded with baskets and parcels of food. They intended coming across to the wire and giving it to any prisoners they saw, but the guards saw them and chased them away. A few minutes later they tried again, but the Jerries were waiting for them and threatened to shoot them if they didn't beat it. They beat it all right, but not very far. When they were out of sight of the guards, they divided themselves up a bit. Just as I got there, all the young and pretty ones suddenly came back along the road. They walked along a little way, then started making love calls to the Jerries. Of course, the Jerries went across to see what it was all about. While the Janes were making passes at them and generally fooling about, the old and not so pretty ones came sneaking through the trees and threw their parcels of food over the wire. When the guards saw what was happening they created hell, but the young ones hung on to them until their mas were safely out of sight.'

'Did you get any of the grub?' Fred asked as he walked up, the more practical side of his character coming to the surface.

'Not a chance,' Lofty replied. 'There were too many there. But it was as good as a pantomime.'

'What about the girls?' I asked. 'Did they get away all right?'

'Sure they did. The Jerries are no match for these Cretan dames.'

Fred lay back and scratched himself. 'I don't know who's the toughest, Greeks or Cretans.'

At this point Lawrie returned from a brief news-collecting trip. 'Heard the latest?' he asked, his face glowing with excitement.

'We'll buy it,' Lofty drawled unkindly. 'What bull have you picked up this time?'

'It's not bull at all,' Lawrie told him. 'It's true. I've seen it.'

'Seen what?' I asked amusedly. 'Has a cow come into the grove?'

Ignoring me, he sat down on his sleeping bag. 'Where's Fred?' I heard him ask Lofty. Lofty didn't know.

'I wonder whether he's heard yet?' he said to Lofty after a brief interval. 'I'll bet he'll be pleased.'

'Heard what?' asked Lofty.

'The latest.'

Lofty betrayed his impatience with a vulgar sniff. 'I don't know and I don't bloody well care,' he said. Then he turned over on his blanket. I glanced over my shoulder. Lawrie was still sitting upright but looking rather less of a prima donna. I cleared my throat, hoping that he'd look round. He did.

'Have you heard about the postcards?' he asked.

'What postcards?'

'They're going to let us write home. They're dishing out postcards.'

I turned and faced him. 'Where did you hear that?' I asked.

'Down by the gate.'

'Is it true?'

'Of course it is,' he said with his usual air of confidence.

'How d'you know? Have you seen them?'

For a moment his self-assurance seemed to desert him. 'Well, I've not exactly seen them. But I've seen a copy of the words we're to use.'

'A copy of the words we're to use!' I repeated. 'It's not writing home if we've to use someone else's words. I think it's a lot of poppycock!'

Lofty turned on his back and began to hum 'Down by the Old Bull and Bush'.

Lawrie moistened his lips and glanced across at him. 'I'm getting browned off with you two,' he suddenly said. 'You think you know everything.' His face began to colour and it was obvious that he was getting angry.

'You believe every bloody rumour you hear,' Lofty said. 'It's time you grew up.'

'They're not always dud, Lofty,' I said. 'He does sometimes get something good.' I was beginning to feel sorry that we'd upset him.

Lofty sat up and slapped his blanket with open palms. From his face I judged that he was feeling anything but sorry for him. 'Picture postcards!' he jeered. 'Picture postcards of what? Hitler's dancing girls?'

'He said nothing about picture postcards,' I reminded him. 'He said postcards.'

He gave another vulgar sniff. 'You're both suckers, if you ask me.'

Then Fred returned. 'Heard about the postcards?' he asked casually.

I glanced across at Lofty, expecting him to explode, but he said nothing. Fred looked at each of us in turn: Lawrie, sulking; Lofty, confounded but arrogant; and me, merely confounded.

'What's been going on here?' he asked. 'It looks like a mummers' meeting.'

'Tell them about the postcards,' Lawrie said. 'I've told them but they don't believe me.'

Fred squatted down. 'Well, it's true enough. I've actually seen them.'

'You really have seen them?' I asked. 'Where?'

'Chiefy Green has ours,' he replied. 'He's collected all the RAF's.'

I got to my feet. 'You're not pulling our legs?' I asked, looking down at him.

His eyebrows lifted. 'Of course I'm not. You can go and have a look at them yourself if you like.'

I glanced across at Lofty. 'Come along,' I said. 'Let's go and see these wonderful postcards. If they really exist, we'll come back and apologize.' I thought he'd be glad of the opportunity to get away, but he refused to move. With a shrug, I set off on my own.

Chiefy Green was sitting cross-legged on the ground, and was checking off a list of names. I looked around him, almost expecting to see a large pile of postcards, but there was none to be seen.

'Is it right about the postcards?' I asked sheepishly.

He looked up and gave a faint smile. 'Yes, it is,' he said. 'But I wish you people wouldn't keep coming here worrying me. You're about the fiftieth who's been here in the last half-hour.'

Despite his mild reproach I suddenly felt excited. We were to be allowed to write home and tell them we were safe! Then I found myself doing some mental calculations. What was the date? When had I last written home? How long would it be before the cards reached England?

'What's the date?' I asked him. 'I know it's Thursday, but that's all.'

Again he looked up. 'It's 21 June. Now go away and stop bothering me.'

21 June! I hadn't realized the time had gone so quickly.

A couple of days later word went round that we were to collect our postcards from Chiefy Green. Everyone was excited as they waited in line, but those who had already drawn their postcards told us as they passed that they'd been warned not to write on them until they were given further instructions.

Soon it was Lawrie's turn to draw his postcard, then Fred's, then mine and Lofty's.

'Don't write anything on them until you're told,' Chiefy said as he handed them out.

'What's the idea, Chiefy,' I asked as I held out my hand.

'Don't ask me,' he replied shortly. 'And keep moving. You're holding up the works.'

'Never heard such a heap of bull,' Lofty remarked contemptuously as we moved away. 'For two pins I'd tear the damn thing up.' Then he held his card high over his head. 'Any offers?' he shouted. There were none, so he stuffed it into his pocket.

I examined my postcard. It was quite plain on the back, but the front was divided by a thin black line, and strange German hieroglyphics indicated that the name and address should be written on the right-hand side, and the number, rank and name of the sender on the left. I pocketed the card, then stood for a moment and watched the other men draw theirs.

'Hello, beardy,' someone said, and I felt a hand slap me hard on the back.

'Hello yourself,' I said turning round quickly. 'You nearly flattened me.' It was Ken Stone, looking very smart and well polished.

'My,' I said. 'You do look beautiful.'

He grinned broadly and looked very proud. 'Yes, I've just had my first shave, how do I look?' He fingered his small moustache and rolled his eyes.

'Beautiful,' I repeated, taking a step backwards and admiring him. 'Too, too beautiful. I see you've had a haircut as well.'

'And my nails,' he said, holding up both hands. Then we both laughed.

'Well, what about it?' I asked, brushing out my whiskers. 'Can't you do something for me?'

He held up his wrist and I saw that he had three watches strapped to it.

'Come along about five and I'll see what I can do,' he said, listening to each watch in turn.

'What *is* this?' I asked in surprise. 'Have you set up as a pawnbroker?'

'No, I'm just repairing them,' he said. Then I remembered that he was the Squadron Instrument Maker.

'Anyway, I'll be along at five,' I said. 'Are you going to use an open razor on me?'

He lifted his eyebrows. 'Good lord, no,' he said. 'And what's more, I'm not going to shave you. It's a Rolls razor and you can jolly well shave yourself. I'll lend you a brush and some soap.'

'Fair enough,' I said with a smile. 'That suits me.' Then again I felt my whiskers. They were about 1½ inches long. 'By the way,' I added; 'I suppose you wouldn't like to go over me with a pair of scissors first?'

He put out a hand and stroked the hair on my face. 'I see what you mean. It is a bit long.' Then he smiled. 'Well, you come round to my tree – he pointed midway between my own tree and the abort – 'and we'll see what can be done. I might even be able to take some of that thatch off as well!' With a cheery, 'Bye', he was gone.

Half an hour later, Lawrie returned to the tree with a copy of the 'message' the Germans had authorized us to use on our postcards. There was a warning that if we varied it by so much as a word, our postcard would be destroyed. It read:

Dear
    I am a Prisoner of War in German custody. I am unwounded and quite well. Please do not write to me until you hear from me again as I am at present only in a Transit Camp.
                                    Love

'So you were right,' I said as I handed it back to him.

He took the card and nodded. 'I suppose they're frightened we'll try and send secret messages,' he said, passing it to Fred.

'Secret message my foot,' exclaimed Lofty sceptically. 'It's because they can't read English. If we all write the same words they can make a template, and if anyone's message doesn't fit they'll know something's wrong. Then they can throw it out.' We all laughed; at least it was an ingenious suggestion.

The next day Fred succeeded in borrowing a stub of pencil, then we took it in turn to write our postcards. I was so excited that my hands trembled. When I finished I realized that I'd written in the date – which wasn't in the authorized version. Would they pass the card? I had no eraser and knew it was impossible to get another card. My excitement evaporated, and it was with a heavy heart that I took my card back.

At five o'clock I made my way to Ken Stone's tree. It was one of the largest in the grove, giving shelter to at least a dozen men. Ken was busy looking at the inside of a watch.

'So that's what you do for a living,' I said. 'Pinching jewels out of watches.'

He looked up and beamed. 'That's right. Have you got a watch?'

'I've flogged it,' I told him. 'At least, it's in the process of being flogged.'

He clicked his tongue. 'What a pity.'

'I suppose you haven't forgotten what I've come for?' I said.

He glanced up. 'Now you come to mention it, I believe I had,' he admitted with a smile. He held up his tweezers. 'Can you wait until I've finished this?'

When the watch was finished and he'd put away his small tin of bits and pieces, he went to his greatcoat and brought out a cloth roll. 'Now we'll see what we can do with your whiskers,' he said. 'Have you a comb, or shall I use mine?'

'I don't possess such a luxury,' I told him. Then I remembered the lice. 'I suppose you don't mind mixing breeds?'

'I don't think you need worry about that,' he said with a smile.

After seating me on a water can, he set to work with a pair of nail scissors and gave me a moderately good haircut. Then he transferred his attention to my beard.

'D'you want the whole lot off, or do you want me to leave a moustache?' he asked.

I stroked my upper lip. Should I keep a moustache? It would break the monotony of an otherwise barren landscape. In fact, why not go the whole hog and keep a small beard? I'd always fancied myself with one, but had not plucked up the courage to do anything about it for nearly 10 years.

'What about a Van Dyke?' I asked. 'D'you think it would suit me?'

He viewed my face with an expert eye. 'Yes, I think it might,' he said. 'You have a long, thin face and your ears don't stick out too far. We can try it, anyway.'

He snipped away merrily for 10 minutes, then produced a piece of mirror. 'What d'you think of it?' he asked, obviously pleased with his handiwork. I took the mirror from his hand and peered into it.

'Holy Mackerel!' I exclaimed, grinning stupidly at my reflection. 'Is that really me?' Though he had shorn a great deal of hair from my cheeks, he hadn't touched the front of my face, and I now looked like some bewhiskered tramp whose head had been caught up in a mechanical potato-peeler.

'Perhaps I better clip a bit more off,' he said, seeing my disappointment.

'A *bit* more,' I said dismally. 'I think you better take the lot off. I look awful!'

For a moment he contemplated my face. 'It's not all that bad,' he said, flattening down the hair. 'Don't forget, Rome wasn't built in a day. I'll tell you what we'll do,' he continued enthusiastically. 'You can't judge what it'll look like until we've finished, so I'll get my shaving kit out and you can go over your chops with a razor, then I'll give you a final trim with the scissors. How'll that suit you?'

With the sigh of a martyr, I agreed to his suggestion.

Half an hour's persistent scraping with the razor left my cheeks and neck clean but bloody. Had the process been less painful, I should have cleaned off my moustache and beard as well. As it was, I again seated myself on the water can and allowed Ken to give me a final trim. With great care he clipped the hair round my mouth, shaped my beard, then gave me a good combing.

'You look really handsome,' he said as he stood back and viewed me. 'All you need now is a wash.'

I brought out the handkerchief and wiped the loose hair from my face.

Looking in the mirror again, I was not so much disappointed this time as frightened. No longer did I look like a bewhiskered tramp. No, far from it! I looked like a rather bald-headed Mephistopheles. With my free hand I felt my whiskers and moustache to make sure they were real – and attached to *my* face. Unfortunately, they were.

'I daren't go round the camp like this,' I said. 'They'll think I'm Old Nick.'

'Old Nick, my ear!' he said with a trace of impatience. 'You look really good.'

I handed him back the mirror. 'Can you imagine what Lofty'll say?' I asked.

'What can he say? At least you look tidy.'

'Tidy, my hat,' I said. 'You don't know Lofty.' I held up my chin. 'Clip some more off – a lot more.'

He grumbled but got busy with his scissors. 'Completely spoils the effect,' he said as he shortened the beard.

With one hand held over the front of my face, I ambled slowly back to the tree. I felt self-conscious and nervous. Why on earth hadn't I shaved the whole lot off instead of getting myself up like some hammy actor? As I trudged slowly along, I tried to avoid the stares of those I passed, using my handkerchief as if I were about to sneeze. But it didn't stop them smiling. At least, that's what they seemed to be doing.

Three pairs of eyes watched me approach the tree. And the same three pairs of eyes watched me as I tried to reach my sleeping bag and sit down without exposing my face.

'It takes all kinds to make a world,' I heard Lofty remark.

I turned my back to them and, chin on knees, idly contemplated the dried-up grass.

Then Lawrie spoke. 'Who did it?' he asked with the same depth of solicitude he'd have shown had I returned with my throat slit.

'What's the matter with it?' I demanded, turning my head.

'Nothing, except that you look sort of funny. I'd got used to your bushy beard.'

'Well, it was getting untidy. I got Ken Stone to clip it.'

'What did he use?' Lofty asked maliciously. 'A knife and fork?'

'You shut up,' I snapped, feeling rattled.

With a short laugh he got to his feet. 'Tut, tut,' he said in mock reproach. 'Remember your new dignity.' Then he sauntered off.

For a time no one spoke. I was feeling far too mad to speak. I toyed with the idea of going back to Ken and asking him to remove the rest of the fungus. I'd never cease to be embarrassed by it, and because of that I would be in a constant state of irritation.

I turned to Lawrie. 'How bad does it look?' I asked.

'The whiskers?'

I grunted irritably. He knew quite well what I'd meant and was just trying to be funny.

'I suppose you look all right. It's just getting used to you.'

'Miss out the "getting used to you" part of it,' I said sharply. 'Does it make me look silly?'

He looked at me uncomfortably, then lowered his eyes. 'I don't think it suits you.'

I rose to my feet. 'Right. I'm going to have the bloody lot shaved off.'

He glanced up at me, and with a mischievous look in his eyes said, 'You might look even worse clean-shaven!'

I gulped and clenched my fists, then with a shrug I turned and made off towards Ken Stone's tree.

Ken was busy trimming someone else's face, but paused when he saw me.

'I want you to take the rest of this mess off,' I told him. 'Just clip it as close as you can, then lend me your razor.'

'But why?' he asked in a pained voice. 'It looks all right.'

'Right or wrong, I want it off. It'll be costing someone their life if I have it much longer.'

'All right,' he said with a disappointed shrug. 'Just let me finish Lofty.'

I looked at the face of the man seated on the water can. It was indeed Lofty.

'You bloody traitor!' I exclaimed in angry surprise.

'Traitor my ear,' he said with a grin, then started to laugh.

'You needn't laugh,' I said. 'You take the mike out of me and make me look the world's biggest fool, then, when my back's turned, you sneak down here . . .'

'Why shouldn't I have my whiskers trimmed?' he interrupted.

I turned to Ken. 'Lend me that razor. I'll give him a bloody trim.'

'If you two want to fight, you better go back to your own tree,' Ken said.

'Fight,' I echoed. 'I don't want to fight. I want to slit his gullet.' Then I changed my mind. 'On second thoughts, I'll keep my face as it is,' I said, glancing at Lofty. 'But make him look as villainous as you can.' Then I tramped off back to the tree.

The following morning, Lofty went out on a news-gathering mission. When he returned an hour later he was unusually quiet and did not seem willing to give us the titbits of news he had gleaned. Eventually Lawrie persuaded him to talk.

'Well, if you really want to know what I heard, I'll tell you,' he said. 'I heard that the Jerries daren't come into the grove again in case we rub 'em out and eat 'em.'

For a moment no one spoke. Then we all burst out laughing. Only Lofty could have come home with such a story.

'I believe you're one of the fiends who starts rumours,' Lawrie told him.

Lofty shook his head. 'It's what I heard. They say three guards have been reported missing so far this week, and they believe we ate 'em.'

Lawrie and Fred started to laugh again.

'I suppose they'll be searching the grove for their bones next,' I said.

He turned to me almost angrily. 'I've just told you, they daren't come into the grove.'

I nodded my head and suppressed a chuckle. Was he play-acting, or did he really believe what he'd just told us? Then I began to wonder why the Germans hadn't come and shanghaied men for a working party. Perhaps what he'd told us was true.

In the afternoon another rumour reached us. It was brought in by Lawrie, and was to the effect that Russia was in the war.

'Where did you pick that one up?' Lofty asked in a voice tinged with sarcasm. Apparently he'd not forgotten how we'd greeted his first rumour.

'Chiefy Green and Abe Zelbard told me,' Lawrie replied.

'I expect they mean America. Russia won't come in,' I remarked.

'They said Russia,' Lawrie emphasized. 'Zelbard's supposed to have got it from a Jerry guard.'

'I thought we weren't on speaking terms with the Huns,' Lofty said. 'Anyway, did they say anything about the other business?'

'About eating Germans, you mean?'

Lofty sniffed menacingly. 'You know quite well what I mean,' he said with some restraint.

Lawrie coloured slightly. 'Chiefy says he knows no more about it than we do.'

26
'It Looks Like a Coffin'

With the aid of a piece of charcoal, I had made a rough sketch on the fly-leaf torn from *Robinson Crusoe* of a framework which I considered suitable for a canoe. I proposed using two of the foot-wide planks as sides and the other two as bottom boards. The battens were to be cut down and used as transverse stays, two each at the bows and stern, and two for a seat amidships.

The framework was to be fitted inside the sleeping bag, and would alter its shape from broad-and-shallow to narrow-and-deep without involving any tailoring to the canvas. The canoe would be blunt at both ends, and I proposed fitting it with a double-bladed paddle, sail and a rudder. The problem of giving it a keel would have to be considered later. My immediate difficulty was getting the battens cut. The wood was an inch thick and very hard, and I would obviously need a saw.

I sauntered down to see Abe Zelbard. 'Hello,' I said when I reached his 'plot'. 'Can I come and sit down?'

He moved over and made room on his greatcoat for me. Then he pulled out his tobacco pouch.

'Smoke?'

I took it from him and filled my pipe.

'I see you still have your watch,' he said, glancing at my wrist.

I returned the pouch and he handed me his lighter. 'I'm still thinking of selling it,' I told him.

He removed his pipe from his mouth. 'Are you still hungry?' he asked with a wan smile.

'I'm starving.' I took off the watch. 'Have a good look at it and tell me how much it's worth.'

'We have talked about all this before,' he said.

'Well, let's talk about it again. What's it worth?'

For a moment he toyed with the watch. Then he felt in his pocket and produced a penknife. 'You don't mind me opening it?' he said.

'No, go ahead.'

He removed the back and peered inside.

'Do you know a lot about watches?' I asked.

'Enough. Yours is a good one. It has 17 jewels.'

'That means it's worth a lot of cigarettes?' I said hopefully.

'Perhaps. It depends on the Jerries. They are the only buyers.'

'Will you try and sell it for me?' I asked.

He replaced the back, then returned the watch to me. 'Why do you wish to sell?' he asked, puffing hard at his pipe.

'Like you, I need cigarettes to buy food.'

He nodded and gave a benevolent smile.

'Will you sell it for me?' I asked.

'Can you not sell it yourself?'

'I can't speak German,' I reminded him. 'I might get swindled.'

He held out his hand and I gave him the watch. 'What is the lowest number of cigarettes you will take?' he asked, slipping it into his pocket.

For a moment I pondered the question. Would 200 be too many to ask? I stroked my whiskers. 200 cigarettes! That was an awful lot; perhaps too many to expect. Well, what about 150? But would a German be able to raise so many? They were supposed to be rationed to five a day. Perhaps I better ask 100. That seemed fair to both sides.

'I'll take 100,' I said at last. 'And that's letting it go dirt cheap.'

He gave a little sigh. 'All right,' he said in a none too hopeful voice. 'I will see what I can do.'

'When d'you think you'll have them?' I asked, feeling that the watch was already sold.

'Come back at six o'clock.'

'But can't you get them before then?' I asked impatiently.

'Do not be too sure that I will be able to sell the watch,' he said, waving the stem of his pipe in my face. 'The Jerries may have no cigarettes to spare.'

I got to my feet. 'I'll be back here at six,' I said. Then I put on my most ingratiating smile. 'Do your best, won't you, Abe?'

'How impatient you are, Meekie,' he said with an amused look.

'I'm impatient and hungry. Cheerio for now.'

I had not gone 10 paces when I remembered something. I retraced my footsteps. 'I'll give you 10 per cent on all you get over 100,' I told him.

He took his pipe from his mouth, and for a moment stared at me. 'That is insulting talk, Meekie,' he said at last. 'I do not want your cigarettes.'

I felt my face colouring. 'I'm sorry, Abe,' I said, lowering my eyes. 'I didn't mean to hurt you.' Then I hurried away. When I got back to my tree, I remembered about the saw.

Promptly at six o'clock I returned to Abe's plot.

'Well, any luck?' I asked hopefully.

He slowly removed the pipe from his mouth and contemplated its stem. His face was expressionless, and he seemed lost in thought. Was he perhaps giving me a lesson in patience? So far he'd not even acknowledged my presence. Then I began to wonder whether he was deliberately ignoring me. Had he really taken my offer as an insult? With a sigh he put the pipe back in his mouth and gently puffed at it.

'What about the watch?' I asked, taking advantage of what appeared to be a break in his thoughts. 'Have you managed to sell it?'

Slowly he looked up at me, then shook his head rather sadly. 'No. I haven't sold it.'

'Oh,' I exclaimed, my heart filled with disappointment. 'What happened?'

Again he removed his pipe and contemplated its stem. 'The Jerry I saw would give only 40 cigarettes for it. I did not sell.'

'40 cigarettes,' I repeated in amazement. 'Why, the bloody robber, it's worth 200.'

He glanced up at me. 'It is not what it is worth that matters, it is what you can get for it. I cannot get more than 40 cigarettes. Perhaps you can do better.'

I seated myself on the ground next to him and brought out my pipe. 'Give me a fill,' I said. 'My nerves are on edge.'

'Have you tried more than one Jerry?' I asked when the pipe was going.

'I have tried all the Jerries this side of the camp. Only one of them was interested.'

'Well, I think they're a shower of thieves,' I said hotly. '40 cigarettes – 2s. They must think we're mad.'

He felt in his pocket and brought out the watch. 'You better have it back. Perhaps you can do better than me.' His voice was slightly reproachful.

I took the watch from his hand and strapped it to my wrist. 'I'll keep it,' I said. 'I'm not all that hard up.'

For a time we smoked in silence. My mind was so filled with hate for the Germans that all other feelings were drowned. 40 cigarettes – I kept repeating it. 40 cigarettes, for a 17-jewel watch. And they called themselves civilized. But gradually the hate subsided and its place was taken by disappointment.

I got to my feet. 'I think I'll trot along now,' I said. 'Thanks for trying.'

'I'm sorry, Meekie,' he said. 'Perhaps you will have better luck.'

I shook my head. 'I don't think I'll try to sell it again.' Then I remembered the saw. 'I suppose you don't know anyone who has a knife with a saw-blade?' I asked him.

He screwed up his eyes. 'A what blade?'

'A saw-blade. You know, a blade for sawing wood,' and I went through the motions of using a hand-saw.

His eyes brightened. 'Ah, yes. I know what you mean.' He turned his head and looked across to a nearby tree. 'A soldier over there had one, but he's not there now. Perhaps he will come back later.'

'What's his name?' I asked.

He smiled and shrugged his shoulders. 'No one seems to know anyone's name, but we call him "Jock".'

I decided to return the next day to find Jock.

Jock proved to be a most obliging man. Not only did he willingly lend me his knife but when I mentioned my plans for escape, he gave me a piece of bed sheet sufficiently large to make a sail.

The saw-blade was only 4 inches long, and the job of cutting the battens and trimming the remainder of the wood was very tedious and took almost the whole of an afternoon. Of course, Lawrie and Fred wanted to know what I was making. Had I been confident that the canoe would be a success, I would have told them. As it was, I put them off by saying that I was trying to make a camp bed. If it was a failure, the fewer people who knew about it, the less my pride would be hurt. With Lofty it was different. He guessed what I was doing – or perhaps remembered Chota's wisecracks about escaping – and asked no questions.

'Any suggestions about what I can use as a hammer?' I asked Lofty. 'My mind doesn't rise above a hunk of rock.'

'Well, there's plenty of that lying around,' he said. 'There's a good one here,' and he put out his foot and kicked a long flint-like object across to me.

I picked it up and examined it. It weighed about 2 lb and was sufficiently slender at one end to afford a good grip. 'It might just do,' I said, walking over to the tree and smacking it against the trunk.

'Are you going to do your nailing now?' he asked.

'No. That'll be the last job,' I told him, stowing away the flint.

I had not yet solved the problem of getting out of the camp and down to the sea, but if I had to go through the wire, then the canoe would have to be reduced to a convenient size and shape and I would be unable to nail the framework together until I was on the seashore. Of course, I'd have to make sure that it could be easily assembled, and I would have to make guide-holes for the nails.

Another problem was how to try out the canoe. I wanted to know that it was watertight, and that it would be sufficiently buoyant to carry me and what little food and drink I could scrounge. I could have rigged it up, then filled it with water, but I considered that too rigorous a test, and was afraid the seams in the canvas would burst.

It was late evening and most of the grove's inhabitants were still away at the singsong over by the well. Lofty and I had remained 'at home'.

'You won't get 400 yards in it, let alone 400 miles.' Lofty said as he contemplated the sleeping bag. I had assembled the framework inside the sleeping bag and pinned it loosely together with nails.

'It doesn't look too good,' I admitted.

'It looks like a coffin, but not half as comfortable.'

'It's the best I can do,' I said with a sigh. 'And at least it should be watertight.' Then I began dismantling it.

'If you want to make a break, why don't you do it in a sensible way?' he asked when I'd finished.

'What d'you mean, a sensible way?'

'Make for the hills.'

'But that won't get me away from the island,' I said.

'Well, you won't last five minutes in that ramshackle outfit.'

For a while neither of us spoke.

'How d'you think you're going to get it down to the sea?' he suddenly asked.

'Over the barbed wire. There's no other way.'

He gave a deep sigh and rolled over on to his back. 'I reckon you're crackers,' he said.

Two days later, my plans for getting down to the sea were considerably simplified by the Germans. They extended the boundary of the grove to include a small patch of seashore in order that we might wash ourselves in the sea, and thus avoid using excessive quantities of well water.

Within an hour of the barbed wire's being moved, I paid a visit to the shore. It proved to be something of a disappointment. The surface of the sea was thick with human excreta, and as each wave gently rolled in and broke, it deposited quantities of the filth on the silvery sand.

'What a bloody sell!' the man next to me said in a tone of disgust.

I drew out a handkerchief and held it to my nose. 'A typical Nazi gift,' I said. 'We might have known there was a catch in it somewhere.'

Breathing as lightly as possible, we walked slowly from one end of the shore to the other in search of a clean patch. But there was none.

'Where has it all come from?' I asked, as we turned to go back into the grove.

'Must be a drain,' he said shortly.

'I didn't know they had drains in Crete. I've not seen a proper lavatory yet.'

'They've got damn all except lice and cicadas.'

'I nodded over my shoulder. 'And that!'

27
The Highway Robber

Daily we were growing more hungry. Fortunately we still had a little of the french chalk left in the tin, and putting aside our suspicions that it would cause us permanent injury, Lofty and I experimented until we could turn out a reasonably tasty 'blancmange'. Thereafter, as each mealtime approached, we borrowed the use of a fire and made a 'glop'. But very soon the tin would be empty and we would be back on bare rations. All this was very worrying in itself, and the worry was considerably aggravated for me by the knowledge that I was unable to save any food for my escape.

One morning I sauntered down to see Abe Zelbard. If he could still get me 40 cigarettes for the watch, I would let it go. The decision had cost me many hours of lost sleep, but I simply had to raise the wherewithal to buy food and equipment if I intended going through with my plans. I was not very happy at the prospect of Abe's reaction. What would he think of me after all that I'd said about the Germans? And was the original offer the best I could get? Furthermore, could I be sure that I would be able to buy food with the cigarettes? After turning the matter over in my mind, I decided that Abe could get more for the watch than anyone else, and that if there were any maps, food or compasses in the grove, cigarettes would buy them.

'Good morning, Meekie,' Abe said when he saw me. 'You are an early caller.'

'I didn't sleep very well,' I told him as I sat down.

'Your stomach?'

'No, that's no worse than usual. I was too hot. And the mosquitoes were busy.'

He handed me his pouch.

'Smoke?'

I nodded and took it from him. 'How much tobacco do I owe you, Abe?' I asked, filling my pipe.

'What is a little tobacco between friends?' he asked with a smile.

'A great deal. Sometimes I think I'd go mad if I didn't have a smoke, and you're the only man I know I can scrounge from.' I got the pipe going, then returned his lighter. 'That's what I've really come to see you about – tobacco.' I lacked the courage to look at him, and kept my eyes on my shoes.

For a time neither of us spoke, and I puffed nervously at my pipe. Suddenly he coughed, and I took the opportunity of glancing up at his face. It was devoid of expression. Damn it, I thought, why doesn't he say something instead of sitting there like a stuffed owl?

Gradually my courage ebbed away and I felt that I would no longer be able to ask him about the watch. I would have to try some other way of disposing of it. Then he spoke.

'So, you have decided to sell your watch for 40 cigarettes.' His voice was quiet and free from ridicule.

I turned my head quickly, and the pipe fell from between my teeth and landed on the ground. I picked it up and tried to recover my composure. 'How d'you know?' I asked, pressing down the smouldering tobacco and burning my finger in the process.

'You said you had come to see me about tobacco.'

I unbuckled the watch from my wrist. 'I expect you think I'm a fool, but I've got to raise some cigarettes somehow, and this is all I have that's of any value.'

He took the watch from my outstretched hand. 'I'll do my best for you,' he said, putting it carefully into his breastpocket. 'But I may get you only 40 cigarettes.'

I nodded. 'When will you be seeing the Jerry again?'

'Some time this morning. Are you still in a hurry?'

'I'm always in a hurry,' I told him with a half-hearted laugh.

'Then perhaps you wait? He may be here soon.'

I had to wait over an hour before the German appeared. He was young, blond, dressed in khaki drill and a soft service cap which was about three sizes too large for him. He came stalking along on the outer side of the barbed wire and, when he was as close to us as he could get, halted. '*Morgen*!' he shouted cheerfully. So this was the young robber who valued my 17-jewel watch at two packets of cigarettes!

Abe got to his feet. 'You won't take less than 40 cigarettes, Meekie?' he said.

I shook my head. 'No, not even 39. I want 40 or I'm not selling.'

Though I was close enough to hear them talking, I was unable to understand a word. At one stage the German appeared to be getting slightly angry.

After pushing his oversize cap to the back of his head, he unslung his gun and started shouting. To my surprise, Abe laughed at him. I looked around to see where the nearest tree was. If there was to be any shooting, I would prefer to view it from a position of safety. Suddenly Abe turned and called to me. I got to my feet and walked slowly to the wire.

'The Jerry says he can give you only 35 cigarettes. That is all he has.'

'Well, tell him I'm not selling,' I snapped. 'My price is 40 cigarettes.'

With a shrug, he turned and quietly spoke to the German, presumably telling him that I would not sell at his price. I watched an expression of disappointment spread over the German's face, and I felt strangely elated. It was quite a new feeling, having the satisfaction of being able to inflict a little pain on a member of the master race!

Again Abe turned to me. 'It is no good,' he said with a shrug. 'He has only 35 cigarettes.'

'Where's the watch?'

'He's still got it.'

'For Pete's sake, you're not trusting him with it, are you?' I said in panic.

He removed his pipe from his mouth and licked his lips. 'Now, Meekie,' he said reproachfully, 'you must not get angry. He is not a thief.'

'Well, you get my watch back,' I said. 'I don't trust these Nazis any further than I can smell them.'

As he turned away from me, the Jerry reslung his gun, then felt in his pockets and brought out two packets. Now what roguery was he up to? Did he think that by dangling cigarettes under my nose he could make me change my mind? He looked across at me and smiled.

'*Zigaretten!*' he said encouragingly.

I shook my head and glared. '*Nein!*'

He shrugged his shoulders, but still smiling, resumed his talk with Abe. Then I saw him open the packets and hold them out. Abe shook his head.

'What about my watch?' I said with mounting anger. 'When do I get it back?'

'You will get it back, so do not worry,' Abe said without turning. Then, 'He is trying to prove that he has only 35 cigarettes, and that he is not trying to swindle you.'

I knocked my pipe against my heel. 'Never mind whether he's trying to swindle me,' I said. 'Just get my watch back.'

They talked together quietly for a few more minutes, then the Jerry turned and suddenly left.

'He has gone to get some more cigarettes,' Abe said with a smile. 'He wants your watch very badly. It is a good one.'

'Where's he gone?' I asked suspiciously.

'He will be back presently,' he repeated, returning to his seat.

I watched the German making his way through the trees towards the road, all the time wondering whether I would ever see him or my watch again.

213

'Come and smoke your pipe,' Abe called out.

'I'm keeping my eyes on that Jerry,' I told him. 'You might trust him, but I don't.'

The German reached the road, then, unslinging his gun, paused for a moment and looked up and down, as if trying to decide in which direction to go. It seemed to take him so long to make up his mind that I began to think he must be waiting for someone. I glanced across at Abe. Should I go and join him in a smoke, or should I wait a little longer? If the Jerry was on guard, he couldn't very well go too far from his post. Perhaps he was waiting for someone – a pal from whom he could borrow cigarettes. I decided to keep an eye on him a little longer. And I was glad that I did.

Two Greek civilians came walking along the road. They were both dressed in worn-out European clothes, and one of them carried a small suitcase. When they caught sight of the German they slowed down. Perhaps they were wondering whether it would not be more prudent to about-turn! But the German had already seen them, so to allay suspicion they continued on their way. When they were within a few yards, the German moved out into the middle of the road and pointed his gun at them. '*Halt!*' I heard him shout. The Greeks stopped dead, and three hands were raised – the fourth was still clutching desperately to the suitcase. The German advanced and in a trice the contents of the case were tipped unceremoniously into the road. But apparently there was nothing of value or interest worth having, and with a couple of deft kicks everything was shot into the ditch at the side of the road.

I turned and called out to Abe. He got up and slowly walked over to the wire. 'Just watch this,' I said, pointing to the German, who was now going through the unfortunate Greeks' pockets. They were both loud in their protest, but apparently without effect.

'That's how he gets his cigarettes,' I said bitterly. 'Highway robbery.'

'How do you know that he is robbing them?' he asked quietly.

'What else d'you think he's doing. Making love to them?'

He removed his pipe. 'He is on duty. It may be his duty to search them.'

'Poppycock!' I said. 'You know bloody well what he's doing.'

Within the next 10 minutes, three more Greeks were held up and robbed. Then the German, wearing a grin that stretched from ear to ear, returned to the wire.

'Do you still wish to sell your watch?' Abe asked.

For a moment I hesitated. To accept the cigarettes was to connive at highway robbery, but what would happen if I didn't accept them? The answer was that someone else would, and could I be sure that I would get my watch back? If he saw that I was being awkward, he was obviously quite capable of keeping it and telling me to go to hell for my cigarettes.

'I'll sell,' I told him. But I had a very heavy heart.

I listened to him as he talked to the German, and I saw him accept the cigarettes. Then, as he continued talking, I noticed that the German was no longer smiling and that his face was angry and red. Presently he left.

Abe turned and walked back to me. 'You better count how many there are,' he said, handing me two packets. They contained an assortment of English, Greek and German cigarettes.

'What a mixture,' I said as I started to count. 'He must be a horrible rogue. I'll bet he even robs his own comrades.'

'He denied stealing them,' Abe remarked as he relit his pipe.

I looked up at him. 'Do you believe him?'

He shrugged his shoulders. 'No. I told him I saw what happened on the road.'

'What did he say?'

'He said it is his duty to search all Greeks who pass along the road.'

'But that doesn't mean he's at liberty to steal from them.'

'He told me he took only English cigarettes.'

'That takes some believing,' I said. 'But what difference does it make? As far as I'm concerned, it's still stealing.'

'The Jerry didn't think so. He said the Greeks could have got English cigarettes only by stealing them.'

I stopped trying to count, and with a sigh put the packets into my pocket. 'Well, I suppose talking about it won't put matters right,' I said. 'Anyway, thanks for getting rid of the watch. Are you sure that you won't accept a few cigarettes?'

He waved a hand in my face.

I spent the rest of the day searching out an Aussie with a tin of bully beef to sell. He asked seven cigarettes for it, and such was my hunger that at a pinch I was prepared to pay his price. But I got him to accept five cigarettes by the simple expedient of telling him that those were all the cigarettes I had.

Then I found a nice quiet patch in the corner of the grove, and in the falling twilight opened the tin and consumed its entire contents. Of course, I had to pay for being such a pig. I was violently sick. That night my conscience was so inflamed that I was unable to sleep a wink until I'd promised myself that the next morning I would go out and buy another tin of bully, to be shared between Lofty, Lawric and Fred.

Alas for my good intentions. I succeeded in getting the bully beef, but because I lacked the courage to tell them the reason for my penance, I had to help them eat it.

28
Trying Out the Canoe

The time had now arrived to try out the canoe. I had made a small sail from Jock's material; the rudder was finished and ready for fitting; and I had managed to construct a doubled-bladed paddle out of two pieces of three-ply and a 6-foot branch from an olive tree. All that remained was to get everything safely down to the sea.

The trial would of course have to be made at night, but I proposed taking the canoe down to the shore piecemeal during the day and concealing it among the rocks. In the late evening I would stroll down to the shore and somehow contrive to hide myself until dark, then I would assemble the canoe and take it out.

I chose the day very carefully. There was no moon, the weather was settled and soon after midday an offshore wind sprang up. This latter point was very important, because if it kept blowing it would reduce to a minimum the chances of the German guard hearing me when I started assembling the framework. I only hoped that it didn't blow too hard and make the sea rough.

During the day I made six trips to the shore, each time carrying some part of the canoe, but I left the rudder and sail behind, my main object being to test the buoyancy and manoeuvrability of the hull. All I needed for this was the paddle.

The sun was low on the horizon when I made my way down to the shore. I had completely emptied my pockets. When the time came to go out in the canoe, I proposed stripping off everything except my vest and shorts. There were still a few men wandering up and down the sand, and I carefully avoided getting close enough to any of them to be trapped in conversation. I didn't wish to have to make excuses for staying on the shore when they were ready to leave.

Watching my chance, I worked my way slowly and unobtrusively towards the rocks where the canoe was hidden. After making sure that it had not been disturbed, I sat down and tried to make myself inconspicuous. The sun sank lower, then vanished from sight. I began to shiver. The wind was cold and the air seemed excessively damp. The sea was lapping quietly on the sand and the masses of excreta were still floating about. I shuddered. It was difficult enough in daylight to pick out a clean path to the water's edge, but in the dark . . .

The last man left and I was alone. In the distance were the sounds of camp life. I heard someone singing, and I could also hear the clanking of buckets on their endless round as someone tried to raise water from the almost empty well. I suddenly felt envious of everyone back in the grove.

Then I began to think of Lofty and the others. Because I hadn't been sure the trial would be a success, I'd deliberately refrained from telling them about it. Would they get worried when they found that I was missing? Lofty would perhaps guess where I was, and in any case he wasn't the worrying kind. But what of Lawrie and Fred? Would Lofty tell them? The fact was, I should have told them all. Perhaps I should even have said goodbye to them . . .

Again I looked down to the sea. The twilight had been brief, and it was now so dark that I could see little but a faint phosphorescence at the water's edge. I glanced up. The sky was like dark-blue velvet. Should I start assembling the canoe now? I shook my head. No, I mustn't get impatient. A stray guard might visit the shore to make sure everyone had returned to the grove. I turned up my tunic collar and wished that I'd brought a blanket with me. I had been tempted to do so, but had decided against it because I knew that if I got too comfortable I might fall asleep.

Back in the grove someone was singing 'Aloha Oe', and my sense of loneliness increased. What a mug you are, I told myself in a sudden fit of depression. If you had any sense, you'd abandon the whole stupid idea and get back to the grove. You don't know when you're well off!

I moved restlessly. 'You better take a grip on yourself,' I muttered aloud. 'This isn't the time to get soft and temperamental. You came out here to do a job of work. Well, get on with it and stop feeling sorry for yourself.'

I tried to bolster up my courage by telling myself that I was already on the road to freedom, that if the canoe was a success – and it *would* be a success – it would enable me to escape. Even without the canoe, you can escape, I told myself. Why, you're practically free now – you're really out of the grove. Yet somehow I couldn't work up much enthusiasm. I made an effort to recall some of the stories I'd heard about other people's escapes. They'd all experienced feelings of excitement when they were planning their escape.

Well, why wasn't I getting excited? Was there something the matter with me? Or were the stories gross exaggerations?

For a while I pondered the question. Exactly why did they get excited? The prospects of success were seldom sufficient to justify more than the mildest optimism. But they had all succeeded. Perhaps that was the answer, that escape was exciting only when you succeeded and so the excitement was strictly retrospective. Yes, that was it.

The singing in the grove died away, and all was quiet except for the faint murmur of water lapping on sand. I snuggled down against the rock and resolved to stop thinking about the canoe and the prospects of escape until it was time to move.

My mind slowly drifted back home. What would they be doing in England – that lovely, mythical country which seemed to belong to another planet? It would still be daylight there, and people would be walking about – perhaps window-shopping. How wonderful to look into well-stocked shops – food shops – and be able to buy just what you fancied to eat.

The silence was suddenly broken by the sound of rattling equipment, and a moment later I heard a guttural '*Verdammung!*' I sank back against the rock and held my breath, praying that I hadn't been seen. No challenge followed; it was probably a prowling guard who had stumbled. I leaned forward, trying to locate him. Then again I heard the rattle of equipment, and judged that its owner was somewhere between me and the water's edge. I listened carefully, trying to pick up the sound of footsteps, but everything was quiet.

Presently I heard some muttering about 30 yards to my right. Again I held my breath. Was he coming or going? A few seconds later I heard him scraping something in the sand, and the next I heard was the challenging voice of a guard at the other end of the shore. For a time I remained motionless, keeping my ears cocked for the slightest sound, but I heard nothing. Perhaps if the guard told his comrades of his misadventure, there'd be no more stray visitors tonight.

I had no means of telling the time, but when I judged it to be eleven, I rose silently. I was so stiff with cold that I could hardly keep my balance, so, climbing carefully down to the sand, I waved my arms about vigorously in an effort to get some circulation going. Then I climbed back to the rocks and listened. If the coast was clear, I would start work. The grove was perfectly quiet, and apart from the faint rustling of leaves from a nearby gorse, I might have been alone in a deserted world.

I dragged out the sleeping bag and carried it down to the sand. Then I brought out the wood, nails and improvised hammer. When I felt the flinty surface of the stone, I regretted not having encased it in a pair of socks. As it was, it would make enough noise to awaken the dead. Opening the sleeping bag, I placed the planks in position inside it. Then I took one of the battens and, after inserting a nail in the hole at one end, fished about until I found the corresponding hole in the plank. Now for the fun, I thought.

218

I picked up the stone and gave the nail a light tap. The noise it made was like an exploding Chinese cracker and almost took my breath away. With a thumping heart, I looked back towards the grove and listened. Surely the Germans must have heard it! I waited, ready to drop everything and run. Not a sound!

I took off my shoes and socks. This is going to ruin them, I thought, as I wrapped the socks round the stone. I got the batten back into position, then gave the nail a very gentle tap. It made little sound, so I gave it another tap, this time putting a little more weight behind it. Again I almost stopped breathing. The nail must have penetrated the wool and made direct contact with the stone. I cocked my ears, expecting to hear the tramp of footsteps as the German guard came running along the shore, but again, nothing.

After taking off the socks, I threw the stone to one side. Any more noise like that and I'd be having a heart attack! Perhaps one of my shoes would do the job. I got the batten back into position, then gave the nail a light blow. This time there was less noise.

Although the shoe proved a very quiet hammer, it was anything but efficient, and it must have taken me at least half an hour to drive home the first nail. Obviously, unless I could speed things up, it would be dawn before the canoe was ready for sea. I set to work with increased vigour and put considerably more force behind each blow. I made much more noise and every few seconds I stopped and listened. After about two hours' hammering, I still had three more nails to put it. To save time, I hammered them only half-way home. I was sure they'd keep the frame secure for the brief test I had in mind. When at last the job was finished, I lay the shoe down on the sand and felt round the sides of the canoe to make certain everything was firm. It was only then that I realized how small it was. My spirits began to ebb, and I began to doubt whether I'd be able to raise the courage to get into the thing even if it floated. With a rather heavy heart, I rolled my trousers up to the knees, then began dragging the canoe down to the sea. I'd heard of magic carpets and flying bedsteads but never before of sailing sleeping bags, and I found myself wondering whether my effort, if successful, would be immortalized in some modern version of *The Arabian Nights*.˙

At the water's edge I paused and listened, then I turned the canoe bows-on to the sea and heaved. I could feel the framework moving within the canvas and wondered whether something had come adrift, then quite suddenly the canoe slipped forward and floated away like a ball in a bath. I waded in after it and, taking hold of the stern, rocked it gently to and fro. Well, at least it floats right side up, I thought, with some satisfaction. I felt its sides to see how deep it was in the water. It seemed to draw about 3 inches at the bows and 6 inches at the stern. I felt inside – perhaps it was leaking. It was perfectly dry. I decided that the framework was badly balanced and that I would have to build more wood into the bows. Again I rocked it. It was exceptionally buoyant and should be safe to carry me. I dragged it back to the shore. I would collect my shoes and socks and dump them on the rocks, then strip off and get the paddle.

I made my way back to where I had done the assembling and searched around in the dark for my shoes and socks. I couldn't find them anywhere. I went down on hands and knees and groped about. Still nothing. At last I gave up the search. I had to remain on the shore until morning, so I could find them then. What would have happened if I'd lost my tunic and trousers ...

I got the paddle from the rocks, then started to strip off my clothing. The wind seemed colder than ever and I was soon shivering. Must I take off all my clothes? I asked myself. The canoe doesn't leak so I'm not likely to get wet. For a moment I stopped undressing. What should I do? A sudden gust of wind decided me. I hitched up my trousers and slipped on my tunic. I had enough to worry about without being frozen; I'd take a chance on the canoe developing a leak.

I pushed the canoe back into the sea. It was as calm as a millpond and what wind there'd been seemed to be dying away. I pointed the bows away from the shore, then carefully leaned over the stern. The canoe began to sink deep in the water and I had visions of it foundering. I slid a hand over the side to see how much freeboard remained. To my surprise, there was about 4 inches, so I gave it a little more of my weight. The canoe sank deeper and deeper, but there was still an inch to spare when I discovered that it was completely supporting me. This is where I should smash a bottle of champagne over her bows, I thought.

Then, as I began to wriggle forward, I discovered how unstable the canoe was. Once the bulk of my weight was removed from the stern, I had to balance myself as if I were riding a bicycle with my stomach on the saddle. Even when I succeeded in turning over and sitting on the bottom, I felt that the slightest movement would cause her to capsize. I picked up the paddle. Perhaps it would help me to balance, I thought, and it did. I was now all set. The canoe floated on a more or less even keel, and she appeared to be watertight. If she could be paddled without capsizing, and was manoeuvrable, then I would consider her a success.

I glanced around to see in which direction the shore lay. At first I couldn't find it, and just as I was beginning to get rather worried, I saw a faint phosphorescence. I turned the canoe broadside on so that I could keep the shore in view, then began to paddle.

Very soon I discovered that my little craft had some shocking vices. For a few yards she would go along quite merrily, then without warning she would start going round in tight circles, sometimes to the left, sometimes to the right. On other occasions she would suddenly start rocking violently, and even though I would immediately stop paddling, she took an uncomfortably long time to regain her stability.

For what must have been an hour, I paddled up and down close to the

220

shore, trying to master my craft, but it soon became apparent that there was insufficient framework in the bows to keep the canvas rigid, and in consequence the front of the canoe was constantly changing shape. Each time this happened she went round in a dizzy circle. Then I felt my seat begin to get wet and cold. I slipped a hand into the bottom of the canoe and discovered water slopping about; it was perhaps only a slow leak, but I decided to take no chances and headed for shore.

As I paddled along, I hoped that I'd land fairly near to where I had first entered the water – I didn't relish having to carry this sodden mass very far. On approaching the shore, I gave a couple of extra hard heaves so that the increased speed would carry me well in. The canoe chose that precise moment to whip round in a tight circle, and I ended up broadside on. Stiff and wet, I climbed over the side and dragged the canoe up on to the sand. Then I tipped it over on its side so that the water could drain out.

As I had no idea which end of the shore I had landed on, I decided to reconnoitre. Setting a course at right angles to the water's edge, I set off, counting each pace so that I would be able to return safely to the canoe. I counted 50, then changed direction right and started counting again. I'd got up to 40 when the light from a powerful electric torch lit up the sand a few yards in front of me. I stiffened and jerked myself to a halt. The light hovered for a moment, then, like an evil eye, began travelling slowly along the sand towards me. Petrified, I stood watching it, then, as it was about to reach me, I regained my wits and decided that I could dodge it quite easily if I didn't panic. Before I had time to move, though, the light was playing around my bare feet. Fear rooted me to the spot, but an inverted sense of pride stopped me from calling out. If I were to be shot, I wouldn't give the guard the satisfaction of knowing how scared I was. With my arms at my sides, I waited for the bullets to come.

Miraculously, the light flicked away. Had I not been seen? For a moment I watched it move slowly along the silvery sand in the direction of the sea. Then I began to wonder about the canoe. If the guard discovered it, he might go off to have a look. I glanced hastily around. Where were the rocks? But again I was too late. The light suddenly swept back across the sand and, with uncanny sureness, caught me full in the face. Half-blinded, I closed my eyes. So this is it, I told myself with resignation.

'*Was ist lose?*' demanded a gruff voice.

I tried to look in the direction of the light, but it was too strong. But I better say something or he'd start shooting. 'I am a prisoner,' I said, blinking painfully. Then to show him that I was harmless, I held both hands above my head.

The light was deflected from my face to the ground at my feet. '*Komm!*'

I knew what that meant and started walking slowly forward, the disc of light preceding me. When I was within a few feet of the guard, he shouted '*Halt!*' I stopped walking.

221

'*Englander?*' he asked, flashing the light on my tunic.

'Yes,' I answered in a shaky voice.

He lowered his torch, and I could see my wet trousers glistening in the bright light. Then he came to my bare feet. Perhaps he would think that I'd been for a midnight paddle! He spoke to me again, but I couldn't understand what he said. Stretching forward, he took hold of one of my arms and pulled it down to my side. I took this to indicate there was no need for me to keep my arms raised, so lowered the other one. Then he flashed the torch around as if in search of something. I followed the ray of light, now hoping that it wouldn't reach my canoe down by the sea. Suddenly the beam picked up two small dark objects about 30 yards away. I peered hard, wondering what they could be. The German had also seen them. '*Komm!*' he said, taking me roughly by the arm.

Long before we reached them I guessed what they were: my lost shoes, and close by were my socks. Now he should be convinced that I'd only been for an innocent paddle. He picked up the shoes and examined them, and while he did so, I retrieved the socks.

'*Ihrige?*' he asked, holding the shoes.

'Yes, they're mine,' I said, taking them from him. Without giving me time to put them on, he again took hold of my arm and marched me to the edge of the grove. Then he let go of me and pointed with his lighted torch to the trees. I nodded. Yes, I would go home to bed – I'd be only too glad to do so.

The next morning I again visited the shore, but there were no signs of the canoe. Like my footprints in the wet sand, it had disappeared.

29

Prison Ship

On 25 July we set off once more for Suda Bay. Our previous attempt to depart, two weeks earlier, had been a shambles. The Germans had assembled everyone at eight in the morning and marched us 15 long miles, only to find there wasn't enough room for all of us on the prison ship. The journey there had been a nightmare – after just a couple of miles my feet were so blistered and swollen I could hardly walk – and the return trip was certainly no better! And now we were to do it all over again.

Before starting, the Germans provided us with a reasonably substantial breakfast, and during the march the guards halted us every half-hour and allowed us to rest. But this time they didn't tolerate straggling. If a man showed signs of falling out, the nearest guard pounced on him and threatened him with his gun.

The pace was almost leisurely, and would have caused distress to no one in reasonably good physical condition. But none of us was in a good condition, and by the time we reached Suda Bay, most of us were exhausted to the point of collapse. We were marched through the dock gates and into a barbed-wire pen, where we were allowed to fall out. I slipped the haversack from my shoulder and let it fall to the ground, then I slumped down, too tired to think.

I was with Charlie Wickended and his Army friend 'Jock' Taylor. I'd met them a couple of days after we'd returned to the grove, and ever since we had somehow contrived to keep together.

'Any signs of the ship?' I asked Charlie.

He turned and looked through the barbed wire. 'I can't see anything of her.'

I stood up and looked across towards the stone jetty. I could see the ship's funnel belching black smoke. 'She's in all right,' I said. 'It looks as if they're stoking up.'

Then Jock returned. 'Come on, laddies,' he said with suppressed excitement. 'Get your kit and come with me. I've found some grub.'

Charlie scrambled to his feet.

It was surprising how our energy returned at the mention of food. We picked up our kit and followed him.

'What kind of grub is it?' I asked as we hurried along.

He turned and put a finger to his lips. 'Shss! We don't want everyone to know about it.'

There were several hundred men in the pen, and they all seemed to be deliberately getting in our way, but at last we reached our objective – a small hole in the barbed wire.

'See those?' Jock said, pointing to a pile of wooden boxes on the other side of the wire. 'They're full of raisins.'

'All right,' I said. 'Let's swipe one. You and Charlie keep watch for the Jerries while I . . .'

'No, I'll get the box. You and Charlie can keep watch. Here goes.' And with the agility of a monkey Jock climbed through the wire.

A couple of men – the only people at this end of the pen – were seated on the ground quite close to us, and began to look scared when they saw Jock on the other side of the wire. 'You'll be getting us all shot,' one of them said in a frightened voice, but I just shrugged, and kept my eyes open for Germans.

In a trice, Jock had lifted up one of the cases and was shaking it to make sure it was full, but Charlie was impatient and not a little apprehensive. 'Come on,' he hissed. 'Don't be all day.'

Satisfied that the case was full, Jock handed it through the wire to Charlie. Then he climbed nimbly back into the pen.

'Bloody good show,' I said. 'Now let's get away from here and open it.' With Jock leading the way, we made for the centre of the pen.

'This'll do,' said Jock, when we came to an unoccupied patch of ground. 'The Jerries won't be able to see us from the wire. Park it down here.' Obediently Charlie dropped the case.

I glanced around. We were completely encircled by a large mob of gaunt and hungry-looking men, and I began to wonder how long it would be before they set about us and stole the box.

'We need a knife,' Jock said, fingering the lid. Then he turned and faced the mob.

'Any of you laddies got a knife?' he shouted. The hands of a dozen men began to move up to belts and into pockets in search of something which would serve to open the box, but only one man produced anything useful – a bayonet!

'Just the job,' I heard Jock say as he walked across to collect the shining weapon. A few deft twists and the lid was off, and there, exposed to our hungry eyes, was a delicious mass of golden raisins.

Charlie let out a low whistle. 'Oh boy,' he said, his face beaming. 'What a feed we're going to have.'

'Be quick and fill your pockets before the mob swoops,' Jock said, sticking the bayonet into the fruit and stirring it round to loosen it.

I grabbed my haversack and untied the straps. 'Just give me 30 seconds,' I said, digging both hands into the box. That was about all the time we had! Like a flock of vultures, every man in sight swooped on us and we were swept over the box and beyond it to the outskirts of the crowd.

When the mob finally dispersed, we found Jock. Each of us had managed to get about the same quantity of the fruit. We made our way silently back to our end of the pen, our jaws too busy chewing raisins for us to be able to talk.

A few minutes later there was another stampede, and everyone began rushing towards the entrance to the pen.

'It's the ship,' Jock said. 'They're letting them on board.'

We got to our feet and went across and joined the rapidly forming queue.

'It's the same ship that took the others,' he announced. 'I can tell by the broken rail near the stern.'

Very soon we were sufficiently close to make out her name: *Katrina Madre*. Slowly the queue shortened and soon we were within a few yards of the gangway. Some Germans were there to check us as we went on board, but this time there was no searching of clothes or kit. When there were only about a dozen men between us and the gangway, the queue suddenly stopped moving.

'Now what's happened?' Charlie asked irritably. 'Don't say they can't get us all on board again.'

'Don't you worry,' I told him. 'They'll pile us all in this time even if they have to hang some of us in the rigging.'

Presently we started to move again. We reached the gangway in single file, with Jock leading, then Charlie, then me. Jock and Charlie went up but then, as I stepped forward, one of the Germans held out an arm.

'*Halt!*'

I was not unduly worried, because I was quite sure there was plenty of room on board, but I was annoyed at the prospect of finding myself in a different part of the ship to Jock and Charlie. After a short wait, a German officer appeared and indicated that the embarkation was to continue. I scuttled up the gangway like a rabbit, hoping that Jock and Charlie would still be in sight, but they had gone. All I saw was a line of armed guards lining the route I was to follow across the deck.

I walked slowly along until I came to the aft cargo hatch. I leaned forward and looked down into the hold. It was so dark that I couldn't see the bottom. A German indicated with his tommy-gun that I was to descend into the hold.

As I looked down into the blackness, I felt a sudden spasm of fear: the iron ladder running down led into the unknown – a broken rung, a slipping hand, might mean death, and there were also deaths, from hunger, thirst or drowning!

I stepped back. Sensing that I was about to refuse to descend, the guards closed in on me, and picked me up and lowered me over the side. In a panic I kicked out, but I soon realized that I had better get my feet on the ladder before they let go of me. With a curse, I began to feel my way slowly downwards.

When I was about half-way down, I suddenly found my legs dangling in midair. Either a lot of rungs or part of the ladder itself was missing. I glanced downwards, but I could see nothing. With aching arms I tried to pull myself up, and in doing so my feet shot forward and came into contact with what felt like the rungs of another ladder. Then a black shadow appeared, and I knew that another man was on his way down.

'Mind how you go,' I shouted up to him. 'There's a break in the ladder. Feel with your toes for the other part – it's a couple of feet further back than this one.'

With a swing that nearly broke my back I succeeded in transferring to the second ladder. Then I began to descend slowly until I reached the bottom. But my difficulties weren't over. The ladder ended on top of a 6-foot-high platform surmounting the main propeller-shaft casing. The casing was warm and greasy, and the only way down was to slide or jump.

With a clatter of noisy feet and a surprised grunt, the second man arrived on the platform. 'Phew! That was a bit of a sod,' he remarked, glancing up the ladder. 'I nearly broke my back manoeuvring that bloody switchback.'

'We're not through yet,' I said, 'How're we going to get down there?'

He looked down at the floor of the hold. 'That's a piece of cake after the ladder,' he said. 'Just jump.' And he did. Then he told me to jump and he'd catch me – an invitation I accepted gratefully. As he planted me carefully on my feet, he said with a laugh, 'You only weigh as much as a smell.'

The first thing that caught my eye was a rolled blanket. As I picked it up, I realized it was mine. Apparently I'd dropped it on deck and the Germans had thrown it down after me. In the dim light I surveyed my new prison. So far it contained only three of us, and there were no signs of either Jock or Charlie – presumably they had been packed into a different hold. It measured about 25 feet wide, and was divided down the centre by the propeller-shaft casing. Only the deck on the starboard side was planked over, and it was on this side that I had landed. For half its height the forward bulkhead was recessed, giving it the appearance of a large inverted step. This accounted for the difference in alignment in the two ladders which had been so difficult to negotiate. The aft end of the hold trailed off into darkness, and from it came a dank, unpleasant smell.

As more and more men were coming down the ladder, I decided to pick out a plot on which to sleep. I chose one alongside the casing, fairly close to the bulkhead. I knew it would be rather warm, but it had the advantage of being near the ladder and as far away from the ship's side as it was possible to be.

The Germans started battening down the hatch and I glanced around to see how many men were in the hold. Excluding any who might be on the other side of the casing, there were about 40. It seemed too good to be true! I'd quite expected them to pack in a couple of hundred.

I stared upwards and watched the patch of daylight getting smaller as they laid more planks across the hatch. When it was nearly closed they opened it again and lowered in a wooden tub.

'What's that for?' I heard someone ask.

'It's our new WC,' was the reply. 'Chrome fittings, mahogany seat and guaranteed anti-splash. Come and give me a leg up and I'll bring it down into the hold.'

Two soldiers got to their feet and helped the third man up to the platform. After releasing the rope, he lowered the tub down to them. They stood it on the deck about 10 feet from my head.

'A pretty crude effort,' one of them remarked, running his fingers round the top edge of the tub. 'Cut your hide if you're not careful.'

'And you'll need a ladder to reach it,' one of the others said. 'It's nearly five feet high.'

'You'll get up all right if you want to go bad enough,' was the comforting reply.

The last plank was put into position across the hatch and we were left in darkness. I lay back on my blanket and tried to relax. Perhaps if I listened carefully I would be able to follow the movements of the seamen up on deck and be able to tell what they were doing.

My nearest neighbours were grumbling about the darkness. 'I guess they'll let us up on deck as soon as we get clear of the harbour,' someone said hopefully.

'You don't know the Jerries,' a melancholy voice replied. 'I'll bet they keep us cooped up all the way to Salonika.'

Turning over on to my side and resting my head in the crook of my arm, I closed my eyes. I tried to shut out the sound of voices around me and to concentrate on the noises up on deck. Judging by the smoke coming from the funnel when we came on board, they were getting up steam. The question was, would the ship sail before nightfall? I strained my ears, but all I heard were the slow, regular footsteps of what might have been a guard close to the hatch. Then I fell asleep.

A pungent odour awoke me from my dreams. From the thum-thum-thum of the engine and the rattling of the propeller-shaft casing, I knew that we were under way. With heavy eyes I sat up and looked around. There was the cause of the odour: perched up on the wooden tub was the trouserless figure of a man balancing himself with all the grace and aplomb of a trapeze artist. Then I glanced upwards and saw that the hatch was open.

'What time is it?' I asked the man on the tub.

He turned his head. 'About half-past-six.'

'When did they open up?'

'Half an hour ago.'

'And everyone's on deck?'

'Yep.'

I sat down again and began putting on my shoes and socks.

'What time did we sail?' I asked.

'An hour or so ago. We've got an Italian destroyer as escort.'

'Escort! Why an escort? Do they think we might seize the ship?'

There was a rustle of paper, and presently he slipped down from his perch. 'The Navy might. It wouldn't be the first time.'

I stood up and surveyed the deck. There was plenty of unoccupied space close to the bulkhead, so I dragged my blanket as far away from the WC as I could.

'Got any fags?' the man asked, hitching up his trousers.

I walked slowly back to the platform. 'No. How d'you climb up this?'

'I'll give you a leg up,' he said. Making a stirrup of his hands he raised me until I could lean forward and grasp the side of the ladder. 'Now pull yourself up,' he said, giving me a final upward heave.

I stood on the platform and looked down. Apparently no one had taken up residence on the other side of the casing. I turned and began to climb. When I came to the switchback, I paused and looked down into the hold. The sense of height made me feel giddy and I clutched tightly at the ladder. Then I began to wonder whether once I was out of the hold I would be able to screw up courage to go down again. But the thought of fresh air urged me on until I reached the top and was able to swing my legs over the coaming and stand on deck.

Almost the first person I saw was Jock. He was sitting on a corner of the hatch, his long fair hair blowing untidily in the breeze.

'So there you are,' he said with a smile. 'I've been scouring the ship for you. Where've they parked you?'

'Down there,' I said with a wave of the hand. 'And you?'

'In the forward hold. There's hundreds of us.'

'Well, why don't you come and live with me?' I asked. 'We've got plenty of room.'

He shook his head. 'They've told us we'll get no grub if we swap about.'

'I don't suppose we'll get much in any case.' I glanced around. 'Where's Charlie?'

'Up on the poop. Come on. Let's go and find him.'

We set off along the gently heaving deck. The first object which caught my eye was a pig – a real, live, very fat pig. It was moored to a ringbolt in the deck, and the rope was just long enough to enable it to reach the ship's side, where it was shaded from the sun. Besides the pig, there were about 50 prisoners accommodated in the well, Greek airmen. We climbed down into the well and walked across to the ladder which led up to the poop.

'What happens if the Greeks kill the pig and eat it?' I asked.

'They'll get killed, and eaten by the fishes.'

Up on the poop deck we stood and watched a party of prisoners and some German guards erecting a scaffolding, although at the time we called it the poop deck, I later realized it was the fo'c'sle. Two baulks of timber, each protruding about 6 feet over the ship's side, were being made fast to the deck. They were about 20 feet apart, and while prisoners held them in position, the guards lashed them to deck fittings. When this part of the work was finished, the prisoners carried what appeared to be a rather thin telegraph pole to the ship's side, lifted it over the rail, then lowered it on to the projecting timbers.

'Do you know what that's for?' Jock asked in an amused voice.

I shook my head.

'Believe it or not, it's the master race's idea of a WC.'

Early next morning word went round that bread was to be distributed and I decided that at all costs I had to get up on deck. With the assistance of two soldiers, I managed to get up on to the platform.

'You better wait until I get to the top before following me,' I told them. 'If I slip, you'll have had it.' I didn't feel too confident.

I set off up the ladder. All went well until I reached the switchback, then I got into difficulties. One half of me was on the lower ladder, the other half on the upper ladder, when I lost my nerve and daren't move either up or down. I began to sweat and tremble, and could feel my grip of the ladder slackening. I closed my eyes. If I looked down into the depths of the hold, I knew that I'd fall straight off. I tried to increase my grip on the rungs, but my hands seemed muscle-bound and just wouldn't do as I wanted.

I was panting hard for breath and felt that my back was about to break, when a voice from below reached me. 'Do you want any help?'

'No thanks, I'll manage,' I replied in a shaky voice.

I made another effort, and, still trembling, found myself on the upper ladder and heading for the hatch opening. At last I stood on deck, blinking nervously in the bright sunlight. That hold'll be the death of me, I murmured, trying to stop myself from shivering. I sat down and wished someone would give me a cigarette.

Presently Jock came strutting along the deck. 'Hello, lazybones. Where've you been all morning?'

'I nearly got killed coming up that bloody ladder,' I said. 'It's a positive deathtrap.'

'Never mind,' he said with a smile. 'They're issuing some bread in a few minutes. You'll feel better after a feed.'

'That's what brought me up on deck,' I said. 'But I think I might have to go along to the poop. Can you get mine if I'm not back in time?'

He nodded. 'I'm getting Charlie's. He's got bellyache. Have you got it as well?'

'Yes, a bit. I never really get rid of it.'

'Not many blokes have.' He glanced along towards the poop deck. 'By the way, they've got a new name for the WC up on the poop. They call it the "poopery".'

'I suppose it's original,' I said, glancing around. 'Anyway, where can I get a drink?'

'Over there there's a tap, if it's not padlocked.'

We walked over to the bridge. Strangely there was no queue, and the tap wasn't locked. The water was warm and tainted, but it slaked my thirst.

'Now I'm off to your so-called poopery,' I told Jock.

I made my way quickly forward. As I crossed the well-deck, I noticed that the pig was still alive. Perhaps the Greeks weren't quite hungry enough yet!

The 'poopery' was full to capacity, so I joined the long queue which wound itself half-way round the deck. I glanced at the faces of some of the men standing close to me. Judging by their expressions of anguish, they were all suffering from bellyache. This conclusion was confirmed every time a space became vacant: the man at the head of the queue literally leapt over the rail and on to his precarious perch.

At last it was my own turn, and it was not long before I found myself hanging over the ship's side with nothing but the wooden pole between me and the deep blue sea.

'Nice and cool out here,' said the man on my left with dreamy contentment.

'I'd call it draughty,' I replied. It felt as if a 30-mile-an-hour wind were blowing. I looked down at the frothy stern wave some 20 feet below and shivered. One slip . . .

The man on my right began to move, and in doing so rocked the pole. A new man climbed out and again the pole rocked dangerously.

'I don't think I like this perch very much,' I said. But whether I liked it or not, I had to use it very frequently before we reached Salonika.

By the time I got back, Jock had drawn the bread. He'd been given a large round loaf, covered with green mould, and it was to last the three of us for two days.

'Aren't they giving us anything to put on it?' I asked.

'You've got some hopes,' he replied, scraping away the mould with his fingernails.

Glancing around the deck to make sure no guards were in sight, he produced a small pocket-knife and proceeded to cut the loaf into three. When he'd finished, he held out the chunks. 'Which d'you want?'

I looked at the bread. 'Pretty grim-looking stuff. I wonder where they dug it up?'

'Well, take your pick.'

I closed my eyes and, after making an imaginary figure-of-eight with my right hand, let it alight. When I opened my eyes I saw that I'd chosen the centre chunk. 'I don't suppose it matters which piece I take – they all look the same size,' I said, taking the break. But there was less mould on it than on the other pieces.

'You'd better choose a piece for Charlie the same way,' he said.

Again I closed my eyes and twirled a hand. 'This'll do,' I said, picking up the chunk my hand had touched. He took it from me and stowed it in his pocket. Then he took a large bit out of the remaining piece. 'Just to make sure they don't get mixed,' he said.

When he'd gone, I sat down and began eating – and wondering what the bread had tasted like when it was newly baked.

30
'You Look Intelligent!'

I awoke with a start. Someone had sat down on the deck next to me, and in doing so had given my leg a hard kick. I turned and looked at the offender, ready to call him a clod, but he didn't have the face of a clod, and my mouth just opened and closed without speaking.

He had a sallow complexion, was clean-shaven and had dark, shining eyes with very long eyelashes. He wore blue service trousers and a khaki drill shirt – just like my own – and I guessed that he was in the Greek airforce. For a long time we just looked at each other, then he broke the silence, speaking in an unintelligible language. When he saw that I was perplexed, he spoke in English. 'Are you an Englishman?'

'An Englishman?' I was rather surprised that there should be any doubt as to my nationality.

There was a trace of embarrassment in his smile as he said, 'I'm sorry, you look like a Greek. You are very dark and your trousers are like mine.'

'It's the sun and I need a shave.' I said, rubbing my hairy cheeks. Then I began to feel quite pleased with myself. It was rather flattering to know that I could pass myself off as a Greek – until it came to speaking their language.

He made himself more comfortable against the coaming, then brought out a pack of cigarettes. 'Will you smoke?'

'Thanks,' I said, taking one. He produced a box of matches and we lit up.

'Where were you taken prisoner?' he asked.

'Crete. I managed to get out of Greece, but they caught up with me.'

'You know Greece?' he asked with sudden interest.

'I was there about seven months. I know Athens quite well.'

'Athens is my home,' he said, confirming my guess as to his nationality.

'Where did you learn to speak English?' I asked. 'You speak it with hardly a trace of an accent.'

'At school,' he said with a smile. 'We all learn to speak English. Do you speak Greek?'

'Just a little. It is not an easy language to learn.'

For a while we smoked in silence. Two of the guards, their tunic sleeves rolled to the elbows, suddenly appeared and walked slowly towards the well-deck. I watched them as they picked their way through the maze of sprawling bodies.

'They go to see whether the pig is still alive,' said the Greek.

I nodded and smiled. 'That's what I was thinking. It's not very nice having a pig living with you, is it?'

'It is better than having one of those Huns living with you. And it is better than being imprisoned down there,' he said, pointing to the hold.

'That's where I sleep,' I said.

He pulled a wry face. 'What will happen to you if we meet a submarine?'

I moved uncomfortably, then took a long pull at the cigarette. The Germans strolled back along the deck; apparently all was well with the pig.

The Greek moved a little closer to me. 'Have you thought of escaping?' he asked quietly.

I turned my head and looked at him. Was this a trap? He might be a Greek, but he could be a traitor. Why should he discuss escaping with a stranger – a foreigner at that?

'Escape,' I exclaimed innocently. 'Escape to where?' Perhaps I could do a bit of pumping.

He glanced around to make sure we couldn't be overheard. 'You know that we are going to Salonika?'

'Of course. Everyone knows,' I replied.

'Well, they are going to release all the Greek soldiers and airmen when we get there and send them home. But they are not releasing Greek officers.'

'Are you an officer?'

'Yes. I am in the Air Force.'

'What rank are you?'

'The same as a Flying Officer.'

'So you'll not be released.'

He shook his head. 'That is why I plan to escape.'

I doused the end of my cigarette. His story might be true. But if he wished to escape, why bring me, a perfect stranger, into his plans? Or was it that he only wanted my help?

The packet of cigarettes again appeared.

'Have you any friends in Athens?' he asked, offering me a light.

My suspicions had been fading, but now they flared up again. Was he employed by the Germans to discover the names of people in Athens who had been friendly with the British? 'I know one or two people,' I admitted cautiously. 'But I'd hardly call them friends.'

'Would they help you if you escaped?'

I turned and looked at him. What kind of a mug did he take me for? Did he really think I'd fall for that? 'I shouldn't think so,' I said. 'I expect by now the Germans have clapped them all in jail.'

He shrugged his shoulders. 'I don't think they would do that unless they had done something wrong.' His faith in Nazi justice increased my suspicion.

'Well, I couldn't possibly ask them to help me,' I said. 'And in any case, if I escaped I wouldn't stay in Athens.'

He blew out a cloud of smoke. 'When I asked if they would help you, I meant would they give you clothing and money.'

'I wouldn't ask them,' I replied. 'I don't know them well enough, and it would be too risky – for them as well as for me.'

I nipped the glowing end off my cigarette and put the half-smoked butt into my pocket.

'You look very much like a Greek,' he said with a smile. 'And you act like one.'

'When I'm clean I look like an Englishman,' I replied caustically.

For a while neither of us spoke. Had I not accepted his cigarette I'd have made an excuse to leave, but now I felt under an obligation to him.

'Do you wish to escape?' he asked at last.

'Of course. Every prisoner wishes to escape.'

'Would you care to come with me. I can help you.'

'Where will you make for?' I asked.

'Turkey.'

'But I can speak nothing but English.'

'That will make it difficult, but we will manage.'

'What about clothes?' I asked. 'And I've no money.'

'You have a watch, perhaps?'

'No. I've nothing except what I stand up in.' That, I calculated, would put paid to any idea he might have of robbing me.

'How much Greek do you speak?'

'Only a few words. I can say good-morning and good-night.'

'Is that all?'

I smiled. 'Perhaps a little more.'

'Have you a tunic?'

'Yes, a blue Air Force one,' and I indicated the tunic draped over the coaming close by his head.

'If I give you some Greek buttons, you can sew them on?'

'But that won't make it like a Greek tunic. It's the wrong shape.'

'It will do.'

'You think it will be easy to escape?' I asked.

He pursed his lips. 'Not easy, but we can do it.'

I turned my head and looked straight at him. 'I want to ask you a simple question,' I said, 'and I want a straight answer.'

He frowned. 'Well?'

'Why have you picked on a strange Englishman to escape with you when there are so many Greeks on board?'

He looked at me with a twinkle in his eyes. 'You look intelligent!'

'Do none of your countrymen look intelligent?' I asked, refusing to be amused.

'Of course,' he replied. 'But I had decided to ask you before I knew that you were English. I really thought you were Greek.'

'Are there no Greek officers on board?'

'No, I am the only one.'

'How do you know?'

He shrugged. 'I just know.'

'Well, the Germans will have you marked.'

He nodded his head.

'And you still want me to come with you?'

'Of course.'

I gave a sigh. I was keen enough to escape, but somehow I didn't feel disposed to commit myself until I knew a great deal more about him. 'Tell me about your plans,' I said. 'You haven't said anything about them yet.'

He spread out his hands. 'It is really quite simple. When we get to the camp at Salonika they will have all the Greeks out on parade and search them. Then they will check their identity, and if they are satisfied, they will open the gates and let them go.'

For a moment I just stared at him. Did he really expect me to believe such a story? I gave a short laugh. 'Just like that,' I said. 'Open the gates and let them all go!'

He looked at me with wide open eyes. 'But of course. Why should they keep us locked up in our own country?'

'Did you ever hear what they did to a couple of million Frenchmen?' I asked.

He shrugged. 'You do not believe me?'

'All right,' I said. 'Let's say that I do believe you. But will you tell me how I'm going to identify myself as a Greek, knowing that I hardly speak a word of your language?'

'Have you heard any of the Germans speaking Greek?' he asked. 'It is awful. They speak it worse than you.'

'You've not heard me yet,' I reminded him.

'Well, no matter how bad it is, you will be able to fool the Germans.' He brought out his cigarettes and handed me one. 'You are the most suspicious Englishman I have ever met,' he said, almost bitterly. 'You believe nothing I say. Perhaps you do not believe that I am a Greek officer.'

I took one of his cigarettes, because to have refused would have offended him.

'Why should I believe you?' I asked quietly, hoping that my forced smile would take the sting out of the words. 'Some of the things you've said are very hard to believe.'

As he struck a match, a shadow fell across him and a voice barked, *'Kommen Sie hier!'*

We both looked up. The two Germans we had previously seen walking up and down the deck were standing watching us, one with a finger on the trigger of his tommy-gun.

'They've heard us talking,' I whispered.

'It's the matches,' he said, slipping the box into a pocket. 'You stay here.' He got to his feet and moved over to the Germans.

'Wissen Sie nicht es ist verboten Streichholzer zu besitzen?' – 'Do you not know that matches are not permitted?'

The Greek shrugged his shoulders, *'Nicht verstehen'* – 'I don't understand.'

The Germans exchanged glances, and one of them proceeded to go through the Greek's pockets. When he found the matches he asked, *'Englischer Gefangener?'* – 'English prisoner?'

'No, Greek.'

'Ah, Grieche Gefangener!' remarked both Germans in unison. *'Komm!'* They took him by the arms and marched him along the deck. When they reached the handrail overlooking the well-deck, they gave him a hard shove and he disappeared from sight.

I slipped the unlighted cigarette into my pocket. Would they come back and search me? But at least I wasn't out of bounds. They came back along the deck jabbering together and laughing. When they saw me, they halted.

'Englischer Gefangener?' one of them asked.

'Ja. Englischer Gefangener,' I said, nodding my head.

'Kommen Sie hier!'

I got to my feet and walked over to them. They went through my pockets but found nothing which was *'verboten'*.

31

Salonika

'I wish they'd be quick and dish out the rest of that bread,' said Charlie in a weary voice.

'And I wish you'd stop talking about the bloody stuff,' replied Jock sharply. 'That's about the tenth time you've mentioned it in the last half-hour.'

Charlie lowered his eyes. He knew that what Jock had said was true, and that it was inevitable that one of us would eventually choke him off. Just the same, I felt sorry for him. He did far less grumbling than either Jock or me, and on this occasion he really had something to grumble about. We'd now been on board the ship four days, and the only food we'd had was the chunk of bread they'd issued on the second day.

'Let's go and get a drink of water, Charlie,' I said. 'That'll help fill you up a bit.'

He looked across at me. 'The tap's been padlocked.'

I glanced in the direction of the bridge, and saw he was right. I took a deep breath and leaned back against the coaming. 'Let's start a mutiny,' I said.

'What about the crew?' Charlie asked. 'And the guard?'

'Throw them to the fishes.'

'And the Eyetie destroyer?'

I looked across the deck towards the sleek destroyer. The only worthwhile armament she appeared to possess was a large gun, facing aft.

'Ram her.'

'If I wasn't so weak, I'd drop over the side and swim ashore,' Charlie remarked.

For a time no one spoke, and I found myself seriously considering Charlie's last remark. The shore was less than 1 mile away, and was flanked in places by small forests which came right down to the water's edge. If one could quietly slip over the side without being seen, it should be possible to swim ashore. But as Charlie had said, we were too weak to undertake such a swim. A pity, because it would not be a difficult feat for a reasonably good swimmer.

I heard footsteps and looked up. It was the Greek.

'Any Germans about?' he asked, scanning the deck.

I turned to Jock and Charlie. 'You know Nicki, don't you? He's a Greek Air Force officer.'

'Yes, we've met,' said Jock. Then he looked closer at the Greek. 'What's happened to your eye?' It was black and blue.

'He got it when the Jerries caught him up here,' I told him. 'This deck is out of bounds to the Greeks. They slung him back into the well-deck. He landed on top of the pig, otherwise he might have broken his neck.'

'What happened to the pig?' Jock asked with poker-faced solemnity.

'It turned round and began to lick me,' Nicki said as he sat himself down.

When he'd made himself comfortable he turned to me. 'Have you heard about the bread?' he asked.

'No, what's happened to it?'

'It was so bad that last night the Jerry guard threw it overboard.'

I leaned forward and looked at Charlie. His face bore an expression of utter hopelessness and misery.

'What're they going to do now?' I asked. 'We'll be dead by the time we arrive at Salonika.'

Nicki shook his head. 'The bread was bad. It would have poisoned us.'

'But can't they give us something else to eat?' I asked. 'What about the crew. Haven't they any spare food? And the Eyetie destroyer, can't they help us?'

'No one worries about prisoners,' he said with resignation. 'They cost nothing and if they die, well, there are always plenty more.'

For a while no one spoke and I half expected Nicki to bring out his cigarettes. Instead, he waited until we had lapsed into a broody silence, then turned to me and said, 'In case we are not dead when we arrive in Salonika, I better start giving you some lessons in Greek.'

Another nightmarish 24 hours passed and we were still without food. Rumour had said that we would dock during Monday night, but it was now Tuesday and we were still ploughing our way steadily northwards.

'See anything?' Charlie asked as I returned from the ship's rail.

'No.' I said as I sat down beside him. 'Only a few caiques out fishing.'

'No orange boxes or dead cats?' asked Jock.

I looked across at him and grunted. I didn't see what he had to joke about.

'I mean it,' he said, leaning forward and smiling. 'You always see orange boxes and dead cats when you're near a port.'

'Well, there's nothing except the caiques.'

'But I can see a seagull,' remarked Charlie, turning his face to the sky.

As he spoke, half a dozen guards suddenly appeared on deck. '*Alles unten! Alles unten!*' – 'All below! All below!'

I climbed slowly down the ladder into the hold, and when the deck had been cleared the guards battened down the hatch and we were left in darkness. Two hours later the hatch was opened again and we were ordered up on deck. We were alongside a dock or pier – we had heard and felt the ship being warped alongside – so when we left the hold we took all our possessions with us.

As I walked down the gangway, I saw that the pier adjoined a promenade and that a large crowd of people was watching us disembark. There were guards everywhere, but instead of carrying tommy-guns they were armed with rifles and fixed bayonets. When we reached the shore, we were made to form up into fives and, when everyone had been cleared off the ship, were counted.

Everything seemed to be going wonderfully smoothly – almost too smoothly. There had been the minimum of shouting, no one had been manhandled, and they had succeeded in getting our correct number at the second count. Just as we thought we were to be marched off, the air was rent by the sound of a raucous klaxon, and a large staff car came tearing along the promenade towards the pier. The crowd of onlookers scattered as, with a screech of brakes, the car came to a halt. Out of it emerged a German officer dressed in a tight-fitting green uniform, jackboots and a tin hat.

'Here comes trouble,' remarked my neighbour. 'Better close your eyes.'

He was right. As Trouble came stalking along the short pier, he unbuttoned his holster and drew out his revolver. '*Feldwebel!*' he roared, flashing the revolver in the air. '*Feldwebel!*'

The *Feldwebel* suddenly appeared. '*Ja, Herr Major,*' he shouted, coming to a halt about a yard from where I was standing and giving a stiff salute.

'*Kommen Sie hier!*'

'With a '*Jawohl, Herr Major,*' the *Feldwebel* broke into a run.

'Scared bloody stiff,' remarked my neighbour.

'Wouldn't you be?'

'*Ruhig!*' snapped a nearby guard.

Half my neighbour's head disappeared down into the oversize collar of his tunic.

Presently the *Major* and *Feldwebel* came marching along the length of the column, the former still shouting and waving his revolver, the latter very red in the face.

'I don't think I'm going to like Salonika,' whispered my neighbour from the depths of his coat.

'Neither am I,' I told him, casting a furtive glance at the nearest guard.

At last an order was given to march and, with a clatter of tin mugs and hobnailed boots, we left the pier. The crowd had again assembled, but as we approached they backed away to make room for us. When we reached the end of the pier, we wheeled right and set off along the broad promenade. As we marched along, people began to leave the shops and line the pavements to watch us. They were in no doubt as to who we were, and several of them timidly waved to us. Then some of them began throwing cigarettes. The guards immediately put a stop to this by threatening to shoot the offenders. Not to be outdone, they gave the cigarettes to some of the children who were watching us, with instructions to walk ahead of the column and drop them in our path. Again the guards roared, this time threatening to shoot any prisoner picking up a cigarette.

About 1 mile along the promenade we came to what I thought I recognized as the White Fort. It was here that a party of school children came into sight. One of them, a boy of about 10 wearing a bright-green shirt, shyly waved his hand. His schoolmates, gaining confidence, also waved. When the *Major* saw them, he shouted for the *Feldwebel* and gave orders for the children to be chased away.

At a street corner further along, the boy in the green shirt again appeared. With him was a girl about his own age and they each carried a brown-paper bag. Waiting until the *Major* had passed – apparently they considered him their real enemy – they both suddenly darted into the road and began handing out oranges to the prisoners. The guards shouted and tried to stop them but, heedless of danger, they wormed their way in and out of the ranks, all the time distributing the fruit.

The column began to get ragged and slow down, and the *Major* turned to see what the trouble was. Then he saw the children. He came tearing back along the column, shouting and waving his revolver. The guards, scared by his ranting, made a concerted effort to catch the children, and very soon had them cornered. The boy was dragged out of the ranks by the scruff of the neck, the girl by her long hair. They were hauled along to the *Major*, who roared at them, then beat them in turn with his clenched fist.

The column got back into formation and began moving forward again. A few minutes later the two children passed us on their way to the head of the column – apparently they were to be taken to the prison camp. The boy, his face screwed up with pain, his eyes filled with tears, was being pulled along by an ear. The girl, screaming and fighting, was being dragged along by her hair.

'For Pete's sake, look at that,' I said to my neighbour. 'Can't we do something about it?'

'What can we do?' he said in a hopeless voice.

240

We eventually reached the camp. It had a pair of large iron gates laced with barbed wire, and just inside was a tall flagpole with the swastika flying. We were marched into the camp and on to a large barrack square.

'Well, here we are,' said my neighbour, dumping his blanket at his feet. 'What happens now?'

I glanced around. In front of us, and cutting off our view of the road, was a huge hotel-like building. Sentries in steel helmets carrying rifles and bayonets were on guard, so I assumed it to be some kind of a headquarters. Behind us and to our left were some large two-storey barrack blocks, and away to the right were four squat stone huts.

'It looks as though we'll have somewhere to live,' I said. 'They've got plenty of barracks.'

'Never mind the barracks,' said my neighbour. 'What about the food?'

Most of the guards had left us at the gate, and now only half a dozen of them remained to see that we didn't wander away from the square. I looked across at the nearest barracks to see if they were occupied. If they were, there was no sign of their occupants.

Then someone started to shout. A small group of men had appeared between two of the buildings, and one of the prisoners was trying to discover who they were. Everyone listened attentively. The group of men were English prisoners, and they'd been in the camp over a month. They were all wounded, which was why they had not been sent out to work. The camp contained about 2,000 prisoners, all from Crete and Greece. Most of them were out at work, and work was compulsory unless the doctor excused you. The food, they told us, was terrible – bad bread, bad soup and bad cheese.

'What time's the next meal?' someone shouted from the square.

'We had it about an hour ago. You'll get nothing to eat today.'

'Hear that?' I said to my neighbour. 'We don't get anything to eat today.'

'Don't take any notice of them,' he said sceptically. 'They're just trying to be funny.' But they weren't. After being searched, we were marched across to the huts and locked up for the rest of the day, with neither food nor water.

I found myself sharing a hut with about 80 other men. The place was completely bare of furniture and fittings, and there were cracks between the floorboards down which a box of matches might easily be lost. I chose a patch of floor close to a window, then laid out my blanket.

I looked at my two neighbours, one an Australian with a long, flowing ginger beard and light-blue eyes, the other a British soldier with an equally long jet-black beard and green eyes. Both of them possessed blankets, and in addition the Aussie had a greatcoat and water-bottle.

'What about a bit of fresh air?' Blackbeard asked. 'It's like an oven in here.'

'Good idea, cobber,' said the Aussie. 'You can get up and open it.'

241

With a grunt Blackbeard got to his feet and, after a short struggle, succeeded in opening the window.

'Any water in that bottle?' I asked the Aussie. So forceful a character was sure to have water.

'Nope, not a drop.'

My opinion of him immediately fell: he was either incompetent or lying!

I wriggled out of my tunic, then removed my shoes and socks.

'You going to have a kip?' asked the Aussie.

'No, I'm trying to cool off a bit.'

'Got any fags?' he asked presently.

'No.' Then out of sheer habit, I added, 'Only an empty pipe.'

'Got any matches, then?'

'No.'

My opinion of him fell even lower.

'I've got a lighter,' said Blackbeard hopefully.

'How did you get it through the search?' I asked.

'Hid it in the sand,' he replied, still looking at the Aussie.

'You don't need many brains to fool these Jerry bastards,' said the Aussie. He felt in his pocket and brought out a waterproof tobacco pouch. 'I've got a bit of 'baccy. D'you know how to roll a fag?'

'Sure,' said Blackbeard, his face lighting up. 'Got any papers?'

My opinion of the Aussie began to rise.

'Bit of Bible,' he said when he saw me watching him unfurl a small roll of paper.

'From Crete?'

'Yep. Want a bit?'

I held out my hand. My opinion of him rose even higher.

He doled out a few shreds of tobacco to each of us, which we rolled into cigarettes. Lighting up, I leaned back against the wall and inhaled deeply. Truly the Aussie was masterful! Then I began to wonder whether it really was a sin to smoke a cigarette made from a page out of a Bible.

When I awoke, it was nearly dark.

'What time is it?'

'About ten.'

'Any grub been dished out yet?'

'Steak and chips, and a pint of old ale.'

'Bloody funny!' I said. 'I hope it chokes you.' I lay back. 'Where are the latrines in this dump?' I asked.

'At the end of the hut,' I was told. 'Just follow your nose.'

I put my shoes on, then set off to find the place. As Blackbeard had said, it was only a case of following one's nose. The latrine measured about 15 feet square, and one side was divided into open stalls. In the centre of each was a large, round hole, on either side of which was a countersunk footprint.

There was a small window, without glass, set high up in the wall. Outside I could hear the guard tramping up and down, and occasionally the beam of a searchlight flashed through the window. It was filthy beyond description.

When I got back to my bed space, I removed my shoes and stood them on the window ledge, they were so foul and stinking.

'I've seen some primitive bogs in my life, but never one to match that,' I told Blackbeard as I got down on my blanket. Making myself comfortable, I noticed that Aussie was still absent, but with that I turned over and fell asleep.

'What the hell's that?' I shouted in alarm as I sat up. The hut was pitch black and I could see neither Blackbeard nor Aussie. I put out a hand to see if either of them was in his bed.

'For Christ's sake,' I heard Blackbeard say in a shaky voice as I touched him. 'What the hell was that explosion?'

'I've no idea,' I answered. 'But where's Aussie?'

I got to my feet. Everyone on the hut was shouting and it was like Bedlam. I felt around on the window-ledge for my shoes but couldn't find them. Then I heard someone making his way noisily along the centre of the hut.

'That you, Aussie?' I shouted.

'No,' came back a reply. A moment later the same voice asked, 'Anyone got a field dressing?'

'What's happened?' asked Blackbeard, and a score of other voices echoed the same question.

'A bloody maniac of a guard lobbed a hand grenade through the bog window and killed half a dozen blokes.'

'Killed 'em?' asked Blackbeard incredulously.

'Yes, killed 'em. Who's got a field dressing?'

A searchlight swung across and its beam shone through the window.

'Get your bloody head down,' someone shouted. 'You'll have the bastards loosing off a few rounds into here if you're not careful.'

I abandoned the search for my shoes, and sat down on my blanket. 'Do you believe what he said about the hand grenade?' I asked Blackbeard.

'Well, it was a hell of an explosion,' he replied. 'But if it killed six blokes, what did he want field dressings for?'

Things quietened down in the hut, then suddenly there was a commotion at the end of the hut.

'Are you there, Aussie?' I shouted.

'Which Aussie?' a voice replied.

'The one with the ginger beard,' I said, wishing that I knew his name.

'Is that you, RAF?' I recognized the voice.

'Yes,' I replied. 'Come on over here.'

The searchlight which had been shining was suddenly switched off, and he was left to find his way in the dark. He threw his boots noisily to the bottom of his bed space. Then I told him of the incident down at the latrine.

'Who said someone had been killed?' he asked.

'It's what we were told,' I replied. 'They said six men were killed.'

'Well, it's a lot of bull,' he replied. 'No one was killed, but three or four were knocked about a bit.'

'Were you there?' asked Blackbeard.

I could hear the Aussie fumbling about with some paper – rolling himself a cigarette, I guessed.

'No, I was having a jaw with a cobber of mine at the other end of the room. When it went off I went into the bog to find out what had happened. Some stupid bloody Kraut lobbed a grenade in through the window.'

I felt him lean across me. 'Lend me your lighter,' he said to Blackbeard.

'You're not going to smoke?' I asked. 'You'll have them lobbing a hand grenade among us!'

'There's no order against smoking,' he said. 'Lend me the lighter.'

Blackbeard handed over his lighter. 'Shelter it as much as you can,' he said. 'I expect there's an order about lights after dark.'

As he flashed the light, he was greeted by a chorus of noisy protests. But he calmly lit his cigarette, then returned the lighter to Blackbeard.

'Like a bunch of crazy bitches out of high school,' he remarked, leaning back against the wall.

'Why did the guard throw the grenade?' I asked.

His cigarette glowed brightly as he pulled on it.

'Must have panicked about something. Maybe thought the blokes were trying to escape.'

'So he just lobbed one through the window?'

'Yes.'

'And no one was killed?'

'I've told you, no. One bloke got it in the face and three or four others got bits in their backsides.'

'What's happened to them?' I asked. 'Have they been taken to hospital?'

'I don't know. There was such a bloody rush to find out what happened that I soon beat it.'

'Didn't the Jerries come in?'

'Not while I was there. Anyway, what the hell are you worried about? You've not been hurt.'

I lay down at full-length on my blanket. So this was Salonika!

The next morning we had confirmation that nearly everything the Aussie had told us was true. We also heard that the man who had been hit in the face was now blind.

244

32
Lost Chance

The next morning I went for a prowl around the camp. It was a large, ramshackle place which, I decided, should have long since been destroyed, preferably by fire. The barracks might have been built at the time of Alexander the Great. They were of the most primitive construction and were now in the last stages of dilapidation. Toilet accommodation was practically non-existent, there was no lighting, seldom any water in the taps and the camp roads were made of compressed flea-ridden sand.

Twice each day all prisoners, except those excused by the camp doctor, had to parade on the square. On the morning parade we were counted, then working parties were picked out and marched away to Salonika. In the late afternoon we were again counted, this time to enable the guards to ascertain how many had escaped during the morning. There were seldom less than a dozen missing, but strangely, nothing ever seemed to be done about it.

I succeeded in dodging the working parties by waiting until the count was over, then quietly slinking away to the edge of the square and hiding behind a tree. Guards were placed in strategic positions all the way around us, but if one of them attempted to stop me, I just said 'diarrhoea', rubbed my middle and pulled a long, miserable face. That always seemed to do the trick, and as long as I didn't leave the square they were quite happy. During the rest of the day I sunbathed. I was already well tanned, but if I were to pass myself off as a Greek, the darker I was the better.

A week passed before I was able to see Nicki. We had made no definite arrangements on the ship about meeting as so much depended on conditions in the camp, and had agreed that our first meeting ashore would have to be left to chance. I soon discovered that the Greeks were confined in an isolated part of the camp, and that the huts in which they were housed were surrounded by barbed wire, but on each occasion I went there the guard chased me away. While I was still trying to devise some scheme whereby I could pass a message to Nicki via the cookhouse, he suddenly turned up. He had succeeded in breaking out and with considerable difficulty had managed to find me.

If it was to be believed, his news was most heartening. The Germans had confirmed that all Greek prisoners other than officers were to be released within a week, and that they would be given 24-hours' notice of the time of their liberation.

'I still think it ranks as one of the seven wonders of the world,' I told him after he had given me his news. Somehow I was still very sceptical.

'But there is nothing wonderful about it,' he said. 'If they keep us caged up, they will have to feed us. If they let us out, we will feed ourselves.'

I nodded. 'But look how much free labour they're losing. It wouldn't cost them much in food to keep you.'

'Well, no matter what you think, we are being released. You should be glad for us.'

'I am glad, especially as I'm coming with you.'

He smiled and brought out his cigarettes. 'Smoke?'

'I'll have to come with you or I'll get no more of these!'

'Do you still remember all the Greek words I taught you?' he asked when our cigarettes were alight.

'Yes. But I'm worried about my accent. It's terrible.'

'Don't worry about that,' he replied. 'The important thing is to be able to tell them your name, age and where you were born – they will need that for your identity card.'

'You've got everything cut and dried, haven't you?' I said. 'I'd no idea they were issuing us with those.'

He felt in his pocket and brought out some Greek Air Force buttons. 'You better sew these on,' he said, handing them to me. 'And it might be better if you stop washing your hands and face: the more you smell, the less time the Germans will spend searching you.'

'That's rather letting the Greek Air Force down, isn't it?'

'No, not really,' he said with a smile. 'You can be one of the dirty sort of airmen. I expect you have them in your Air Force. There is always one man in each squadron who is filthy, and usually very stupid.'

I gave a short laugh. 'What one has to do in the name of freedom. You'll have me rubbing garlic in my whiskers next.'

'No, I will not ask you to do that. But you will have to try and appear very stupid. That is most important.'

Before he left, he gave me final instructions and full details of his plans for our escape. My story was that I came from Larissa but, as my home had been destroyed in the recent earthquake, I was now going to my uncle's farm in eastern Thrace, where I hoped he would give me work. Nicki's story was that he was returning to his home, also in eastern Thrace, where he expected to get his old job back as a leather worker. As our respective homes were within 50 miles of each other, and little more than 50 miles of the Turkish border, we would be able to keep to our stories for most of the journey. After promising that he would come and tell me as soon as the Germans had given them their 24 hours' notice, he set off back to his own part of the camp.

Two days passed with no news from Nicki. On the third day I awoke after a bad night's sleep with a violent headache and pains behind the eyes. I went along to see the Medical Officer. His diagnosis was that I had sand-fly fever. He gave me a chit excusing me from parades and ordered me back to bed. He had no medicine, but he cheered me up by telling me that I would be better in a very few days, as the fever seldom lasted more than three days.

Jock and Charlie frequently visited me, and the Aussie drew my daily rations – a bowl of filthy soup with a scum of olive oil floating on its surface, about 4 oz mouldy bread, a minute portion of stinking cheese and half a pint of mint tea.

The fourth day came and still no news from Nicki. The pain at the back of my eyes was now so bad that I never opened them unless it was absolutely necessary, and I had completely lost my appetite. I was glad, though, that I'd not heard from Nicki and ardently hoped I wouldn't see him for at least three more days.

On the evening of the fifth day he came and told me that they were being released the following morning. Of course, he was very disappointed when he discovered I was on the sick list, but we both realized it would be foolhardy to attempt travelling in my present state.

'I do not wish to leave you behind,' he said sadly. 'Is there nothing we can do?'

'I can't think of anything,' I replied. 'It's just my rotten luck to go and get ill at a time like this. But I can't travel. I'd be an awful hindrance.'

He wriggled about uncomfortably. 'What can we do?' he asked, almost in despair. 'If I had friends here in Salonika I would ask them to look after you until you were better, but I have none.'

I closed my eyes. There was just nothing we could do, unless he would wait until I was better.

'Will you go home before trying to get to Turkey?' I asked.

'No. It would not be good for my family if the Germans knew that I had visited them.'

'Well, could you find somewhere to hide in Salonika until I'm fit to travel?' I asked. 'When I'm off the sick list I could go out with a working party, then escape and join you.'

He considered the idea for a few moments, obviously without relish. 'You would have no identity card, and it would be very difficult travelling without one,' he said at last.

'Then I don't think I will be able to come with you,' I told him.

He looked at me with sad eyes. 'It is bad luck,' he said, 'very bad luck. In two, perhaps three, weeks you might have been in Egypt.'

'Don't rub it in,' I said, holding my hands against my eyes. 'I want to come badly enough, but how can I come like this?'

'Perhaps you will feel better tomorrow.'

'Judging by the way I feel now, I don't think I'll ever get better,' I told him in a sudden fit of depression.

I felt him putting a cigarette into my hand. 'Perhaps a smoke will cheer you up.'

'I don't think I dare smoke,' I said. But I put the cigarette between my lips and waited for him to give me a light.

'If I'm feeling better in the morning I will be able to make it,' I said presently.

'You sound better already,' he said. 'Be quick and smoke some more.'

'It's good to have another smoke,' I said. 'But I expect it's doing me more harm than good.'

'How long have you had the fever?'

'This is the third day.'

'Then tomorrow it should be gone,' he said hopefully.

'That's what the doctor told me.'

'Are you better now than you were yesterday?'

'No, I feel ten times worse,' I told him truthfully.

He gave a deep sigh. 'I suppose it will not be wise to try and escape if you are ill.'

I took a pull at the cigarette, then doused it. 'Have they given you all the details about tomorrow?' I asked. 'D'you know what time you go, and where you have to parade?'

'Yes, we have to be on the square at nine. They will search us, then check our identity, then we go.'

I sat upright and opened my eyes. Could I make it? Couldn't I somehow get out on the parade and go through the preliminaries? Once out of the camp, I was sure I could hide up until I was fit to travel. But the throbs in my head. I lay back against the wall again.

'If I were fit, do you still think I could get away with it – pass myself off as a Greek?'

'If you remember all the words I have told you, yes.' Then I heard him chuckling. 'Do you remember your Greek name?'

Yes, I remembered that all right. 'Vasili Papagos,' I said, trying to smile. Then for good measure added, 'I'm a peasant from Larissa – a bloody ignorant peasant, because I can neither read nor write.'

I painfully opened my eyes and looked at him.

248

'But you must say it in Greek,' he said. 'And do not forget what I told you if they say something you do not understand. Start coughing, and spit as much as you can, spit everywhere – the Germans do not like that.'

I suddenly felt more confident of myself: I remembered all the words he had taught me; and I could cough and spit – nothing would give me greater pleasure than spitting . . .

'I'll try to come, Nicki,' I said. 'If I feel any better, I'll definitely come. But if I'm not, I won't attempt it. I would be an awful nuisance if I were sick.'

He gave me two more cigarettes, then, after shaking hands, he left me.

The next morning I felt infinitely worse. At nine o'clock I dragged myself up to the window and for almost an hour watched the Greeks being searched and having their identities checked. Periodically I crawled back to my bed space and tried to get dressed – perhaps I could somehow get out there on the square and go through with it – but inwardly I knew that my chances of joining them had long since passed. I was too weak even to stand upright. Now all that remained was for me to watch them with hurting eyes, and weep with disappointment as they marched towards the gates and freedom.

33
'Your Name is on It!'

At eleven o'clock the Aussie brought me my ration of soup.

'Take it away,' I told him. 'I'm past eating. You have it.'

I could hear the spoon rattle every time he dipped it into the tin, and every rattle seemed like a needle being poked into my eardrums. 'Must you make all that noise?' I asked pettishly.

'Sorry.' Then, 'Haven't you any appetite at all?' he asked presently.

I thought for a moment. What would I like to eat? A slice of chicken? A poached egg? No. Just a bowl of porridge.

'I'd like some porridge,' I told him. 'What d'you make of that?'

I heard the rattle of his tin mug as he put it down, and the rattle of mine as he picked it up.

'D'you know what I think?' he answered. 'That you haven't got sand-fly at all. You've got yellow jaundice. Quite a few blokes have got it across in the barracks at the other side of the camp, and that's what they all ask for – a bowl of porridge.'

I moved restlessly on the floor, but couldn't get comfortable. 'I think you're talking a lot of poppycock,' I told him. 'Since when have I looked yellow?'

'That comes later,' he said. 'If you'd had sand-fly you'd be better by now.'

'Well, I have all the symptoms of sand-fly,' I argued. 'Besides, the MO should know the difference between that and jaundice.'

'Have you seen the MO lately?' he asked after a pause.

'No, but when I did see him he said there was nothing he could do for me. He's got no medicines.'

'Well, take my tip. Go and see him again. You'll find you've got jaundice.'

I dragged myself back until I was leaning against the wall. 'Well, there's certainly something wrong somewhere. I'm nearly too weak to move, and this is the fourth day.'

He put down his empty mug and licked his spoon clean. 'Shall I try and get the Doc to come and see you?' he asked.

I rolled up my shirt sleeves and looked at my arms. There wasn't a trace of yellow in them, 'I don't think it's jaundice,' I said but I thought I'd go and see the MO in the morning. However, when the time came I was too weak to stand, so the Aussie carried me on his back to the little room in the barrack block at the far end of the square which served as the surgery.

There were about a dozen other men in the room but when the doctor saw me carried in, he left the patient he was attending and came and helped the Aussie lay me on the floor.

'He's in a bad way, Doc,' the Aussie said. 'Can't even stand up.'

The doctor was down on his knees beside me. 'Any pain?' he asked.

'No. I just feel all in. I even feel too weak to breathe properly.'

He sounded me with his stethoscope, then rolled back my lower eyelids. 'I've seen you before,' he said.

'I was here a few days ago with sand-fly fever.'

'You've still got it,' he said, getting to his feet. 'When did you last eat?'

'He's not eaten anything for a week,' the Aussie said.

'Aren't you hungry?' the doctor asked.

'I'd like a bowl of porridge.'

He got down on his knees again and repeated his sounding with the stethoscope. 'You've got jaundice as well,' he said at last. Walking across to a small table, he picked up a small chit of paper.

'There's a room in the next barrack block full of jaundice cases. You better move in with them. I haven't any medicine to give you, so you'll just have to take things easy. You'll get over it all right. You ought to go on a diet, but all we can get is rice. That's all you are to eat for the present.' He tucked the chit into my breast pocket, then asked the Aussie to take me to my new home.

The Aussie picked me up and carried me out of the room. 'Some people have all the luck,' he said. 'I wish they'd put me on a rice pud diet!'

I smiled at him weakly. 'I'm sorry I'm leaving you.'

'You'll be back in a few days,' he said cheerfully.

The room in the barrack block contained about 40 men, and the Aussie found me a patch of floor about half-way along on the left-hand side. After putting me down, he went off to collect my blanket and haversack. When he returned, he helped me off with my tunic, laid out the blanket and moved me on to it.

'I'll come and see you each day,' he promised as he tucked me up.

He'd been gone less than half an hour when I began to itch. At first I thought it was the heat, then I remembered that I still had lice. Still, they'd never bitten me quite so hard before. I began to scratch.

'What's up, mate?' the man next to me asked. 'The bugs getting at you?'

I glanced wearily at him. He was as yellow as a guinea.

'I think it's the lice,' I told him. 'I never got rid of them all.'

'You from Crete?'

'Yes. Are you?'

He nodded. 'And now we've got bugs to contend with. They're a bloody sight worse than lice.'

'Are there really bugs here?' I asked in surprise.

'Millions of 'em.'

'Well, I was told that if you had lice they kept the bugs away.'

'They don't here. They mate and breed by the million. Their offspring are as big as ladybirds.'

I sank back exhausted. I was itching in so many places at once I just couldn't cope.

'You got the jaundice?' he asked.

'Yes. I feel half dead.'

'You'll be OK in a few days. I felt like that when I first came here.'

I closed my eyes and wished he'd stop talking. But he hadn't finished yet. 'Have you fixed up with someone to bring your rice?' he asked.

'No. Don't they bring it round?'

'You have to fetch it yourself, unless you can get someone to collect it for you.'

I turned restlessly on to my back. What a cock-eyed organization. But what did it matter? I wasn't really hungry.

'Shall I fetch yours?' he asked.

'If you will, please. What time do you get it?'

'Twelve o'clock and again at four. Have you got the chit the MO gave you?'

I gave him the paper from my tunic pocket and he read it. 'Yes. I'll give it in at the cookhouse for you.'

For a time he was quiet, and the low buzz of voices in the room began to fade away. Just as I was about to fall asleep, though, a new batch of bugs arrived and brought me back to full consciousness. This was intolerable. I thought I would never sleep.

Still, it was after noon when my neighbour awoke me with a plate of boiled rice. It had been boiled in water, then strained. It contained neither sugar nor salt, but I enjoyed every mouthful of it and could have eaten twice as much as I was given. When I'd finished he took my plate away and, after washing it, put it with his own on the window ledge.

'How d'you feel now?' he asked.

'Much better. A few more meals like that and I'll soon be on my feet again.'

'There's another RAF bloke somewhere in the next barrack,' he said as he pulled the blanket over his shoulders. 'I wonder if you know him. He's a bit of a shortarse and looks as miserable as sin.'

'That's a hell of a description,' I said. 'Don't you know his name?'

'No, and I only know he's in the RAF because he sometimes wears a tunic. More often than not he's just in his shirt tails.'

'Perhaps he's not RAF. I've seen plenty of army men in Air Force uniform.' I was suddenly wondering whether it might not be Chota.

'He's RAF all right,' he said. 'And he's got something the matter with his guts. He's got a pipe hanging from a hole in the side of his belly. Looks ghastly.'

'Sounds ghastly too. But I don't expect I know him. They've got quite a few RAF prisoners, you know.' I was now feeling quite sure it wasn't Chota – his wound was in the neck.

At four o'clock I had my second plate of rice.

'Who looked after you when you first came here?' I asked my friendly neighbour as I began to eat.

'The chap next to me. He was here nearly a month before they let him out.'

'Where is he now?'

'Packed off to Germany. They pack us all off when we're better.'

During the evening he helped me along to the latrine. It was even worse than the one attached to the hut, and I could hear the rats scurrying about in the open drains.

'You don't want to spend much time in here,' my neighbour told me. 'If the rats get the idea you have any flesh on your bones, they'll come up and go for you.' I didn't disbelieve him, for the two I saw were as big as medium-sized cats.

My neighbour looked after me like a mother for a whole week, till I decided that I'd had all the bed I could take in one dose and got up. I felt bruised from head to foot, and the bugs and lice seemed to have drawn off huge quantities of my blood.

We spent most of our days sitting in the shade of the trees near the cookhouse, which was run for the Germans by men who I thought were ordinary British soldiers but turned out to be medical orderlies from the Society of Friends. We had been told that they voluntarily gave themselves up to look after the wounded, thus becoming prisoners, as an act of humanity. And a good bunch of chaps they were.

We talked about food, home, escaping and Crete. At mealtimes we were nearly always at the head of the queue for our rice – there were many others besides us who were on a limited diet of rice as a result of jaundice. If there was ever any left over, we were always first to hear of it.

Then I heard that the ginger-bearded Aussie had been sent off to Germany. The news left me feeling very sad; he hadn't even had time to come and say goodbye. But I felt even sadder when my neighbour was also sent away.

I went into the barracks next door to see if I could find this mysterious RAF type with the pipe hanging out of his abdomen, but no one was able to tell me. Perhaps he also had been sent to Germany. Wandering off in the direction of the cookhouse, I saw a small figure approaching, dressed only in a short khaki shirt, with his hair hanging over his forehead. The shortarse RAF type who looked as miserable as sin, I thought. Now I'll see whether I know him. When he was about 10 yards away, I suddenly recognized him. It was Dingle Bell!

I hurried forward. 'Dingle,' I said. 'What's been happening to you?'

'Oh, Micky!' he exclaimed, holding out his hand. His face was drawn and thin, and there was little more of him than a skeleton. 'I've got appendicitis,' he said. 'They don't seem to know what to do with it.'

'Appendicitis,' I repeated. 'But surely they can fix that easily enough. And what about the wounds?'

'They patched those up in hospital in Athens. This other business only came on since I came to Salonika. They say they can't operate, so they're draining it off.' He lifted up his shirt and showed me his discolored abdomen with the small rubber tube sticking out of one side of it.

'But that's bloody ridiculous,' I said. 'Why can't they operate?'

He gave a tired sigh. 'I don't know. I expect the truth is that they haven't a proper operating theatre.'

'Well, what about the tube?' I asked. 'They had to cut you open to put it in.'

'They only gave me a local anaesthetic.'

I lifted his shirt and had another look at the hole in his side. 'What are they going to do now? You can't walk around like this for ever.'

'The MO says they're going to fly me to Berlin tomorrow.'

I looked at his spidery arms and legs, and at his bony chest. It seemed a wonder that he had the strength to stand up.

'You got jaundice?' he asked.

'Yes, but I'm getting over it now.'

'You look pretty yellow. Have you seen yourself lately?'

'No thanks,' I said with a smile. 'I feel bad enough without seeing what I look like. Where are you living?'

'In here,' he said, pointing to the nearest barrack block. 'It's supposed to be a hospital. There's hundreds of us in it. It's just like a doss house. The stink, and the bugs!'

'We've got bugs too. And rats as big as cats. I'm in the next barrack. You should see the lavatory!'

'That's just where I'm going,' he said. 'I've got a touch of diarrhoea.'

I shook my head. 'I'm not surprised. What keeps the bugs from crawling up the tube?'

'The stink, I expect,' he said with a weak smile. 'Now I've got to go. I'll see you in the morning.'

'What time are you supposed to be going?' I asked. 'I don't want to miss you.'

'I don't know, but it won't be very early, if I go at all.'

But Dingle did go. At nine o'clock I was outside his barrack block keeping watch for him. As he hadn't turned up by half past nine, I went inside and asked for him. They told me he'd gone at eight.

Again I began thinking about escape. I was still far from fit, but there seemed no reason why I shouldn't start making some plans. I nosed around the camp in search of a racketeer who might be able to help me. Two days of cautious inquiry brought me to an English-speaking Yugoslav who worked in the cookhouse. He specialized in maps, railway tickets, Greek money and civilian clothes. The fact that such a useful person existed in the camp was a great surprise. The best I had hoped for was someone who could furnish me with a map and some oddments of clothing.

Before discussing terms, the Yugoslav demanded to know my name and service number. This made me suspicious, but he refused to help me until I gave him the information, I told him who I was, but even that wasn't enough. He told me he'd have to check my identity and that he would see me the following morning.

I spent the rest of the day trying to work out how I would meet his terms, as I was quite destitute. Then I hit on the idea of charging everything up to the Air Ministry. I would promise him anything within reason in the way of money, payment to be made when I was safely home. If he refused these terms there was no alternative but for me to go out with one of the working parties and try to get away.

That night I found it very difficult to sleep. What exactly would the Air Ministry say when I told them that I'd committed them to paying a racketeer a couple of hundred pounds for having helped me to escape? They might think it such a bad bargain that they'd pack me off back to Salonika on the first neutral boat!

When I met the Yugoslav next morning, I received a shock. 'You are sure this is your right name and number?' he asked, tapping a sheet of foolscap.

'Of course,' I replied. 'Why shouldn't it be?'

He shrugged and looked down at the paper. 'This is a list of men going to Germany tomorrow. Your name is on it.'

34

Food for Seven Days

As the Yugoslav had forewarned, I was later told by the Germans that I was to parade at eight o'clock the following morning with all my kit. They didn't give any reason. At the appointed time I paraded with several hundred others, and after being counted, identified, searched and generally bullied by a pack of irate guards, we were each issued with half a loaf of black bread and a small tin of meat paste – our rations for a week!

As we marched off the square and out through the gates, I felt almost free again. Behind us were all the horrors – not least of which were the rats, bugs and sand-flies – of a typical Nazi transit camp (as it was called). But as we marched along, there loomed up the now familiar and rather frightening spectre of the unknown. What would Germany hold for us?

We marched through Salonika to a railway siding close to the main-line station, where a train of cattle trucks was already drawn up to receive us. Each truck was about 25 feet long and 7 feet high, and there was a sliding door in the centre. There was also an aperture measuring approximately 18 inches by 12 just under the roof, heavily laced with barbed wire, which served as a window.

We were not allowed to enter the trucks immediately. Instead we were again searched, though on this occasion the guards were very lax. While the search was in progress, half a dozen lorries entered the siding, and I was surprised to see prisoners climbing out of them.

'What've they got that we haven't?' asked the man next to me.

'They must be special prisoners,' I said. 'Maybe they've just come from the local lock-up.'

But we soon knew all about them. They'd been brought from the camp in lorries because they were all either sick or wounded.

'I didn't know they moved hospital patients in cattle trucks,' my neighbour remarked. Neither did I, but I wasn't surprised. I glanced along the length of the train to see if there were any special coaches into which they could be loaded, but I saw none.

Despite the efforts of the guards to prevent us talking to the new arrivals, we soon got into communication with them. Most of them had recently arrived from hospital in Athens and were being sent into Germany for further treatment. The MO in Salonika had apparently remonstrated with the Germans about moving them, but he'd been overruled, and, like us, they were to be packed into cattle trucks and sent to a prison camp.

Suddenly I heard someone shouting my name. 'Micky! Micky! It's me. Over here. Look!'

I looked in the direction of the voice. It sounded strangely familiar, but the excited tones made it hard to recognize. Then I saw him, right in the middle of the sick and wounded. Chota! The bandage was gone from his neck, but he was as pale as a ghost and painfully thin.

I stood on my toes and waved. 'Chota!' I shouted. 'What are *you* doing here?'

He quickly edged his way to the front of the crowd and, had it not been for a guard who pushed him back, he would have come across to where I was standing.

'They're sending us to Germany,' he shouted. 'Where're you off to?'

'The same place. In one of these trucks. How's the neck? Is it better?'

'It's getting better. How're you?'

'Fine. Can't we get into the same truck?'

He glanced at the nearby guard. 'I don't think they'll let us. Did you manage to make your canoe?'

'Yes. But I got picked up while trying it out. How've they been treating you?'

'Pretty good. Where's Lofty?'

'I don't know. He left Crete before I did. I expect he's in Germany by now. How about trying to get into the same truck? I think we could manage it.'

'I haven't any grub. They issued it in bulk and it's being put on the train. If I don't keep with the others I'll get nothing to eat.'

An officious *Unteroffizier* appeared from nowhere and started screaming at us. Apparently he wanted us to stop talking. At first we ignored him, but when he drew his revolver on us we decided that we had better be quiet. For a short time there was comparative silence in the siding, but the moment he was gone everyone started talking and shouting again.

'How long will it take us to reach Germany?' Chota shouted.

'They gave us food for seven days,' I replied.

257

'What did they give you?'

'Half a loaf and some meat paste – enough for one good meal!'

The *Unteroffizier* again appeared, so we stopped talking. Following him was a party of Yugoslavs carrying small wooden boxes. They were directed to unload them into a truck close to where I was standing.

'Grub,' said my neighbour, who had been taking quite an interest in my talk with Chota. 'They must be putting some of the wounded in there.'

Another party of Yugoslavs came into sight carrying more wooden boxes. But they went past us towards the far end of the train.

'Looks as if you might be travelling in this one,' I shouted to Chota when the *Unteroffizier* had gone.

'I'll try and get into it,' he replied. 'You make for the one next door.'

My neighbour nudged me. 'If that's your mate, why don't you try and get into his truck?'

For a moment I considered the suggestion. If the Germans counted us as we entered, they might notice that I was not one of the wounded and throw me out. And there was the question of space. If I did get in with them, I might cause a certain amount of overcrowding. .

'I don't think I better do that,' I said. 'I expect they'll be overcrowded as it is.'

'But if they count you as wounded, it won't make any difference,' he replied.

I scratched my head. No, I suppose it wouldn't.

Then a German officer appeared. Despite the heat of the day, he wore a long black-leather coat and a pair of jackboots.

'I guess we're on the move,' whispered my neighbour, picking up his rolled blanket from the floor. He was right. We were told to get into our 'fives', then they started loading the trucks. Everything was managed by the officer and three of the guards. They loaded one truck at a time, and into each they packed 40 men. As each truck was filled, the sliding door was closed and locked.

Everything was so quiet and well managed that I was afraid of shouting to Chota to watch which truck I went into, but I felt sure he had his eyes glued on me and would know where I was.

Another sliding door clanged to and was locked, and they started loading the next truck. Then it came to my turn, and I found myself packed into a truck with 39 complete strangers. My neighbour had allowed himself to get pushed out of the ranks and would be one of the first to enter the next truck – artful dodger! But I was in the truck I would have chosen had there been any choice – next to the one apparently reserved for the wounded.

The moment the door was slammed and locked, everyone started grumbling. Those who had been first in had seized the best patches of floor, and they were now laid out like ladies of luxury, surrounded by their much-cherished possessions. But there was a Sergeant Major in the truck. He was quiet but firm, and without having to quote his rank, he very soon got things organized. Half of us were lined up on each side of the truck, then he ordered us all to remove our boots or shoes.

'Now, everyone who has a blanket, spread it out on the floor,' he ordered. We did as we were told. 'You'll all sleep with your heads against the walls of the truck,' he told us. 'Everyone will have someone else's feet round his waist, but that can't be helped. At night, try and not move about too much. If someone happens to accidentally kick you, don't start shouting about it – you're all in your stocking feet so you won't get hurt. And if you have kit-bags or haversacks, keep them off the floor. Hang 'em up or do what you like with them, but keep the floor clear for lying on. And try and keep the place clean. We're here for a week and we haven't got a dustpan and broom.'

Slowly we got ourselves sorted out, and all our oddments of luggage were somehow hung up under the roof. I was in second place from a corner of the truck, and was parked in between two Australians. As they appeared to know each, I offered to change places so that they could be together, but they declined. Later I discovered why. One of them snored very loudly, and his friend knew!

The one in the corner was known as Spadger. He was tall, well built and had a long fair beard. His friend – judging by the colour of his skin he'd recently had jaundice – we just called Cobber; it was he who snored.

'I guess it's time we had something to eat,' said Spadger when we had settled down.

'Too soon yet,' said Cobber. 'Better wait until we're on the move. It's got to last a week.'

Spadger shrugged his shoulders, then opened his home-made haversack and brought out his half loaf. 'Might as well eat it now. There's only enough for one meal.'

'You're surely not going to eat it *all*,' I said. 'You better keep a bit for later on.' As these were my first words to him, I had an idea he'd tell me to mind my own business, but I knew what the result would be if he ate all his rations: every time Cobber and I ate, we would have to share ours with him.

He turned and glared at me. 'How long have you been in the bag?' he demanded.

'Long enough to know what it's like to be hungry,' I answered.

With a growl he pushed the bread back into the haversack, then peeled off his tunic.

I edged slightly away from him.

Spadger got to his feet and hung his haversack and tunic under the roof. 'This is going to be a nice comfortable little trip,' he said with venom.

The first warning we had that we were about to move was when the engine backed into the train. This it did with such violence that everyone in truck was thrown into a heap at one end.

'That's the driver, the spiteful bastard,' said Spadger when we got settled down again. 'I expect he knows we're prisoners.'

Cobber joined the group of men who were standing and peering out of the small window.

'See anything?' I asked him.

'A few Krauts and civvies. 'D'you know what time it is?'

'Well, we've been here for hours. I expect it's about four o'clock.'

'It's half past five!'

'Any women about?' asked Spadger.

Cobber turned and looked down at him. 'You and your women. What d'you think this is? The Rome Express?'

Presently the German guards came along the length of the train, trying all the doors to make sure they were locked. Then someone blew a whistle, there was a lot of shouting and the train began to move.

With the exception of a brief stop to take on fuel and water, our first main halt was not for 23 hours. At times we travelled along like an express; at others we went so slowly that it would have been quicker to get out and crawl. Now we had stopped, and could hear the engine being uncoupled.

'I guess we're in a station,' said Cobber, as he climbed wearily to his feet and looked out of the window. For his sake, as well as for the rest of us, I hoped he was right. He was suffering from diarrhoea.

With Spadger and several others, I joined him at the window. Our view was rather limited, but we could see some German soldiers and civilians on the platform.

No one had any idea where we were; we didn't even know what country we were in. Then came the unmistakable sound of truck doors being opened.

'I reckon we've arrived,' someone said excitedly.

'We're not in Germany yet,' he was told. 'At the speed we've been travelling I don't expect we've covered more than a couple of hundred miles.'

Then I noticed a large flat platform truck full of churns being wheeled towards the train.

'I guess they're going to feed us,' said Cobber when he saw it.

'You mean they're going to feed the guards,' said Spadger.

'I think they're going to feed us,' I said. 'Here comes a truck load of boxes.'

The trucks were dragged across to the train and passed out of our sight.

'There goes your grub,' said Spadger, resuming his seat on the floor.

Suddenly an elderly nurse appeared at the window. We blinked our eyes in disbelief, but she was real enough. 'Hello, boys. We have some soup and biscuits for you. I expect you are hungry.'

Immediately everyone began searching for something to collect his soup in. I turned to Cobber. 'She speaks perfect English, so why don't you tell her about your diarrhoea. She might be able to give you something for it.'

He shook his head. 'She might tell me to lay off the soup.'

'Oh, bull,' I said. 'If you don't ask her, I will.'

He turned and pushed his way back to the window. 'Hi, nurse,' he bawled. 'Have you anything for diarrhoea?'

Half a dozen startled faces turned and looked at him. How could he be so crude with a complete stranger – a woman at that?

'Oh dear,' the nurse said with a sympathetic frown. 'I don't know what I can give you. We have nothing left.' Then she smiled. 'Do you think aspirins will help? I only have about two left, but you can have them.'

'I'll be OK, thanks,' said Cobber, shaking his head. 'It's not too bad.'

Two aspirins – her entire stock – and she was willing to give them to an unknown prisoner.

She gave a smile and added, 'I don't think you'd better have any hot soup. I'll try to get you an extra biscuit.'

The door of the next truck opened and we could hear the prisoners scrambling out into the fresh air.

'It will be your turn next,' the nurse said as she left us to walk along the platform.

I squeezed closer to the window, anxious to know if Chota had been in the truck, but there were no signs of him.

'You're a helpful bastard,' Cobber said. 'You've just cost me my soup.'

I turned and looked at him. 'Well, I like that. It isn't me who's stopping your soup – it's the nurse. And I agree with what she said.'

'Well, it was you who suggested I spoke to her.'

'You bet it was. D'you think we like having someone in the truck who has diarrhoea?'

He ran his fingers round the inside of his empty bully-beef tin. 'Well, I'm going to have my full whack, nurse or no nurse.'

I shrugged my shoulders. 'That's up to you. But I hope it doesn't make you worse. If it does, it'll be worse for all of us.'

Spadger, standing close by, had been an observer so far but now he broke his silence. 'I thought I was the only hungry-gutted bastard in this outfit,' he said.

'You still are,' snapped Cobber. 'Now get back to your kennel.'

Spadger wiped his nose on the back of his hand. 'If you hadn't got bellyache ...'

Cobber turned and faced him. 'Well, just forget that I have.'

The Sergeant Major appeared. 'Break it up, boys,' he said in a fatherly voice. 'We don't want any more trouble. We've got enough with the Germans.'

With a shrug Spadger turned and sat down.

Presently the truck door was unlocked and opened, and we climbed down on to the platform. I stood in the short queue with Cobber, and when we reached the truck containing the churns I saw him hold out his bully-beef tin and get it filled. As he passed me on his way to collect his biscuits, I saw him glancing around for the nurse, but she was nowhere to be seen.

The soup was thick with vegetables and tasted very good. And the biscuits were the largest I had ever seen, measuring about 6 inches square.

I joined Cobber on the step of the truck. 'You are a hungry-gutted bastard,' I said. 'And you'll get shot if the nurse sees you.'

'I'll take a chance on that. This is too good to miss,' and he continued spooning the soup into his mouth as fast as he could.

I glanced along the train. The guards were making the men in the next truck but one get inside again. Apparently they allowed only three trucks open at once. I kept a sharp look out for Chota, but he must have been in one of the trucks at the other end of the train.

'I'm going to save my biscuits,' I told Cobber. 'I've still enough of that stinking bread for two more meals.'

'I'm going to save mine too,' he replied. 'They're enormous bloody things. I wonder where they've come from?'

'There were red crosses on the boxes they hooked them out of, so I expect they came from the Red Cross.' I scraped the bottom of my mug clean. 'By the way, what's the name of this place? I intended asking the nurse.'

'Belgrade. I thought you knew.'

I looked up in surprise. 'Is it really? Who told you?'

'Someone in the truck?'

I got to my feet and stretched. 'Good old Belgrade,' I said. 'All we need now is a smoke and a cup of tea. I'm as thirsty as hell.'

'Maybe we can get some water.' He glanced across at a nearby station building. 'See a tap anywhere?'

'No. But there might be one inside that place.'

He leaned back and threw his empty tin inside the truck. 'D'you reckon I could get across there without being seen by the Jerries?'

'It's a bit risky. Why don't you ask if you can go to the lavatory?'

'I don't want to go now, and if I did, I wouldn't be able to swipe anything if I had a guard with me.'

'Well, you better be careful how you go or you'll be getting a bullet in your backside.'

'It might be worth it if I can swipe a bucket. I'm not doing another trip in that train without some water.'

He glanced up and down the platform. There were plenty of guards about, but they also were having soup and biscuits.

'Here goes,' he said, getting to his feet. 'If I'm not back in five minutes you'll know I've deserted.'

He set off towards the nearest platform building. Luck and audacity saw him through. Within two minutes he was back inside the truck with a large bucket of water.

'Where did you find it?' I asked, amazed by his speed.

'It was just waiting to be picked up,' he said. 'I expect some poor old dear got it ready to do some scrubbing. It was in a waiting room.'

'Did no one see you?'

He shrugged his shoulders. 'I don't know. I didn't wait to see. Where's my bloody bully-beef tin?'

Everyone on the train had been fed and we were now back in our trucks. The whistle sounded and, with a great deal of clattering from the couplings, we began to move.

'Good old Belgrade,' said Cobber as we stood together, looking out of the window. 'I'm coming back here after the war to tell the folk how much I like them.'

'That's just how I feel,' I told him, clutching my two biscuits affectionately.

Suddenly the train slowed, then, with a jerk, stopped.

Cobber went to the window. 'It's the nurse,' he said after a brief pause. 'I'm sure it's her running along the platform.'

A moment later a hand appeared at the window. 'Here you are. I nearly missed you.'

'Thanks, nurse,' Cobber said. 'You shouldn't have bothered.' He blushed to the roots of his long hair as he took the large biscuit and stuffed it inside his shirt.

'Did they stop the train for that?' I asked him.

'I expect the signal's against us,' said one of the other men at the window.

Then another hand appeared. 'Here you are, boys. Share them out.' Cigarettes shot like confetti through the window.

The Sergeant Major came forward and ordered that the cigarettes be picked up and handed to him. After counting them, they were shared out equally between all the smokers in the truck – three each.

'After that, I'm coming back here to live when the war's over,' said Cobber. I think everyone in the truck felt the same.

Half an hour later the train again stopped. This time we were on the outskirts of the city. We could hear the doors of the trucks at the other end of the train being opened, and soon discovered that we were being let out 'to relieve nature'! This was, in fact, the only reason we were ever allowed out again until we arrived in Germany. Once each day the train stopped on some quiet stretch of line and, truck by truck, we were let out to seek what privacy we could behind the wheels of the trucks or some small shrub by the side of the track. We were given no more food or drink, and the further we got into Germany the colder it got. When at last we arrived at our destination, we were so exhausted that it was only the soreness of our bodies that kept us conscious.

35
Then the Gates Closed

We arrived at Annahof, the railway station for Stalag VIIIB, Lamsdorf, in Upper Silesia, at five o'clock in the morning. It was wet, miserable and very cold. The train had drawn into a siding, and as the trucks were opened we were told to get out and form into fives at the front of the train.

During the latter part of the journey I had been greatly worried about Chota. Unless he had been treated very much better than we had, he was likely to be in a pretty bad state. As soon as the truck was opened, I decided to walk back along the track in the hope of finding him.

'I'm going to look for a pal of mine,' I told Cobber as I climbed out of the truck. 'He's one of the sick, and I want to make sure that he's all right.'

'You don't want to worry,' he said. 'I expect they'll supply transport for all the sick. They did at the other end.'

'Well, just the same I'm going to try and find him.'

'I'll come with you,' he said, picking up his kit and following me out of the truck.

'But what about Spadger?' I asked. 'Aren't you ...'

'He can look after himself,' he interrupted. 'He's big enough.'

We walked along the length of the train, and when we'd almost reached the last truck I saw Chota. He was still seated and was propped up against the edge of the open door, both hands held to his neck.

'Hello, Chota,' I said. 'So you've made it.'

He gave a sickly smile. 'I'm glad you've come. I can't move.'

'What's the trouble?' I asked, moving closer. 'Your neck?'

He screwed up his face. 'Yes, partly. But I feel so weak.'

Cobber dropped his blanket. 'I better lift you out,' he said. 'Where's the best place to get hold of you?'

Chota pushed himself round until he was facing the doorway. 'Just grab me round the waist and pull.'

When he'd been deposited on the ground he was so unsteady on his feet that Cobber had to keep hold of him.

'I think I better go along and see if there's any transport for you,' I said.

'Don't bother, Micky,' he replied. 'I'll manage. The fresh air'll soon put me right.'

'You know bloody well it won't,' I said. 'You're as weak as a kitten.'

'I'll manage all right,' he insisted. 'I don't expect we'll have all that far to go, so just collect my bits and pieces and hand them to me.'

After retrieving his blanket and haversack, I asked him what had happened to all the other men who'd been in the truck.

'They all beat it as soon as the Jerries opened the door,' he replied.

'Miserable shower of bastards,' remarked Cobber. 'Come on, I suppose we better start moving.' We each took an arm, then set off to join the rapidly forming queue at the other end of the train.

From their appearance, we could tell that our guards for the march were from the camp. They were all elderly soldiers, dressed in shabby, ill-fitting green uniforms, down-at-heel jackboots and faded service caps. And instead of carrying tommy-guns, they were armed with 1914-vintage rifles.

'What a worn-out bunch,' remarked Cobber in disgust, as the guards began taking up their positions around us. 'I reckon Hitler must be losing the war.'

'They look worn-out all right,' I said. 'I only hope they haven't gone sour as well. They'll be worse than the young ones if they have.'

The counting was undertaken by two German officers – the one in the black leather coat who had accompanied us from Salonika and one from the camp. They each went along the ranks twice, counting. Then they got together and compared notes. Satisfied with the results, they saluted each other, about turned and disappeared from sight.

'*Hoch! Hoch! Mein Gott*, what a bloody fine lot,' said Cobber to Chota. 'Aren't you glad you're not a goddamn Kraut?'

Presently an English-speaking German called us to attention and, after warning us that we would be shot if we tried to escape, gave the order 'Quick march'.

The march to the camp was a painful nightmare. Though we had over 2 miles to cover, we were not allowed a single rest, and the guards were brutal to the extreme. They didn't wait for a man to fall out of the ranks before using their rifle butts; they watched until they saw him falter, then used them. Chota was quite incapable of walking. Indeed, it is doubtful if he was even capable of standing, and Cobber and I practically carried him the whole way. But despite this, we each received more than one bashing for not keeping properly in the ranks.

When at last we reached the camp, they halted us on a large patch of waste ground close to the main gates. Through the almost solid wall of barbed-wire which surrounded the camp, we could see row after row of long, squat, black huts. And a swastika, rain-sodden and indecent, its folds clinging like streaks of red and black slime to the flagpole, had been put out in our honour.

We lowered Chota gently to the ground.

'He looks about all in,' said Cobber.

I stooped down and put a rolled blanket under his head. 'He'll be all right when he's had a rest.'

Cobber felt in his pocket and brought out a piece of dirty rag. 'What're they going to do with us now?' he asked, wiping some of the rain from his bearded face.

'I don't know,' I said dismally. 'I wish they'd be quick and get us into the dry.'

Then the camp gates opened and a large party of helmeted soldiers in green marched towards us. Half of them were armed with bayoneted rifles, the other half carried revolvers. Following them were some German officers.

'What the hell,' exclaimed Cobber. 'The whole Nazi army's coming to look at us.'

The English-speaking guard called us to attention. I stooped down. 'Come on, Chota,' I said. 'You've got to stand up.' Cobber helped me to get him to his feet. 'Just lean on us,' I told him. 'You'll be all right.' But his face was grey, his lips blue.

The Germans were drawn up in two columns facing us, those with rifles in front. One of the officers ordered them to load. There was a clatter of bolts, then silence. Another order was given, and the soldiers with rifles marched away to take up positions around us. There now seemed almost as many Germans as prisoners on parade.

Chota opened his eyes and glanced around. 'What's happening?' he asked in a hoarse whisper. 'Are they going to shoot us?'

'Of course not,' I replied, trying to keep my voice under control. 'I expect they're going to search us again.' But I didn't feel too happy.

Chota began to sway drunkenly and we had great difficulty in preventing him from falling. I was about to suggest to Cobber that we lie him down again when one of the officers began speaking to us in English. He told us that we were to spread our belongings on the grass and we would then be searched. If anyone resisted, or attempted to run away, he would be shot. It was the same old ritual.

'Now you can lie down again,' I said to Chota. We began lowering him to the ground, but we ourselves were so weak that he fell most of the way, landing in a heap on our kit.

'What the hell do they expect to find?' grumbled Cobber as he laid out his few possessions. 'A box of hand grenades or something?'

'I don't know,' I said with a sigh. 'I just don't understand the Jerry mentality.'

'He hasn't got any mentality to understand. He's not even human.'

The search started at the opposite end of the column and progressed very slowly. Frequently a guttural voice could be heard shouting angrily, and we guessed some unfortunate prisoner was going through the mill for being in possession of something which was deemed '*verboten*' (prohibited).

The search party was still some distance away when the camp gates opened again and a small party of khaki-clad men carrying stretchers appeared.

'Someone passed out?' asked Cobber, glancing around.

I looked down at Chota. 'We'll all be passing out if they don't soon get us into the dry.'

There was a lot more shouting, and the stretcher party moved out of sight at the other end of the column. When they reappeared a few minutes later, they were going back towards the camp gates, their stretchers loaded.

'How're you feeling now?' I asked Chota, readjusting the blanket roll at his head.

He mumbled something, then began to cough. Even the effort of coughing didn't restore any colour to his face.

I looked at Cobber. 'D'you think we could get the Jerries to move him inside the camp?' I asked. 'I'm sure he's as ill as any of those they've just carried inside.'

'We can try,' he said, glancing towards the nearest guard. 'Shall I shout for one of these lugs to come over?'

Before I could answer, Chota started coughing again. I held his shoulders until, gasping for breath, he stopped. 'You'll be all right,' I told him, gently patting him. 'Just take it easy.' After a time he began breathing regularly and I thought he was asleep.

Suddenly he opened his eyes. 'You won't leave me, will you, Micky?' he whispered.

I peered at the thin, grey face. How old he had grown in the space of a single hour.

'No,' I said quietly. 'I won't leave you.' He tried to smile, then closed his eyes.

I bent over and looked at his neck. The old wound seemed to be almost completely healed, but close to it was the red scar of another and more recent wound.

His right hand began to move and found mine. 'I'm sorry about the canoe,' he murmured weakly. 'It's a pity you couldn't make it.'

I gently squeezed his hand. 'It's all in the luck of the game.' Then, 'What's the other scar on your neck? Have you had an operation?'

As he started to answer, he had another coughing fit. 'I think I'll try to get the Jerries to take you into the camp,' I said. 'It's too cold and wet for you out here.'

He clasped me with both hands. 'No,' he said. 'I don't want to go inside the camp. I'm all right here.'

'But it's so cold. Besides, you're soaked to the skin.'

For a moment he stared at me, then, closing his eyes, he turned his head away. I felt a sudden inward chill. Those eyes, that strange stare. Was it he or I who had had a premonition?

Cobber moved closer and, with an involuntary shudder, I sank back on my haunches.

'What's up?' asked Cobber, getting down on his knees. 'Doesn't he want to go inside?'

'No,' I said with a sigh. 'He doesn't want us to leave him.'

Cobber shook his head. 'I think he should be made to go.'

'So do I, but ...'

'But what?'

'There's something about him I don't understand. He's really ill, and I don't know what it is.'

'Well, the Doc'll soon find out.'

I shook my head, then stood up. 'Chota knows what it is.'

'You're talking in riddles. What d'you mean?'

Again I shook my head. I could hardly admit to myself what I believed to be the truth, let alone admit it to him.

The search party drew closer and finally reached us. Between us we managed to get Chota to his feet, but now he was an absolute dead weight and his head dropped forward on his chest.

'Is this man sick?' the German officer asked in clipped English.

'Yes, sir,' I said. 'Very sick.'

With an effort, Chota raised his head. 'I'm all right,' he mumbled weakly.

'Lie him down,' ordered the officer. 'I will call a *Sanitator*.'

We did as we were told, and one of the guard was sent off to the camp at the double. Then we were searched. On going through Chota's pockets they discovered a petrol lighter. Had I known he possessed anything '*verboten*' I would have hidden it for him. With a slightly embarrassed look, the officer ordered it to be confiscated. When they'd finished with us and moved away, I heard Cobber give a sigh of relief. He'd got away with his lighter! We repacked our kit, and I put the folded blanket back under Chota's head.

'How're you feeling now?' I asked him.

He opened his eyes and tried to smile. But his eyes were dull and tired and I wasn't sure that he'd even heard what I said. Then I saw that he was trying to speak, so I got closer to him.

'What is it?' I asked.

He made another effort.

'I can't hear, Chota,' I said, putting my ear close to his mouth. 'Try to speak louder.'

Then I caught his whisper, so faint that I hardly heard it. 'Don't leave me, Micky,' he said. It was like listening to a sick child.

I turned and looked at him. 'I won't leave you.'

A smile flickered across his face, then his eyes closed.

Trying to stop my mind from thinking, I got to my feet. 'Where the hell's that stretcher party?' I said, looking towards the gates.

'It soon won't be worth their while coming,' Cobber said. 'There's only another dozen blokes to be searched.'

It was still raining and the sky seemed to be getting darker. I looked back at Chota. The rain was running in rivulets down his face. I brought out my handkerchief and, going down on my knees, wiped some of it away. Poor kid, I thought. If they ever get you to hospital, you'll be there for the rest of the war.

At last the search was over and we were called to attention. I bent down. 'We're on the move, Chota,' I said. 'Bed's the next stop.'

He remained motionless. I felt his wet forehead. It was icy cold.

I turned and looked up at Cobber. 'I think he's fainted.'

He knelt down and joined me at Chota's side.

'He looks sort of queer,' he remarked, glancing at Chota's face.

I loosened his wet clothing and put my hand over his heart.

'Feel anything?' asked Cobber in a whisper.

'No. You try.' I was suddenly feeling very frightened.

'There's something wrong here.' he said after a moment. 'Which side's your heart?'

'Left. Let's try his pulse.'

I held his wrist and put a finger lightly between the bone and tendon. There was no pulse. What I had feared seemed to have happened.

A nearby German began shouting. Cobber got to his feet. 'What're we going to do?' he said in a shaky voice.

'You go on,' I said. 'I'll stay with him.'

He picked up his kit and made as if to go. Then he suddenly let it drop to the ground again. 'I guess I'll stay with you,' he said.

The column wended its way towards the camp gates, and soon the last man was gone. Then two of the guards who had been left behind to collect up the things which had been confiscated began shouting at us and one of them came running towards us waving his gun. When he reached us, I pointed to the inert figure at my feet.

'*Was ist lose?*' he demanded.

Again I pointed to Chota. He laid his rifle on the ground, then went down on one knee. A moment later he stood up. '*Tot,*' he said. '*Ihr Kamerad ist tot.*'

I looked at Cobber. 'He says he's dead.'

'But he can't be,' said Cobber with a frown. 'He was talking a few minutes ago.'

I gave a sigh. That was how I was feeling about it. It seemed impossible that he could have slipped away so suddenly. Again I got down on my knees, and this time I held an ear to Chota's mouth, but there were no signs of life.

I stood up and shook my head. 'I'm afraid he has gone.'

Still unconvinced, Cobber got down to the ground. 'Let me feel his heart again,' he said, sliding a hand under the wet clothing. Presently he got to his feet. 'Poor little sod,' he said with feeling.

I looked down at the body, so small, so neat, so young.

'He once told me he'd never go to a POW camp. He was right.'

The guard wouldn't let us carry Chota into the camp, but said they would send a stretcher party for him. So we had to leave him, his head still propped up on the folded blanket, a faint smile on his face. In silence and with heavy hearts we walked slowly towards the camp gates. While we still had a few yards to cover, Cobber suddenly stopped.

'At least he's escaped all this,' he said, pointing to the barbed wire.

I nodded. 'Yes, and he's escaped from that as well,' I said, looking up at the rain-sodden swastika.

We continued on our way. When we reached the gates, a guard opened them for us and we walked slowly in. Then the gates closed.

Afterword

Within a couple of days of my arrival at Stalag VIIIB at Lamsdorf, I was interrogated by the Germans, given a POW number and provided by the Red Cross with some items of clothing I needed badly. I was then transferred to the RAF compound.

Here I met a number of 30 Squadron men, none of whom I knew particularly well. In common with all other new prisoners in the compound, I was asked to tell how I became a POW. It was known as 'line shooting', and one was expected to make the story as colourful as possible. I told exactly what happened, and everyone agreed that Lawrie was the hero of the event.

Some weeks later a number of other members of the Squadron arrived in the compound. They had all been transferred to Stalag VIIIB from various other POW camps, and among their number were Lofty Bond, Bunny Austin and Lawrie. One day Lawrie came up to me and started an argument. He wanted to know what exactly I had told the other prisoners about our capture. I told him what he must have already known, but he denied the truth of the story, or at least the part concerning his argument with the German paratrooper corporal about his intention to shoot us all and Lawrie's refusal to be shot without a German officer present. I argued with him, and eventually called on Lofty Bond and Tom Yeomans to confirm my story, but he still refused to accept it. Unfortunately he continued to deny the story, and told me not to shoot such a stupid line involving him. I asked him to tell me exactly what did happen, but he was unable to remember the events, so the matter was left there, unresolved.

Despite promises to keep in touch with each other when the war was over, few of us did. I lost touch with Lawrie until about October 1982, when we were put in touch with each other by a mutual friend. I sent him a photostat copy of the first 90 pages of my manuscript, hoping that he would be able to reconcile it with his own memories of early POW days. He acknowledged the manuscript and remarked on its accuracy, but there was no mention of his earlier denial of any of the events.

Shortly afterwards I was in the Nottingham area, and telephoned Lawrie to ask if I might come across to see him. He agreed, and in due course I met him and his wife. I had taken the entire manuscript with me and gave it to him to read. His wife apparently knew little about Lawrie's capture and was glad of the opportunity to read about it. She later told me that her husband had acted exactly as she would have expected all the way through the chapters dealing with our actual capture. I told her that Lawrie was not prepared to believe what I had written about him.

Apparently they sat up half the night reading the manuscript, and when we met at breakfast the following morning, Mrs Lawrie soon told me they had sorted things out. They had had a deep discussion and decided my account was accurate and that Lawrie must have suffered from amnesia. This I am quite prepared to believe. The events leading up to our capture were indeed traumatic, and for most of the time Lawrie had been at the sharp end of events. For a man of his character to be accused, even if jointly, of mutilating and killing German wounded must have shaken him to the soul. Probably after that awful episode, his mind decided to blank out the terrible events, and unlike me he would not revive his memory of them periodically by retelling the story to his wife and family.

End Note

R. J. Lawrence (always known as Lawrie) was a regular, having joined the RAF in 1937 at the age of 19. Surviving the war, he left the Service in 1946, after spending two months in hospital. He went to a Teachers' Training College from 1947 to 1949, then to the Birmingham School of Music towards the end of 1949. From 1949 to 1980 he taught music and other subjects. From 1960 to 1963 he was deputy head of the Snaith County Secondary School, and thereafter Headmaster of the Snaith Comprehensive School until his retirement in 1980. Concurrently he was musical director and conductor of the Doncaster and District Choral Society, which continued until 1986. He was also director of the Doncaster Police Male Voice Choir from 1957 until 1976. While a POW in Germany, he formed his own choir and was its director until the end of the war. Lawrie and his choir were in constant demand and took part in most of the camp entertainments.

Tom Yeomans, Albert Bond, Bill Williams, Albert Bell and G. R. Burwell were all regulars. Bill Williams met his end from a shower of German bullets when he tried to make a getaway on realizing that his party was surrounded. The author has lost touch with Bond, Yeomans and Burwell and does not know what happened to them. They were last seen at Stalag VIIIB, Lamsdorf, at the end of the war.

Albert Bell (Dingle, as he was known) appeared to have vanished from the scene. None of the others met him in Germany and it seems that the author's sighting of him in Salonika was the last time he was seen. However, on writing to the Air Historical Branch, the author learned that Dingle was in fact flown into Germany, survived the war and was liberated from Stalag IIID in May 1945.